SC

Massachusetts, Rhode Island & Southern New Hampshire

POCKET GUIDE

SIXTH EDITION

RICHARD BARNETT, EDWARD SOOMRE AND WILLIAM COBB, EDITORS

Printed in USA

SCANNER MASTER CORPORATION
Post Office Box 428, Newton Highlands, MA 02161

Ask for your free copy of our all-new catalog!

SCANNER MASTER

The catalog is filled with products and services, such as F.C.C. data online, data on disks, and data on CD-ROM!

Our line of publications include:

Massachusetts Guide -5th edition (the "Big Book")
Maine, New Hampshire & Vermont Pocket Guide;
New York Metro/No. New Jersey Guide -5th edition;
New York Metro Pocket Guide; Ohio Pocket Guide;
Grtr. Philadelphia/So. Jersey Pocket Guide 3rd ed.;
Virginia/Metro D.C. Guide -3rd ed.; Illinois Guide;
Florida Guide; Monitor America -3rd edition...

and loads of other products from Scanner Master and other publishers.

Call 1-800-722-6701 Today!

CONTENTS

Massachusetts Communities	1
City & Town Section Notes & Abbreviations	85
MA State, County, Federal Communications	86
Rhode Island Communities	126
RI State, County, Federal Communications	139
Southern New Hampshire Cities & Towns	148
NH State, County, Federal Communications	171
Vermont & Connecticut Major Systems	181
Massachusetts Ambulance Frequency Sort	186

Copyright © 1994, Scanner Master Corp. (1st Printing Nov., 1994)

All rights reserved. Reproduction in whole or in part without the written permission of the publisher is strictly prohibited. "Coded" information has been included to detect infringement of the copyright. Cover photo by Bill Noonan, BFD.

Section 605 of the Communications Act of 1934 states that it is illegal to divulge or make use of the information heard over the airwaves. It is also illegal to interfere in any way with public safety officials who are performing their duty.

Scanner Master Corporation and the editor disclaim any liability or any misuse of the information contained herein and any responsibility for incorrect, missing and/or misspelled data. This publication was as up to date as possible at presstime.

SCANNER MASTER, Box 428, Newton Highlands, MA, 02161

Abington
PL tone

Freq	Description	Call	PL
483.0125	Police "X1" (PLC)	KAB239	203.5
33.800	Fire (2/SE)	KCD823	203.5
33.800	Fire -Station #2	KTE698	203.5
154.355	Fire -mobile repeater	reported	203.5
158.805	Highway Department	WNKK780	103.5
158.805	DPW/CD/Police-Fire tie	WQL493-7	103.5
158.895	Water Department	WQQ344	

Acton

Freq	Description	Call	PL
154.815R	Police -F1- ops. (SOM)	KCB875	173.8
155.250	Police -F1- repeater input	KCB875	173.8
154.815M	Police -F2- simplex ops.	KCB875	173.8
155.010	Police -F3- area tie	KCB875	107.2
153.815	Police -F4- Littleton tie	KCB875	151.4
154.785	Police -F5- car to car	KCB875	173.8
153.995	Police -F6- also DPW	KCB875	CSQ
153.875	Police -F7- car to car	KCB875	107.2
158.880	Police -F10- car to car	reported	173.8
155.880	Police -data terminals	reported	CSQ
155.475	Police -regional	KCB875	123.0
46.500	Fire -operations (6/14)	KCD310	100.0
46.400	Fire -F2- Regional net	KCD310	CSQ
153.815	Fire -officers' Littleton tie	reported	CSQ
153.995	DPW/Emerg. Mgmt./PD6	KFI544	CSQ
153.995	Water & Building Depts.	WNPD274	100.0
462.700	Emergency Management	KAD5995	114.8

Acushnet

Freq	Description	Call	PL
482.8125	Police (BRC)	KZM468	203.5
45.600	Fire (3)	KCK996	CSQ
46.180	Bristol County Fire Net	KNDN830	CSQ
45.600	Highway/Water Depts.	KNDN832	CSQ
39.500	Acushnet EMS "309"	WNCD309	
39.820	Dog Officer/Civil Defense	KNDN833	
461.4375	Public Schools	KB73456	

Adams

Freq	Description	Call	PL
155.130	Police (BEC)	KNDA824	107.2
156.210	Police -North Adams tie	KNDA824	107.2
154.445	Fire	KNGY914	107.2
154.310	Fire -PD dispatch (12)	KNGY914	107.2
154.310	Fire (12)	WNQM572	107.2
156.225	Highway Department	KNIQ430	107.2
155.220	Adams/Town Ambulance	KNFL539	

Agawam

Freq	Description	Call	PL
153.980R	Police -primary	KNFX711	91.5
155.895	Police -input to repeater	KNFX711	91.5
155.790	Police -detectives (WEM)	KNBU292	91.5
153.980M	Police -simplex operations	KNFX711	91.5
154.235	Fire -F1- primary (11)	KNGN400	91.5

153.890	Fire -F2- fireground	KNGN400	91.5
155.055	Fire -F3- adm./muni tie	KNGN400	91.5
154.280	Fire -F4- area intercity	KNGN400	82.5
33.520	Fire -Agawam Fire Tower	KE9550	CSQ
467.9875	Town Ambulance	KA89582	
155.055	DPW/Fire Adm./Aux. PD	KCK524	91.5
462.550	School Department	KAE5143	
151.715	Agawam Soccer Assoc.	KB70710	
154.600	Northeast Pro Racing	KA92832	
464.925	Riverside Park -security	KKJ487	141.3
464.525	Riverside Park -operations	WNNJ287	141.3
464.825	Riverside Park -operations	WNIR574	141.3
464.5625	Riverside Park -operations	KA81836	141.3
154.625	Riverside Park -Paging	WNCG779	

Alford

154.740	Berkshire County PD Net	mobiles	107.2
153.965	Berkshire County PD Net	mobiles	107.2
154.310	Fire/Berkshire County Net	KJ5411	107.2
156.120	Highway/Ambulance	WNFS213	

Amesbury

482.8375	Police "788" (NES)	KCB788	146.2
158.955R	Fire -F1- operations	WNEC686	203.5
154.145	Fire -F2- Seacoast Area	KCV354	CSQ
154.070	Fire -F3- District 15 net	KCV354	CSQ
154.190	Fire -F4- Seacoast Net	KCY354	CSQ
154.280	Fire -F5- fireground	KCV354	CSQ
154.010	Fire -F6- regional tie	KCV354	CSQ
155.805	Fire -F7- DPW tie		123.0
155.100	Fire -F8- Emrg. Mgmt. tie	KNJN401	127.3
153.875R	Fire -F9- N. Shore CD		127.3
155.220	Fire -F10- N. Shore backup		203.5
153.965R	Fire -F11- MEMA tie		203.5
158.955	Fire -F12- operations		203.5
153.995	Fire -F13- AMCARE Ambulance		CSQ
155.340	Fire -F14- Exeter Hospital		82.5
154.400	Fire -F15- Exeter Fire		136.5
156.800	Fire -F16- USCG channel 16		CSQ
155.100	Emrg. Mgmt. -F1- Local Ops.		127.3
153.875	Emrg. Mgmt. -F2- North Shore Net		127.3
153.875R	Emrg. Mgmt. -F3- North Shore Net		127.3
155.220	Emrg. Mgmt. -F4- Local backup		127.3
153.965/R	Emrg. Mgmt. -F5/6- MEMA tie		203.5
158.955	Emrg. Mgmt. -F7- Fire Dept. tie		203.5
154.145	Emrg. Mgmt. -F8- Area Fire Net tie		CSQ
154.070	Emrg. Mgmt. -F9- District 15 Fire tie		CSQ
154.190	Emrg. Mgmt. -F10- Seacoast Fire tie		CSQ
154.280	Emrg. Mgmt. -F11- Seacoast fireground		CSQ
155.805	Emrg. Mgmt. -F12- DPW tie		123.0
155.805	Highway Dept./Housing	WRG827	123.0
464.425	Amesbury Sports Park	reported	D-423

Amherst

460.150	Police	(WEM)	WBC488	173.8
460.175	Police -F2- foot beats		WBC488	173.8
460.325	Police -F3- tactical		WBC488	173.8
154.370	Fire	(10)	KCH729	127.3
153.890	Fire -fireground		WZY360	127.3
159.300	Fire -future dispatch		KCH729	127.3
154.855	Fire -administration		reported	114.8
33.540	Fire -Tri State Network		KCH729	123.0
458.0375	Ambulance -mobile rptr.		KB49457	
159.135	Highway Department		KSV881	141.3
153.845	Municipal Services		WNCX922	146.2
45.080	Council on Aging		KXC730	
154.540	Amherst Pelham Schools		KNIB852	CSQ
155.175	Amherst Pelham Schools		KNHY926	D-244
464.425	Amherst College		KNGV613	D-703
151.685	Amherst College		KJR855	141.3
464.875	Hampshire College		KUN283	
463.850	U. Mass. -Campus Police			173.8
464.525	U. Mass. -Security		WNBW706	141.3
464.825	U. Mass. -Security		WNBW706	141.3
150.995	U. Mass. -Facilities		KRM930	110.9
151.085	U. Mass. -Facilities		KRM930	110.9
464.325	U. Mass. -Facilities		KNAF897	88.5
464.675	U. Mass. -Facilities		WNBW706	141.3
45.920	5 Colleges Regional Trans.		WNWU585	141.3

University of Massachusetts (additional licenses)
156.075/154.515/151.715/153.905/159.075/453.1375/
453.400/453.8125/453.8875/462.100/464.925

Andover

482.6125	Police	(NEM)	WIE665	146.2
483.5875	Fire "892"	(15)	WII892	146.2
483.7625	Fire -fireground		WII892	CSQ
33.660	Fire -regional	(6)	KCF313	CSQ
151.130	Highway Department		KCZ912	173.8
39.100	C.D./Community Dvlpmnt.		WZN232	103.5
453.900	Water Treatment Plant		KNHF451	100.0
464.975	Phillips Academy		KNIG353	141.3
464.475	Phillips Academy		WNAX357	
463.9375	Phillips Academy		WPBN506	123.0
463.9625	Phillips Academy		WPBN506	
464.875	Rolling Green Inn		WQW984	
464.9375	Courtyard by Marriott		KD34746	

Arlington

471.1625	Police	(BAPn)	KZN839	131.8
460.600	Fire	(13)	KSL418	82.5
460.550	Fire -mobiles		KSL418	82.5
465.600	Fire -car to car		KSL418	
483.6625	Fire -auxilliary		reported	131.8

158.760	DPW/CD/Fire Ambulance	KBC888	CSQ
158.805R	Civil Defense -F1-	KNBZ682	141.3
158.760	Civil Defense -F2-	KBC888	141.3
159.090	Civil Defense -F3- input	KYB896	141.3
153.875M	Civil Defense -F4- mobiles		127.3
153.875R	Civil Defense -F5- regional		127.3

Ashburnham

39.220	Police -F1- dispatch	WNJK574	110.9
39.340	Police -F2- car to car	WNJK574	110.9
33.820	Fire (8)	KCB404	118.8
33.820	Fire -South Station	KCF249	118.8
33.780	Fire -Winchendon tie	reported	123.0
33.740	Fire -Base 500 tie	reported	CSQ
154.415R	Fire/Amb. -mobile repeater	KCB404	CSQ
45.200	Highway Dept./Power	WNAV831	CSQ
463.950	Cushing Academy	WNXZ530	173.8

Ashby

155.715	Police/Fire/Highway (8)	KFF298	CSQ

Ashfield

39.160	Police "2" (FRC)	KSM919	141.3
33.540	Fire/Tri-State Net (9)	KCE577	123.0
154.995	Highway Department	WRC877	82.5

Ashland

483.1125	Police "327" (SOM)	KNCE706	123.0
484.3875	Fire (14)	WIH877	123.0
46.460	Fire -area town tie	KCF945	114.8
155.340	Fire -ambulance -F1- to Hosp.-Frmgm		CSQ
155.280	Fire -ambulance -F2- to C-MED		CSQ
155.160	Fire -ambulance -F3- to Hosp.-Natick		107.2
158.940	Highway/Muni/PD-FD tie	KQR329	CSQ
484.8125	School Department Maint.	WIG368	103.5
158.265	Water Department	WNSS721	

Athol

453.225	Police (some scrambling)	KCA682	100.0
39.220	Police -area regional	KCA682	141.3
33.480	Fire -dispatch "3" (8/9)	KCD598	123.0
33.920	Fire -secondary	KCE598	123.0
158.775	Highway Department	KGY295	
39.580	Municipal Services	WNRM792	123.0

Attleboro

39.740	Police -F1- primary	KCA887	CSQ
39.540	Police -F2- regional	KQL655	CSQ
39.640	Police -F4- secondary	KCA887	CSQ
453.4375	Police -mobile extenders	reported	123.0
453.4625	Police -mobile extenders	reported	123.0
154.385R	Fire -primary	KCC341	100.0

159.300	Fire -repeater input	KCC341	100.0
46.320	Fire -Headquarters (3)	KCC341	100.0
46.320	Fire -Newport Ave. Station	WZX844	100.0
46.320	Fire -So. Main St. Station	WZX855	100.0
46.320	Fire -Park St. Station	WZX843	100.0
153.890	Fire -Fireground portables	reported	100.0
72.180	Fire -Alarm boxes	WGC972	CSQ
154.280	Fire -RI Intercity tie	KCC341	CSQ
47.500	Emergency Management	KWL648	CSQ
156.165	Public Works Department	WZU212	CSQ
451.700	Water Department	WPDU906	
151.685	School District	WPDI413	
154.600	Bishop Feehan High	KB73551	
453.400	Attleboro-Taunton Transit	KNJT995	110.9

Auburn

45.140	Police "A"	(WOR2)	KNDD874	167.9
155.550	Police -portables		KNDD874	167.9
155.550	Police -mobile data		KNDD874	CSQ
154.385	Fire	(7)	KBT465	82.5
158.760	Highway Department		KAT540	136.5
153.980	Housing Authority		KB83342	CSQ
153.445	Water District		KUI345	127.3
462.100	Auburn Mall		WPCD705	192.8

Avon

453.9625	Police -temporary use	WPCP832	
154.785	Police	KCI271	CSQ
155.730	Police -area regional	KCI271	CSQ
46.240	Fire (SE)	KCD727	136.5
46.140	Fire -secondary/regional	KCD727	136.5
158.925	Public Works Department	KTI570	
158.895	Rockland/Abington Water	WYE340	
158.955	Rockland/Abington Water	WYE340	

Ayer

158.895R	Police -F1/A- "3"	WNBG942	167.9
155.610	Police -input to repeater	KCF802	167.9
154.830	Police -F2/B- backup	KCF802	151.4
158.790R	Police -F3/C- special	WNBG942	151.4
154.785	Police -input to repeater	KCF802	151.4
155.475	Police -F4- area net	KCF802	151.4
155.505	Police -F5-		151.4
154.950	Police -F6-		151.4
153.815	Police -F7-		CSQ
155.850	Police -F8- Littleton tie		151.4
155.535	Police -F9- Shirley tie		131.8
153.605	Police -F10- special ops.		151.4
155.580R	Police -F11- Groton tie		151.4
159.090R	Police -F12- Harvard tie		107.2

Frequency	Description	Call	Tone
158.790	Police -F13- simplex	KCF802	151.4
159.105	Police -F14- Highway tie	KCX309	151.4
39.420	Police -area base network	KCF802	CSQ
161.400	Police -Railroad PD tie	reported	CSQ
46.140	Fire	KAQ921	CSQ
159.105	Highway/Water/Police tie	KCX390	151.4
155.340	Nashoba Community Hosp.	KNCP977	CSQ

Barnstable

Frequency	Description	Call	Tone
855.2125	Police "EASY" (BAR)	KCA374	D-445
158.835	Police -Marine patrol	WNKW713	110.9
155.535	House of Corrections	KNDN805	173.8
453.700	County radio techs/maint.	KJF772	114.8
33.480	Fire -Barnstable Village (1)	KCB781	114.8
33.840	Fire -Osterville	KCD760	114.8
33.840	Fire -Centerville	KCF358	114.8
33.840	Fire -Marstons Mills	KZQ731	114.8
33.940	Fire -Hyannis	KCD454	114.8
460.5875	Fire -Hyannis mob. rprtr.	KCD454	114.8
33.560	Fire -Cotuit	KNHD618	114.8
33.480	Fire -West Barnstable	KCF481	114.8
460.625	Fire -Investigations/Adm.	KCO454	123.0
453.575	County Transit Authority	WYC873	141.3
37.260	Highway Department	KGK599	114.8
37.100	Solid Waste Division	KNGE576	
153.815	Water Pollution Control	KD28862	
153.650R	Barnstable Water District	WNKQ310	
158.265M	Barnstable Water District	WNKQ310	
47.740	Barnstable Water Co.	KQW738	CSQ
37.480	Cotuit Water Department	WNHN737	114.8
155.745	Airport Security/Maint.	KRK985	CSQ
154.515	Cape Community College	WPEV692	156.7
154.540	Cape Community College	WPEV692	
461.0875R	Cape Cod Mall Security	WNQS623	123.0
464.425	Cape Cod Hospital	WNMK279	100.0
464.150	Cape Cod Hospital	WPDS283	
464.675	Hyannis Regency Inn	KNCC908	

Barre

Frequency	Description	Call	Tone
153.980	Police/Ambulance/DPW	WNMD772	146.2
33.740	Fire -F1- Operations	KJW733	CSQ
33.700	Fire -F2- Mid-State	KJW733	CSQ
37.260	Fire -inactive	KJW733	
45.780	Police (limited use)	WNMD772	146.2
453.5625	Highway Department	WNSY480	
154.570	Quabbin Regional High	KB75739	

Becket

Frequency	Description	Call	Tone
154.740	Berkshire Cty. PD Net	KW9168	107.2
465.100	Police -mobile repeater	WPEC575	
154.310	Fire/Berkshire Cty. Net	KNCJ825	107.2
151.115	Highway Department	WQN746	151.4

Bedford
482.7125	Police	(NEM)	KAA999	146.2
154.340	Fire	(6)	KBT205	131.8
153.935	Highway Department		KBI783	141.3
484.3625	Middlesex Cmty. College		WIE966	

(See military bases for Hanscom frequencies.)

Belchertown
158.820	Police "52"	(WEM)	KUG782	179.9
155.145	Fire/State School	(10)	KCW396	127.3
154.370	Amherst Fire Dispatch		KCW396	127.3
155.925	Public Works Department		WNNG464	118.8
155.145	Municipal Services		KDG401	127.3
153.965	State School		KNIT448	100.0
154.600	Chestnut Hill School		KD23637	CSQ

Bellingham
155.910R	Police "B"	WNHY207	103.5
154.680	Police -input to repeater	WNHY207	103.5
155.475	Police -regional	WNHY207	
155.460	Police -car to car	WNHY207	
33.540	Fire	KEP595	CSQ
37.940	Highway Department	KUS492	CSQ
155.220	Town Ambulance	KYK489	
451.6625	Water Alarms	WNYS696	CSQ

Belmont
471.4125	Police	(BAPn)	KAN840	131.8
154.130	Fire	(13)	KCD849	100.0
153.770	Fire -Fireground		KCD849	100.0
156.195R	Highway Department		WPAW967	100.0
151.070	Highway Department -input		WPAW967	100.0
153.620	Town Power Department		KCG543	131.8
155.805	Aux PD/School Bus/Aging		KSJ346	136.5
151.805	McLean Hospital Paging		WNNS359	156.7
155.340	McLean Hospital		KLR318	
155.265	McLean Hospital Security		KLR318	173.8

Berkley
483.5375	Police	(BRC)	WEC762	203.5
483.0625	Police -Taunton tie		WEC762	203.5
46.180	Fire/Bristol County Net		KFZ756	CSQ
151.130	Highway Department		KNFN756	
154.570	School Department		KD47687	

Berlin
37.100	Police	(SOM)	KNFW788	CSQ
33.700	Fire/Mid-State Net		KCB778	CSQ
33.640	Fire -Future Dispatch		KCB778	
453.375	Highway Department		KEM417	
154.600	Spooky World			110.9

Bernardston
39.160	Police "4" (FRC)	KZT529	141.3
453.2125	Police -mobile extenders	KD22645	123.0
33.540	Fire/Tri-State Net (9)	WRX664	123.0
453.6625	Fire -mobile extenders	KD43974	141.3
39.180	Highway Department	WNML863	141.3

Beverly
471.3375	Police (BAPn)	KCA875	131.8
45.480	Fire (5)	KCG966	CSQ
484.3875	Fire (possible future use)	WIK892	
150.995	Highway Department	KCF953	CSQ
153.980	C.D. -F1- local primary	WXP310	CSQ
153.875	C.D. -F2- No. Shore Emerg.	KNBV916	127.3
153.875R	C.D. -F3- No. Shore Emerg.	KNBV916	127.3
155.985	C.D. -F3- Repeater input	WXP310	127.3
155.220	C.D. -F4- No. Shore Backup	KNBV916	127.3
153.965R	C.D. -F5- State Network	KNBV916	203.5
153.980R	C.D. -F10- Local repeater	WXP310	127.3
155.055	C.D. -F10- Repeater input	WXP310	127.3
45.480	C.D. -Fire Department tie	WXP310	CSQ
155.280	C.D. Ambulance	WYC540	
150.790	C.D. Mobile Rptr. (45.48)	WYC540	CSQ
462.575	Senior Citizens Council	KAC6950-2	
154.115	Elder Vans	KNCJ883	127.3
155.205	Public Schools	KKD372	
155.340	Beverly Hospital	KGT586	
154.600	Beverly Hospital	reported	
453.450	N. Shore Cmmty. College	WNFK960	
151.715	Endicott College	KGV907	
461.725	Endicott College	reported	

Billerica
483.0875	Police (NEM)	KEC445	146.2
482.6625	Police -Tewksbury tie	KEC445	146.2
154.995	Police/Fire -auxiliary	WZM911	118.8
33.660	Fire/No. Middlesex Net	KCF312	CSQ
33.760	Fire -secondary	KCF312	CSQ
154.205	Fire -mobile tie to Lowell		186.2
154.995	Public Works/Water Depts.	KJV270	82.5
155.895	Municipal Services	WNNI774	118.8
483.8125	Valley Ambulance	WIG284	151.4
462.575	Civil Defense	KAC3814	
47.500	Public Schools	KNFU627	D-516
47.540	Public Schools	KNFU627	D-516
464.4875	Billerica Mall	WPEZ613	136.5

Blackstone
155.790	Police "B"	KCI228	CSQ
33.620	Fire/So. Worcester Net	WQY368	131.8
33.540	Fire/Norfolk Cty. area tie	WQY368	CSQ
159.120	Highway Department	KNGJ601	162.2

Blandford

453.575	Police/Fire/Highway	KDW495	141.3
33.460	Fire/Hampden County Net	KTZ395	CSQ
154.310	Fire/Berkshire County Net	WPBI544	107.2
157.560	Springfield Ski Club	KD41520	
157.680	Springfield Ski Club	KNCQ857	
157.620	Blandford Ski Area	KD40565	

Bolton

37.380	Police (SOM)	KBC209	*CSQ
33.700	Fire/Mid-State Net	KBA887	CSQ
33.700	Fire -mobiles	KBA887	131.8
37.100	Ambulance	KBC209	CSQ
37.260	Highway Department	WNVS351	118.8•
157.680	International Golf Club	WSO389	

* mobiles are PL 118.8/• mobiles are CSQ

BOSTON

Boston Police

All frequencies- Call Sign: KCA860 Tone Code: 118.8
(Note: The BPD may use a new channel configuration in the future.)

460.350	-F1-	-Citywide- Emergency/Tactical/Special Events
460.450	-F2-	-Area "A" (ALPHA) Operations
460.225	-F3-	-Area "B" (BRAVO) Operations
460.400	-F4-	-Area "E" (ECHO) Operations
460.500	-F5-	-Area "D" (DELTA) Operations
460.175	-F6-	-Area "C" (CHARLIE) Operations
460.300	-F7-	-Car to car/Station to car
460.125	-F8-	-"Harry Base" Information requests
460.075	-F9-	-Investigators (VICTOR)
460.250	-F10-	-Administra./Command (YANKEE)
460.375	-F11-	-Investigators/Radio Techs
460.475	-F12-	-Investigators (scrambled)
159.210R	-F18-	-Paging/Mobile phones
158.910R	-F28-	-Miscellaneous services
853.5625R		-Mobile Data Terminals
154.860, 154.890, 154.950, 453.200 Invest./Unknown use		
856-860.7625		-Limited Use (also 856-860.9375)

Area "A"	(ALPHA)	-Downtown/Waterfront/Beacon Hill East Boston/North End/Charlestwn (Districts 1 and 7)
Area "B"	(BRAVO)	-Mattapan/North Dorchester Roxbury/Mission Hill (Districts 2 and 3)
Area "C"	(CHARLIE)	-South Boston/Dorchester (Districts 6 and 11)

| Area "D" | (DELTA) | -Back Bay/South End/Fenway Allston/Brighton/Kenmore Square (Districts 4 and 14) |
| Area "E" | (ECHO) | -Jamaica Plain/Hyde Park Roslindale/West Roxbury (Districts 5,13 and 18) |

Boston Fire

483.1625	-F1-	General Communications	118.8
483.1875	-F2-	Fireground 1	118.8
483.2125	-F3-	Fireground 2	118.8
483.2375	-F4-	Fire Alarm Constr./Ground 3	118.8
453.650	-F5-	Apparatus Page Dispatch	131.8
153.890	-F6-	Subway Radio	
154.220	-F7-	Metrofire (simulcasted on 483.2875)	

Health & Hospitals Emergency Medical Services

Boston "EMS" staffs two dispatch elements: Boston C-MED –the EMS service within the city of Boston– and Metro Boston C-MED which is the control point for ambulance to hospital coordination within metropolitan Boston. Primary UHF PL tone is 151.4. Future 460 MHz splinter frequencies will be used. A state-of-the-art Global Positioning System (GPS) is in use by the agency.

462.975		"Citywide 10" Boston Operations
453.775		Repeats Citywide 10 (156.7)
462.950	-Tac 9-	On-scene/Working
460.550	-Tac 11-	Second On-scene/Working Radio Techs/Phone Interconnect Possible Future Division #2
460.525	-Ch. 12-	Command (DES) "Secure 12"
463.050	-MED 3-	Ambulance-hospital channel
463.075	-MED 4-	Common Calling Channel -C-MED channel assignments
463.125	-MED 6-	Ambulance-hospital channel
463.175	-MED 8-	Ambulance-hospital channel
155.295	"295"	Boston Ambulance Squad
155.340	HEAR	Amb-Hosp. outside greater Boston
155.280	HEAR	Amb-Hosp. within greater Boston C-MED to C-MED communications Boston Hospitals Disaster Network
155.040R	"040"	Paging/Portables/Misc. Use

Notes: All Med 1-8 channels are available to C-MED and may be repeaterized.

Miscellaneous City Agencies

Other than the police, fire and EMS departments, most Boston's city services use an 800 MHz trunked radio system for their communications. Agencies on the system include Housing Authority Police, Municipal Building Police, Park Rangers, the Transportation Department, Department of Public Works, Senior Services, and city supervisors. Public safety units may also have access.

856-860.7625	City Services Trunked Network	
856-860.9375	City Services Trunked Network	
851.0875	Transportation Department	
851.1125	Transportation Department	
851.5375	Unknown (& 851.4875, 851.7125, 852.1875)	
453.300	Old Citywide Radio -F1- Housing	118.8
453.350	Old Citywide Radio -F2- Pagers	CSQ
482.9375	Public Schools Police (changing)	151.4/131.8
482.9625	Public Schools Police	151.4/131.8
483.0875	English High School	
453.725	Water & Sewer Department -F1- Svc.	74.4
453.825	Water & Sewer Department -F2- Meter	74.4
155.115	City Paging/Administration	CSQ

Hospitals

464.475	Beth Israel Hospital	127.3
453.600	Boston City Hospital Security	167.9
464.175	Boston City Hospital	
464.325	Brigham & Womens (464.825/463.475)	88.5
151.805	Carney Hospital Security/Administration	
855.0875	Children's Hospital	141.3
855.3125	Children's Hospital	
461.375	Dana Farber Cancer Institute	
484.2875	Deaconess Hospital Security	107.2
483.8125	Deaconess Hospital (& 483.9375)	
155.265	Faulkner Hospital Security	
464.625	Faulkner Hospital	
472.7875	Mass. General Hospital Security	131.8
464.975	New England Baptist (& 155.205, 464.1375)	
462.675	St. Elizabeth's Hospital (& 151.655)	
472.0125	Tufts New England Medical Center Security	
464.775	Tufts New England Med (& 464.825, 464.975)	
155.235	University Hospital (& 154.570)	
154.570	University Hospital	

Colleges & Universities

472.1375	Boston College Campus Police	127.3
472.1625	Boston University Campus Police	131.8
464.850	Boston University Services	107.2
471.8125	Harvard University Medical School	
464.925	Berklee College of Music	
463.875	Emerson College	103.5

461.475	Emerson College (& 463.625)	
151.685	Emmanuel College (& 151.715)	
461.425	Massachusetts College of Art	88.5
464.975	Northeastern Univ. Campus Police	127.3
464.125	Northeastern Univ. Student Patrol	127.3
464.675	Northeastern Univ. Services	
464.325	Roxbury Comm. College (& 464.950, 463.750)	
464.300	Showa Woman's University	
463.650	Suffolk University Campus Police	127.3
463.250	Suffolk Univeristy Operations	
154.600	Suffolk University Maintenance	
483.8375	Simmons College Security/Admin.	141.3
463.850	University of Mass. Boston Security	141.3
464.225	University of Mass. Boston Athletics	
463.775	Wentworth Institute of Technology (WIT)	
151.775	WIT (& 151.805, 151.895, 151.925, 461.525)	

Attractions & Production Companies

151.280R	Arthur Fiedler Memorial (159.285 in)	151.4
484.0125	Aquarium Security (156.975 Boat Docking)	
461.9125	Aquarium (& 463.2875/154.570 Parking)	
461.400	Christian Science Center (& 463.750, 462.850)	
464.375	Fanueil Hall Security	
471.9375	Franklin Park Security	136.5
462.625	Boston "First Night" (also 464.550)	
464.575	Isabella Stewart Gardner Museum (& 464.775)	
151.745	Museum of Fine Arts (& 151.835, 154.600)	
464.575	Museum of Science (& 462.0625/464.850)	
461.100	Symphony Hall	
152.930	Mugar Productions	
464.925	Capron Lighting & Sound (& 461.5125)	
152.960	Capron Lighting & Sound (& 856-8.8375)	

Sports & Events

463.325	Boston Red Sox -Security- ch. #1	103.5
464.075	Boston Red Sox -Security- ch. #2	103.5
463.3625	Boston Red Sox -Park Operations	71.9
463.3875	Boston Red Sox -Concessions	71.9
463.4125	Boston Red Sox -Media Coordination	
154.600	Boston Garden Security/Operations	136.5
154.570	Boston Garden Concessions (154.625 also)	
49.830	Boston Bruins -Coaches (other 49 MHz chnls)	

State & Federal Agencies

460.025	Former Capitol Police (Now State PD)	118.8
460.0875	Former Capitol Police -F2- simplex ops.	
417.200	Government Buildings Security (GSA)	
166.950	National Historic Park (166.775 also)	
165.2625	US Coast Guard Security (& 165.3375)	
164.9875	US Postal Svc. (& 164.2/168.225/166.375)	

Hotels
463.550	Back Bay Hilton Security	
463.225	Boston Harbor Hotel	
484.5625	Bostonian Hotel Security	
154.570	Collonade Hotel Security	
464.575	Copley Place Security (464.350 also)	
463.925	Copley Plaza	141.3
462.025	Copley Plaza (& 154.570)	
154.570	Copley Plaza Hotel	
151.745	57 Motor Hotel	
464.675	Four Seasons Hotel Security	
151.745	Holiday Inn	
464.475	Hotel Meridian Security (& 464.925)	
461.350	Hyatt Harborside Hotel	
464.4375	Lafayette Place Hotel Security	
154.515	Logan Airport Hilton (& 154.540, 463.800)	
464.350	Marriott Copley Place	
464.825	Marriott (& 463.800, 464.2875, 464.450, 464.825)	
463.800	Marriott Convention Services	
151.865	Park Plaza Security (& 151.745)	
464.500	Parker House Hotel (& 464.525)	
463.950	Ramada Inn (East Boston) (& 462.900)	
464.775	Ritz Carlton Security	
461.225	Sheraton Boston (154.570/464.725/464.750)	
464.925	Suisse Chalet Motor Lodge	
462.125	Westin Hotel Security (& 462.875, 463.350)	

Realty & Property Management
463.625	Center Plaza Associates	
461.2875	Charles River Park (& 463.5625, 151.715)	
154.570	Bay Village Neighborhood Association	
462.575	Fenway Area Institutional - "Street Safe"	
464.725	Hancock Building (& 461.725, 463.500, 464.850)	
461.5875	Harbor Towers	141.3
464.675	Lafayette Place Security (& 464.425/461.475)	
464.425	Long Island Shelter	
464.625	One Post Office Square Assoc. (& 154.540)	
472.0625	Prudential Center (& 484.0125, 461.50) 131.8	
464.3375	Rowes Wharf Associates (& 464.600)	
464.300	South Station Management	
464.800	World Trade Center (461.9125-.9625/462.1625)	

Bourne
851.1625	Police "YOKE"(BAR)	WNHW401	D-445
33.640	Fire (1)	KNAW393	114.8
72.660	Fire -Alarm boxes	WNKH899	CSQ
156.195	Highway Department	KNBV300	192.8
155.520	Game Warden/Resources	reported	
46.520	Water Department	KCH355	
47.740	Water District	KCH355	CSQ
155.265	School Department	WNQR408	
464.550	Mass. Maritime Academy	reported	

Boxboro

153.815	Police	KYK414	151.4
154.725	Police -unused	KMK588	CSQ
155.010	Police -Concord area tie	KMK588	CSQ
154.815R	Police -Acton repeater	KMK588	173.8
159.090R	Police -Harvard tie	KMK588	107.2
458.550	Police -mobile repeater	reported	CSQ
46.500	Fire/Amb. -Acton Dispatch	KNFP294	100.0
46.400	Fire -area secondary	KNFP294	CSQ
154.600	Fire -mobile rptr. for 46.50	reported	100.0
151.625	Fire -mobile rptr. for 46.40	reported	141.3
46.580	Highway Department	KYK414	CSQ
464.375	Boxboro Host Hotel	WQM590	162.2

Boxford

154.800	Police	KJD278	123.0
153.845	Fire (15)	KJD277	CSQ
45.080	Highway/Civil Defense	KJU382	123.0
155.265	Town Ambulance	KKV605	
151.745	Masconomet School Dist.	WNGC989	

Boylston

45.620	Police "B" (WOR1)	KEV420	167.9
37.100	Police -area tie	KEV420	CSQ
33.700	Fire/Mid-State Net	KCF337	CSQ
48.380	Town Power	KCG321	
467.8875	Mt. Pleasant Country Club	WPEC295	

Braintree

471.5375	Police (BAPs)	KSS950	131.8
474.56375	Police -F5- car to car	KSS950	
483.5125	Fire -F1- (13/SE)	WII887	131.8
483.5125M	Fire -F5- direct	WII887	131.8
158.880	Highway Department	WPFC988	
47.760	Town Light Department	WZQ742	136.5
463.500	So. Shore Plaza -security	KNAL764	D-632
154.540	So. Shore Plaza -maint.	WYZ895	118.8
461.5875R	So. Shore Plaza -maint.	WNYW340	131.8
467.750	So. Shore Plaza -Jordans	reported	CSQ
464.475	So. Shore Plaza -Filenes	reported	173.8
464.525	So. Shore Plaza -Sears	reported	
464.875	Sheraton Tara	WNPB576	

Brewster

155.955	Police/Fire/DPW "KING"	KYQ454	CSQ*
155.640	Police -backup/area tie	KCC419	110.9
33.520	Fire (1)	KCD845	114.8
460.6375	Fire -mobile repeater	KD46628	114.8
465.6375	Fire -mobile repeater	KD46628	114.8
465.625	Fire -mobiles	KCD845	
37.940	Highway Department	expired	CSQ

154.995	Building Department	WNLZ766	CSQ
47.740	Water Department	KVG654	CSQ
451.1625	Water Dept. Tank Sensors	KB91848	210.7
39.880	Youth Forestry Camp	KSZ658	CSQ
151.325R	Nickerson Park (159.42 in)	WNYI895	
464.9125	Ocean Edge Condos	KB78514	110.9

* Mobile PL = 110.9.

Bridgewater
484.7875	Police "J" (PLC)	KAB237	203.5
482.6125	Police -E/W Bridgewater	KAB237	203.5
33.720	Fire (2/3)	KCB281	203.5
33.980	Fire -Taunton tie	KCB281	203.5
460.5125	Fire -link for 33.720	KCB281	203.5
465.5125	Fire -link for 33.720	KCB281	203.5
37.180	Highway Department	KFR604	203.5
483.9375	State College Campus PD	WII458	203.5
153.905	State College Maintenance	KSR983	
472.6125	State Hospital	WIK218	210.7

Brimfield
154.445R	Police/Fire	KUV641	94.8
158.880	Police/Fire -repeater input	KUV641	94.8
158.880	Police/Fire -secondary	KUV641	82.5
33.460	Fire/Amb. (N.B. Disp.) (11)	KCF790	131.8
158.880	Highway Department	KUV641	114.8

Brockton
482.7125	Police "B" (PLC)	KAB240	203.5
482.8625	Police -secondary	KAB240	203.5
482.3875M	Police -F5-	KAB240	203.5
154.310	Fire (SE)	KNBH632	203.5
153.890	Fire -fireground/FA maint.	KNBH632	203.5
33.420	Fire -old channel/training	KNBH632	203.5
453.325	Highway/Water Depts.	KRL401	192.8
453.575	Housing Authority	WXY577	192.8
155.835	Civil Defense	KUV538	
472.5375	B.A.T. Transit	WRE287	192.8
155.925	B.A.T. Transit	WRE287	192.8
484.1125	Westgate Mall -F1-	KNR858	136.5
484.9875	Westgate Mall -F2-	KNR858	136.5
154.515	Cardinal Cushing Hospital	KNCD205	203.5
155.400	Brockton Hospital	WNJR234	
469.3125	Massasoit Cmmty. College	WNRM730	
464.3125	Massasoit Cmmty. College	WNRM730	
151.925	Explorer Post 701	WPEZ495	
461.0375	Holiday Inn	WPCJ461	
469.3125	Massasoit Cmmty. College	WNRM730	

Brookfield
155.310	Police/Ambulance	KYK309	131.8
33.620	Fire/So. Worcester Net	KNEN321	131.8
45.520	Public Works Department		CSQ

Brookline

471.0125	Police (BAPw)	KUJ724	131.8
483.4375	Fire (13)	WIE734	131.8
151.055	Highway Department	WNAW987	110.9
151.055	Water Department	WNAW987	CSQ
463.325	Brookline High School	KD23053	
463.9125	Brookline High School	KD23053	
463.350	The Country Club	WNDB857	
466.3125	The Country Club	WNXH489	
151.865	The Brook House	WNVV287	
462.125	Hampton Place	KD27173	
151.895	1200 Beacon St. Hotel	KYZ493	
469.375	Bournewood Hospital	KNER645	
461.650	Dexter School	WNWH891	
462.0625	Hebrew College	WPCS364	
151.835	Hellenic College	WPDG672	
464.925	Pine Manor College	WNMB490	D-365

Buckland

39.160	Police (FRC)	WNRT477	141.3
39.080	Police -F3-	WNRT477	141.3
460.0875	Police -mobile repeater	WNRT477	141.3
465.0875	Police -mobile repeater	WNRT477	141.3
33.540	Fire/Tri-State Net (9)	KNCL523	123.0
460.5875	Fire -mobile repeater	WNUG355	123.0
465.5875	Fire -mobile repeater	WNUG355	123.0
153.920	Highway Department	KA81958	141.3

Burlington

482.4875	Police (NEM)	KYL886	146.2
483.3625	Fire (6/13)	WIJ384	131.8
154.340	Fire -old freq./area tie	KAX310	CSQ
156.240	Highway Department	KBA744	CSQ
155.085	Civil Defense	KNIH674	127.3
153.875R	No. Shore Emergency Net	KNIH674	127.3
155.220	Emergency Management	WNAV485	
154.600	School Department	KA57041	
464.375	New England Exec. Park	WNCS371	
463.425	Marriott Hotel	KNEL339	
464.825	Burlington Mall	WNMK701	D-734

Cambridge

470.3125	Police (BAPn)	WIE468	131.8
471.3125	Police -Tac 5- secondary	WIE468	131.8
154.355	Fire -simulcasts 800 MHz	KNEQ454	146.2
854.4875	Fire -fireground #16	KNEQ454	D-125
852.2625	Fire -fireground #14	KNEQ454	D-125
856-60.787*	Fire/other city services	WNGH670	D-125
153.830	Fire -fireground/area tie	KNEQ454	
155.085	City Paging	KNEG753	
159.135	City Paging/Cemetery Dept.	KNEK313	CSQ
158.250	Cambridge Electric Light	KCB850	131.8

153.515	Cambridge Electric Light	KCB850	Data
456.1375	Cambridge Electric Light	KCB850	131.8
453.9375	City Golf Course Sprinklers	WPCI641	Data
471.0625	Harvard U. Campus Police	KFN287	131.8
463.850	Harvard University	WNJD225	141.3
484.0625	Harvard University	WIG358	136.5
484.8125	Harvard Fogg Art Museum	WIG424	107.2
461.200	Harvard Coop Society	KLK788	146.2
484.1875	Radcliffe College	KXN407	127.3
484.2625	Radcliffe College	KFN287	127.3
464.675	JFK School of Government	WNYC256	
472.5375	M.I.T. Campus Police	KZA726	131.8
461.250	M.I.T. Services	KWG774	173.8
461.575	M.I.T. Services	KRW863	85.4
462.7625	M.I.T. Services	WPFA764	
464.3625	M.I.T. Services	WPFA764	
464.825	Lesley College	KNFP774	127.3
464.325	Whitehead Institute	WNYF647	88.5
33.400	Buckingham Brown & Nichols	WPDY834	67.0
464.4375	Galleria Mall Security	WNSN358	D-664
464.875	Cambridge Marriott	WNGL366	146.2
464.975	Cambridge Marriott	WNGL366	
463.375	Hyatt Regency	WPBB615	
154.570	Hyatt Regency	KQ2835	
464.650	Sheraton Hotel	WNAT851	
154.515	Sonesta Hotel	KNIS532	67.0
154.540	Sonesta Hotel	KIX513	67.0
463.600	Mt. Auburn Hospital	WNBL309	167.9
154.540	Sancta Maria Hospital	KNDB402	
463.9375	Athenaeum Group	KD39231	
464.825	River Front Office Park	WNRE353	

* Fire & City Services Trunked Frequencies:
853.2625, 856.7875, 857.7875, 858.7875, 859.7875, 860.7875

Canton
471.6625	Police	(BAPs)	KZN838	131.8
453.525	Fire		WNZR387	D-051
465.5125	Fire -fireground		reported	D-051
33.500	Fire -old main/reg. (4/SE)		WSZ316	CSQ
458.0625	Fire -33.50 mobile rptr.		reported	136.5
453.875	Highway Department		KSQ423	136.5
156.060R	Highway Department		WNHH273	
154.600	Blue Hills Regional School		KN9990	

Carlisle
154.830	Police	WQL891	107.2
155.010	Police -area tie	WQL891	107.2
33.660	Fire/No. Middlesex Net	KCF311	CSQ
33.440	Fire -secondary	KCF311	CSQ
46.500	Fire -tie to Concord area	KCF311	CSQ
156.105	Highway Department	KNIY669	107.2
153.905	School Department	WNDZ408	100.0

Carver
483.3625	Police "D1" (PLC)	KZV262	203.5
33.440	Fire (2)	KCA661	203.5
39.160	Emergency Management	& GMRS	
155.880	Public Schools Transport	WNHU903	D-023

Charlemont
39.160	Police "7" (FRC)	KZT531	141.3
453.5125	Police -mobile repeater	KD22636	141.3
33.540	Fire/Tri-State Net (9)	KWE619	123.0
33.780	Fire/Tri-State Net	reported	
151.010	Public Works/Fire backup	WNLN399	127.3

Charlton
155.070R	Police	KCB296	114.8
158.790	Police -input to repeater	KCB296	114.8
33.620	Fire/So. Worcester Net	KCD975	131.8
156.105	Highway Department	KRX815	173.8

Chatham
155.640	Police "FOX" (BAR)	KCA368	110.9
155.115	Police -mobiles	KEF953	151.4
33.620	Fire -Main Station (1)	KCD594	114.8
33.620	Fire -South Station	KRG649	114.8
155.115	Highway & Sewer Depts.	WRG854	151.4
155.115	Emergency Management	KEF953	151.4
47.740	Water Department	KUD797	CSQ
451.575	Water Department	WPED481	

Chelmsford
482.5125	Police "703" (NEM)	KEF703	146.2
155.700	Police -backup/auxiliary	KAA370	192.8
33.660	Fire/No. Middlesex Net	KCF310	CSQ
33.760	Fire -secondary	KCF310	CSQ
155.835	Water Department	KNFM345	CSQ
156.225	Highway Department	WNDI466	192.8
156.045	Highway Department-supv.	WNDL466	192.8
158.805	Cemetery Department	WNSX406	192.8
45.520	Elderly Transport	KYJ327	127.3
173.350	N. Chelmsford Water	WNBX977	127.3
461.275	High School	KD30509	
469.5625	McCarthy Middle School	KD53486	
469.8625	McCarthy Middle School	KD53486	
464.925	Lighthouse School	KD29289	
47.620	Merrimack Valley Ed Ctr.	WNPW553	110.9

Chelsea
470.8875	Police (BAPn)	KZR406	131.8
471.2375	Housing Authority Police	WIG960	141.3
154.325	Fire (13)	KDD985	114.8
153.830	Fire -fireground	KDD985	114.8
155.745	DPW/CD/Electric/Schools	KLE837	151.4

153.875R	No. Shore Emergency Net	KNBV916	127.3
151.805	Soldier's Home	reported	167.9
154.570	Williams School	WPCP780	
461.075	Mystic Mall	WNHU837	107.2

Cheshire
154.740	Berkshire Cty. PD Net	KX4859	107.2
154.415	Fire (12)	KNBU762	107.2
151.070	Highway Department	WNAG896	107.2

Chester
39.500	Police/Highway Dept.	KYU933	CSQ
33.460	Fire/Hampden County Net	KCH549	CSQ

Chesterfield
154.115	Police/Municipal Services	KNAG226	127.3
154.370	Fire/Hampshire Cty. Net	KCM620	127.3

Chicopee
155.490R	Police (WEM)	KCA996	141.3
158.910	Police -input to repeater	KCA996	141.3
158.805	Police records/backup	KYF300	141.3
154.160R	Fire -F1- dispatch	KDQ358	141.3
158.865	Fire -F1- repeater input	KD29332	141.3
154.340	Fire -F2- fireground	KDQ358	141.3
154.160M	Fire -F3- talkaround	KDQ358	141.3
154.280	Fire -F4- area intercity	WNND402	82.5
456.700	Fire link to Blandford	WOV78	131.8
154.995	Highway Department	KNHE476	141.3
37.660	Chicopee Light Company	KCA936	94.8
37.680	Chicopee Light Company	KCA936	94.8
158.805	Civil Prep./Auxiliary PD	KYF300	141.3
154.570	Public Schools Dept.	KB36930	D-143
154.600	Public Schools Dept.	KB36930	D-143
453.600	County Animal Control	WNHT950	131.8
464.425	Housing Authority	WNQR324	141.3
464.575	Fairfield Mall	WNLW825	88.5
469.575	Fairfield Mall	WNLW825	88.5
468.2625	Our Lady of the Elms Coll.	KD36955	
154.570	Chicopee Country Club		CSQ

Clarksburg
154.740	Police (BER)	WQF451	107.2
155.055	Police -car to car	WQF451	
154.310	Fire/Berkshire Cty. Net	KJU245	107.2
153.980	Public Works Department	WNFA523	

Clinton
37.100	Police -F1- dispatch	KNEN299	118.8
37.340	Police -F2- mobiles	KNEN299	CSQ
154.310	Fire (8)	KCH246	82.5

153.830	Fire -fireground	KCH246	
46.580	Highway/Elder Transport	KNFW450	141.3
453.2625	Housing Authority	WNNG536	118.8
155.745	MEMA Area III Net	WNXS673	100.0
154.570	Clinton Hospital	KB83527	

Cohasset
482.9875	Police "R4"	(PLC)	KNR436	203.5
154.265	Fire	(SE)	KNFW924	203.5
154.190	Fire -regional		KNFW924	203.5
153.830	Fire -fireground		KNFW924	203.5
153.875	DPW, Parks, CD, Fire tie		WQG897	

Colrain
39.160	Police "8" (FRC)	KNCG512	141.3
33.920	Fire	WNLY226	
33.540	Fire/Tri-State Net (9)	KCE879	123.0
460.5125R	Fire -mobile repeater	KCE879	123.0
151.025	Highway Department	KNDJ506	123.0

Concord
482.3375	Police (NEM/SOM)	WIK795	146.2
155.010	Police -area tie	KCA685	107.2
155.100	Police -secondary	KCA685	107.2
483.5375	Fire	WIJ880	D-054
483.7125	Fire -future regional	WIJ880	250.3
46.500	Fire -F1- area net (6/14)	KNBP838	100.0
46.400	Fire -F2- secondary	KNBP838	100.0
155.100	DPW/Water/Light/PD -F2-	KBS973	107.2
151.625	Light Dept. -wire pulling	reported	
155.775	Council on Aging	expired	107.2
153.875R	Civil Defense	WNEB984	127.3
164.425	Minuteman National Park	KCA724-30	CSQ
482.4375	Regional School Buses	KNO928-9	D-116
151.625	Concord Schools	reported	
154.570	Concord Area Special Ed	WPFD993	
154.600	Concord Area Special Ed	WPFD993	
464.5375	Middlesex School	KD34074	71.9
464.5125	Concord Academy	reported	136.5
461.100	Emerson Hospital	WNYX653	
462.700	SpotNet	KAE4366	114.8

Emerson Hospital: Med channels 1, 4, 5 and 7   167.9

Conway
39.160	Police "9" (FRC)	KZU980	141.3
33.540	Fire/Tri-State Net (9)	KMA859	123.0
159.120	Highway Department	KNDD852	141.3

Cummington
154.845	Police	WQA819-20	127.3
154.370	Fire/Hampshire Cty. Net	WXT896	127.3
156.060	Highway Department	KNDD852	CSQ

154.540	Swift River Inn	WNYG771	
154.600	Shire Village Camp	KD20804	

Dalton
154.875	Police (BEC)	KXQ866	107.2
153.815	Fire	KDO270	107.2
154.310	Fire/Berkshire Cty. Net	KCD784	107.2
45.800	Highway Department	KEV474	167.9
33.080	Central Berkshire School	WNLP981	

Danvers
472.3125	Police (BAPn)	KED938	131.8
483.3375	Fire (5/13)	WIG837	131.8
46.120	Fire -backup/training	KCI243	
45.640	Highway Department	KAZ872	CSQ
47.800	Water/Electric Depts.	KCI244	CSQ
45.600	Council on Aging	WNSD953	CSQ
155.715	Lyons Amb.-Hunt Hospital	KNDM207	127.3
153.875R	No. Shore Emergency Net	reported	127.3
30.800	St. John's Prep High	WNLZ753	
155.325	State Hospital	KYT276	
154.570	State Hospital	KB82395	
155.880	Police to Liberty Tree Mall	KUN453	CSQ
464.950	Liberty Tree Mall Security	WNBR769	D-546
463.950	N. Shore Community College	WPFE860	
464.6875	Marriott Hotel	KD47008	

Dartmouth
155.250R	Police (BRC)	KCA937	85.4
155.595	Police -input to repeater	KCA937	85.4
155.475	Police -regional/backup	KCA937	
46.180	Fire -Headquarters	KCC952	CSQ
46.180	Fire -N. Dartmouth Station	KTV678	CSQ
46.180	Fire -District #1 -primary	KCC452	CSQ
46.340	Fire -District #1 -fireground	KCC452	CSQ
46.180	Fire -District #2	KNFF850	CSQ
46.180	Fire -District #3	KCC922	CSQ
46.340	Fire -Town fireground	WNVN328	
453.5375	Fire -mobile repeater	KCC452	
458.5375	Fire -mobile repeater	KCC452	
155.025	Highway Department	KFZ749	167.9
158.745	Public Works Department	WNXC444	
453.9125	Municipal Services	WNXC444	
33.400	School Department	KB86214	
154.965	SE Mass Univ. -Security	KTY961	97.4
153.905	SE Mass University	WPED307	
152.480	Southeastern MA Univ.	KNFR583	

Dedham

470.9625	Police/Sheriff (BAPs)	KZN841	131.8
155.580	Police -auxiliary/detectives	KMK948	151.4
158.850	Police -auxiliary/detectives	KMK948	151.4
153.950	Fire	KCH551	CSQ
861-5.6125	Public Works Department	KNIS502	CSQ
861-5.2625	Public Works Department	trunked	CSQ
154.600	Dedham High School	KB83511	
464.825	Noble & Greenough School	WPFA552	
451.200	Dedham Water Company	WNZI268	118.8
464.550	Dedham Mall		D-306

Deerfield

39.160	Police "10" (FRC)	KZU981	141.3
33.540	Fire/Tri-State Net	KNEU520	123.0
33.540	Fire -So. Deerfield Station	KBB990	123.0
33.480	Fire -secondary (9)	KNEU520	123.0
156.225	Highway Department	KNDT811	162.2
155.940	So. Deerfield Water Dist.	WPAC860	
151.895	Deerfield Academy -maint.	KRN459	71.9
463.3625	Deerfield Academy -sec.	KRN459	179.9

Dennis

155.985	Police "ITEM" (BAR)	KYY951	110.9
33.860	Fire -Main Station (1)	KCD492	114.8
33.860	Fire -North Station	KCG831	114.8
453.5125	Fire -Fire Alarm TX link	KCD492	210.7
458.5125	Fire -Apparatus TX link	KCD492	114.8
37.900	Highway Department	WNAE320	CSQ
154.980	Town Admin./Beach Patrol	WNGN297	CSQ
155.805	Council on Aging	WNML833	D-025
155.805	Town Golf Course	WNIM717	D-025
155.805	Housing Authority	WNVU916	103.5
453.575	Cty. Elderly Transport B-Bus	WFE629	141.3
47.740	Water Department	KCF328	CSQ

Dighton

483.5875	Police (BRC)	KZM470	203.5
482.3375	Police -Smrst/Swansea tie	KZM470	203.5
46.180	Fire -Headquarters	KNDU339	CSQ
46.180	Fire -Communication Ctr.	KNDU338	CSQ
46.180	Fire -North Fire Station	KNDU337	CSQ
460.6375	Fire -mobile repeater	KNDU337	
465.6375	Fire -mobile repeater	KNDU337	
45.280	Public Works Department	KFV834	107.2
45.280	Water District	KNCJ918	107.2

Douglas

39.600	Police	KCB775	110.9
39.980	Police -regional network	KCB775	118.8
33.620	Fire/Tower/So. Worc. Net	KAY985	131.8
37.920	Highway Department	KXG854	100.0

Dover
155.310	Police	KCG758	167.9
33.500	Fire (4)	KCA303	CSQ
150.995	Highway Department	KCF978	131.8
45.960	School Department	KIL305	
154.540	Regional School District	WNDE541	

Dracut
482.8875	Police (NEM)	KYR953	146.2
482.4625	Police -Methuen tie	KYR953	146.2
155.415	Police -backup- unused	KTC808	
154.400	Fire (6)	KCB745	146.2
154.205	Fire -mobile tie to Lowell	reported	186.2
155.055	Highway Department	KFT496	107.2

Dudley
155.430	Police	KCC416	179.9
154.340	Fire	WNGM830	127.3
33.620	Fire/So. Worcester Net	KCH427	131.8
159.105	Highway Department	KNIJ417	
151.775	Nichols College	WNJR829	
154.570	Nichols College	KB212389	

Dunstable
155.580R	Police "5"	KB30201	151.4
154.680	Police -input to repeater	KB30201	151.4
155.475	Police -secondary/regional	KB30201	151.4
39.420	Police -area network	KB30201	CSQ
33.660	Fire/No. Middlesex Net	KJS918	CSQ
150.995	Highway Department	WNIQ944	
45.520	Ambulance/Pepperell tie	reported	141.3

Duxbury
482.4125	Police "01" (PLC)	KZU624	203.5
482.4625	Police -Kingston tie	KZU624	203.5
33.480	Fire (2/SE)	KCA351	203.5
33.480	Fire -Ashdod Station	KJZ993	203.5
460.575	Fire -new channel	WPFD963	
155.775	Public Works Department	KNBW697	CSQ
47.540	Duxbury Beach Park	KNEQ201	

East Bridgewater
482.6125	Police "J1" (PLC)	KZV264	203.5
33.720	Fire (2/SE)	KCC350	203.5
153.980	Highway/Police-Fire tie	WNHS444	CSQ

East Brookfield
45.820	Police	KYO334	CSQ
453.5375	Police -mobile repeater	KYO334	
33.620	Fire/So. Worcester Net	KCF803	131.8

Eastham
155.640	Police "DAVID" (BAR)	KCB710	110.9
33.820	Fire (1)	KCD574	114.8
45.840	Public Works Department	KNAU486	CSQ
155.820	Building Department	WPAK831	
151.955	Nauset Regional Schools	WNRM911	

Easthampton
460.025	Police (WEM)	KCB230	173.8
460.125M	Police -tactical operations	KCB230	173.8
853.5625	Police -mobile data	reported	DATA
154.415	Fire (10)	KCH431	127.3
158.760	Highway Department	KNIT776	179.9
153.875	Council on Aging	KNGR879	100.0
464.475	Williston-Northampton Schl.	WNML906	

East Longmeadow
155.550R	Police (WEM)	KVP496	114.8
158.925	Police -input to repeater	KVP496	114.8
155.475	Police -regional	KVP496	
155.760	Fire/Municipal Svc. (11)	KCH462	114.8
153.830	Fire -fireground	KUB896	
159.105	Highway Department	KNHZ593	114.8

Easton
852.2875	Police -operations	WNMY548	D-026
807.2875	Police -car to car	WNMY548	D-026
155.730	Police -old area net	KCF692	CSQ
33.580	Fire -Station #1 (4/SE)	KCA627	107.2
33.580	Fire -Station #2	KCG574	107.2
33.500	Fire -regional net	KCA627	107.2
453.925	Highway Department	KNBF359	156.7
153.875	Municipal Svcs./C.D.	WNIL344	
155.205	Public Schools Transit	WPAN840	
462.125	Stonehill College	KXK823	
464.375	Stonehill College	WNRV922	
151.715	So. Easton Vo-Tech	KSR296	
154.570	Easton Country Club	KD47317	

Egremont
154.740	Berkshire County PD Net	KX4870	107.2
154.310	Fire/Berkshire County Net	KX4870	107.2
156.120	Highway Department	WNFM317	

Erving
39.160	Police "11" (FRC)	KNDR814	141.3
453.3875	Police -mobile repeater	KD23941	141.3
33.540	Fire/Tri-State Net (9)	KCE564	123.0
33.640	Fire -Montague tie	KCE564	
39.180	Highway Department	KB53538	141.3

Essex

155.820	Police/Fire/Muncipal (5)	KCI370	CSQ
155.895	Police -limited use	reported	CSQ
156.165	Highway Department	WNPP725	CSQ
151.835	Cape Ann Golf Course	WNSO247	

Everett

470.8125	Police (BAPn)	KZR400	131.8
154.310	Fire (13)	KCH424	107.2
153.830	Fire -fireground	KCH424	CSQ
154.265	Fire -fireground/training	KCH424	
155.805	Highway & Wire Depts.	KLY958	156.7
153.875R	No. Shore Emergency Net	KNIB536	127.3
464.825	Whidden Memorial Hosp.	WYT418	

Fairhaven

482.8125	Police (BRC)	KZM463	203.5
46.180	Fire -Washington St. (3)	KCB836	CSQ
46.180	Fire -Adams St. Station	KTK784	CSQ
46.180	Fire -East Fairhaven Sta.	KTY971	CSQ
460.5375	Fire -mobile repeater	WPAV858	
465.5375	Fire -mobile repeater	WPAV858	
39.820	DPW/CD/Water/Dog Offcr.	KCA703	136.5
39.980	Civil Defense -old ch.	KD43120	136.5
464.125	School Department	WPET520	

Fall River

482.3625	Police (BRC)	KWJ364	203.5
482.6875	Police -secondary	KWJ364	203.5
482.3125	Police -detectives	KWJ364	203.5
33.820	Fire (3)	KCB275	CSQ
33.740	Fire -administration	KCB275	CSQ
46.180	Fire -F2- Bristol County	KNFF610	CSQ
154.400	Fire -mobiles	WPEE272	
482.4375	Housing Authority	WIG414	127.3
482.4375	School Dept./Misc. Svcs.	KNO479	118.8
453.525	Municipal Services	WNVN492	
453.375	Municipal Services	KRO335	
458.425	Municipal Services	KRO335	
461.200	School Buses	KNFB649	88.5
156.225	Highway Department	KJW540	CSQ
155.775	Council on Aging	KMA465	110.9
47.840	Water Department	KFC332	
37.100	Wastewater Plant	KNAY949	
464.850	Community Development	WSA795	
44.460	SE Regional Transport	KKD355	136.5
44.460	SE Regional Transport	KKD355	186.2
464.775	Bristol Community College	KO8985	
464.0125	Bristol Community College	WPAK679	
464.850	Project Headstart	WSZ240	
453.5125	Corrigan Reg. Health Ctr.	KD41053	
458.5125	Corrigan Reg. Health Ctr.	KD41053	

Falmouth

855.4625	Police	WNNP305	D-445
33.780	Fire -Headquarters (1)	KCD244	114.8
33.780	Fire -East Station	WXY444	114.8
33.780	Fire -West Station	WXY445	114.8
33.780	Fire -North Station	WXY446	114.8
72.640	Fire -Fire Alarm Boxes	WNPA551	CSQ
153.860	Fire -Fire Alarm Maint./Adm.	KAW742	CSQ
153.860	Housing Authority	KNGN956	
37.940	Highway Department	KNIR366	
46.520	Water District	KSM898	
47.740	Water District	KCF290	
155.235	Public Schools Transit	WNFA502	
453.575	Elder Transport	WYC873	141.3
156.350	Steamship Authority	marine	CSQ
155.175	Washburn Island Preserve	KNBU348	
151.805	Seacrest Resort Center	WPDY733	
154.570	Seacrest Resort Center	WPDY733	
154.600	Seacrest Resort Center	WPDY733	

Barnstable County Fair

464.325	Fire/Ambulance	110.9
464.025	Parking/Security	110.9
461.775	Administration	110.9
154.570	Concessions	
151.625	Concessions	
151.625	Billy Burr's Fun-O-Rama	DPL

Fitchburg

453.425	Police	KNAF257	186.2
154.250	Fire (8)	KNJX299	192.8
154.175	Fire -F2- administration	KNJX299	192.8
460.6125	Fire -mobile extender	KNJX299	151.4
33.800	Fire -Mid State Fireground	WPAB671	
33.940	Fire -Mid State Fireground	WPAB671	
45.600	Highway Department	KBS469	CSQ
153.740	School Department	KKO864	
155.745	Civil Defense	WNBD952	192.8
155.355	Burbank Hospital ALS		192.8
453.5875	Water Treatment Plant	WNUQ215	192.8
453.800	MART -Buses/School Buses	KNBY247	107.2
453.800	MART -Elder Vans	KNBY247	127.3
453.0125	Airport Operations	KD46329	123.0
458.0125	Airport Operations	KD46329	123.0
453.200	Fitchburg State College	WNHH206	173.8
451.125	Fitchburg Gas & Electric	WNNC445	110.9
154.540	Montachusett Reg. Vo-Tech	WQO340	

Florida

154.710	Police -F1-	KNAK487	107.2
154.740	Police -F2- Berkshire Cty.	KNAK487	107.2
154.310	Fire/Berkshire Cty. Net	KNCW959	107.2
151.130	Highway Department	WRB839	107.2

Foxboro

Freq	Description	Call	Tone
471.1375	Police (BAPs)	KCA855	103.5
471.2375M	Police -secondary	KCA855	131.8
471.2375	Police -detectives	KCA855	103.5
484.6625	Fire	WIK835	D-023
33.500	Fire -regional (4/SE)	KCF297	
33.460	Fire -Mansfield tie	reported	CSQ
72.580	Fire -Alarm boxes	WBG480	CSQ
460.6125R	Fire -Low Band mob. rptr.	reported	100.0
45.760	Highway Department	KLV944	
154.600	New England Raceway	KA35487	
154.570	Normandy Family Camp	KB46890	
461.1375	Day's Inn Hotel	KD26085	
464.9375	Courtyard by Marriott	KD48659	

Foxboro-New England Patriots/Stadium

Freq	Description	Call	Tone
464.950	Security -F1-		D-132
464.775	Security -F2-		
464.725	Management Staff		
463.7375	Miscellaneous Use		
463.7625	Miscellaneous Use		
154.600	Miscellaneous Use	KA77940	
154.570	Operations -channel #1	KA77940	
154.625	Operations -channel #2	KA77940	
800 MHz	State Police System/National Tactical Freqs.		

Framingham

Freq	Description	Call	Tone
471.7625	Police (BAPw)	WIG750	131.8
39.380	Police -So. Middlesex Net	KCA458	123.0
483.7625	Fire -F1- dispatch (14)	WII729	114.8
483.7625	Fire -F2- backup rptr	WII729	167.9
483.7625	Fire -F3- simplex	WII729	CSQ
483.5875	Fire -F4- fireground	WII729	CSQ
33.560	Fire Prevention/Maint/.CD	KCC457	CSQ
33.020	Highway Department	KLY299	136.5
151.685	School Department	WXH204	210.7
453.4125	Housing Authority	reported	210.7
151.955	LIFT Vans	reported	91.5
155.985	Inter-department/Inactive	KLE838	CSQ
155.340	Ambulance to Hospital	KTZ460	CSQ
151.805	So. Middlesex Reg. VoTech	WNCK399	
155.055	Framingham State -Security	KAG378	77.0
153.860	Framingham State -Maint.	reported	77.0
461.600	Shopper's World (disc.)	KJR756	110.9
154.570	Framingham Mall	WNYI878	CSQ
154.600	Framingham Mall	WNYI878	CSQ

Franklin

Freq	Description	Call	Tone
39.420	Police -F1- "F"	KCA462	123.0
39.200	Police -F2- secondary	KCA462	123.0
33.540	Fire (4)	KCY582	CSQ
159.015	Highway Department	WNKN336	162.2

154.515	Dean Jr. College	WPBB556	D-423
154.570	Dean Jr. College	KN5363	CSQ
464.325	Dean Jr. College	KNDW672	D-155
464.375	Dean Jr. College	KNHL574	D-731

Freetown

483.5875	Police -F1- Primary	WIJ239	203.5
482.5125	Police -F2- Bristol Cty. Net	WIJ239	203.5
482.3875	Police -F3- Car to car	WIJ239	203.5
482.3375	Police -F4- Area tie	WIJ239	203.5
482.8875	Police -F5- Plymouth Cty.	WIJ239	203.5
482.4875	Police -F6- Area tie	WIJ239	203.5
482.5375	Police -F7- Area tie	WIJ239	203.5
482.8125	Police -F8- Area tie	WIJ239	203.5
46.180	Fire/Bristol County Net	KCG726	CSQ
460.625	Fire -inactive	WNNT775	
45.280	DPW/Schools/Bldgs./C.D.	KIB971	118.8

Gardner

155.730	Police	KNGX461	192.8
154.130	Fire (8)	KCB308	192.8
154.355	Fire -fireground	KCB308	192.8
159.165	Highway Department	KCE897	179.9
156.165	Public Works Department	WPEX802	
154.055	Housing Authority	WZU918	
453.850	Montachusett Transport	WNAA584	100.0/110.9
155.295	Woods Ambulance	WNXJ533	192.8
155.805R	MCI Gardner Prison	KNCP300	192.8
154.965R	Mt. Wachusett College	KWZ773	192.8

Georgetown

154.710	Police	KFN667	210.7
154.010	Fire (15)	KCD690	CSQ
155.040	Fireground/PD 19/Elder Vans	WNKT388	156.7
45.680	Highway Department	KTC861	

Gill

39.160	Police "12" (FRC)	KZU984	141.3
460.0375R	Police -mobile repeater	WNWX712	141.3
155.985	Police Mobiles/Highways	KT8398	91.5
33.540	Fire/Tri-State Net (9)	KJE253	123.0

Gloucester

471.5875	Police (BAPn)	WIK792	118.8
155.550	Police -old channel	KNFJ319	127.3
154.830	Police -mobiles	KNFJ319	127.3
154.160	Fire (5)	KNCN367-70	127.3
155.775	Housing Authority	KNBD921	127.3
154.980	Highway Department	KDZ446	151.4
153.875R	No. Shore Emergency Net	WQS284	127.3
151.745	School Department	WNRX279	
155.220	Cape Ann CD Council	WNBW691	127.3

155.295	New England Beach Patrol	WZY302	
472.7625	Cape Ann Transit Authority	WIG344	

Goshen
154.115	Police -F1- operations	KAR947	127.3
154.055	Police -F2- secondary	KAR947	127.3
154.370	Fire -F1- ops./county	WXP638	127.3
154.190	Fire -F2- ambulance	WXP638	127.3
154.115	Fire -F3- police tie/DPW	KAR947	127.3
154.310	Fire -F4- Berkshire Cty.	KQI374	107.2

Grafton
45.100	Police "G" (WOR2)	WNQW338	167.9
45.400	Fire (7)	KAS759	167.9
153.485	Water Department	WNUH273	123.0
151.955	Job Corps Center -F1-	WNDK429	D-205
151.625	Job Corps Center -F2-	WNDK429	D-205
461.6625R	Tufts Veterinary School	KD28825	192.8
463.325	Tufts Veterinary School		192.8

Granby
155.250	Police (WEM)	WQJ319	114.8
155.040	Fire/DPW/School/PD (10)	KDT390	114.8
151.040	Highway Department	WPBA599	114.8

Granville
39.180	Police/Fire/Municipal	KDX307	141.3
33.520	Fire (11)	KTZ509	114.8
33.940	Fire -secondary, CT tie	reported	CSQ
154.310	Fire -Berkshire County tie	reported	

Great Barrington
155.775	Police -F1- (BER)	WNPS475	107.2
154.785	Police -F2-	KXH270	
154.310	Fire -F2- /Berkshire Cty. Net	WNPQ624	107.2
155.760	Fire -F1- /Highway Dept.	KBA482	
458.175	So. Berkshire Vol. Amb.	KA34410	
157.620	Simmons Rock College	KB43944	
173.225	Berkshire Eagle	reported	D-114
154.515	Butternut Basin Ski Area	KNDY699	
155.175	Butternut Basin Ski Area	KNEA839	
155.220	Butternut Basin Ski Area	KNEA839	
155.340	Butternut Basin Ski Area	KNEA839	

Greenfield
156.330	Police (FRC)	KCB221	151.4
156.030	Police -secondary	KCB221	151.4
39.160	Police -regional/Cty. Jail	KCB221	141.3
33.700	Fire "13" (9)	KCB884	CSQ
33.700	Fire -Brookside Station	KSJ335	CSQ
33.540	Tri-State Mutual Aid #1	KCE358	123.0
33.480	Tri-State Mutual Aid #2	KCE358	123.0

33.840	Tri-State Mutual Aid	WNVY938	123.0
453.925	Housing Authority	WNKQ412	103.5
155.805	Highway Department	KRR965	141.3
155.115	Municipal Services	WNMV687	CSQ
453.400	Franklin County Jail	WPDQ325	141.3
458.5875	Franklin County Jail	WPDQ325	141.3
464.825	Community College	KNDX296	
44.540	County Transit	KDC248	141.3
44.460	Greenfield-Montague Transit	KNAJ388	136.5
155.385	Mercy Ambulance	WZV430	136.5

Groton
155.580R	Police "1"	WSB835	151.4
154.680	Police -input to repeater	WSB835	151.4
155.475	Police -F4- sec./regional	WSB835	151.4
39.420	Police -area network	KCA580	CSQ
155.130	Police -tactical	reported	
153.860	Fire -shared with DPW	KCH423	151.4
46.140	Fire -regional tie	KAP589-90	CSQ
33.660	Fire -North Middlesex tie	KE7235	CSQ
154.055R	Ambulance/Rescue	KNAI426	151.4
155.985	Amb./Rescue -input to rptr.	KNAI426	151.4
153.860	Groton Electric Light/FD	KNGD353	151.4
154.570	Groton School	KB23728	151.4

Groveland
154.710	Police	KAW496	131.8
154.010	Fire (15)	KCF251	CSQ
156.195	Highway Department	KTN328	
153.620	Town Power	KJN976	

Hadley
155.415	Police (WEM)	KNJP772	127.3
158.940	Police -mobiles	KNJP772	127.3
154.100	Police -secondary	WNKQ575	127.3
33.540	Fire/Tri-State Net (9)	KBF372	123.0
154.370	Fire/Hampshire Cty. Net	KBF372	127.3
154.100	Highway Department	WNKQ575	156.7
158.820	So. Hadley Water District	WZW243	
461.8125	Hampshire Mall	WNZD671	D-245

Halifax
482.7875	Police "T2" (PLC)	KZV266	203.5
33.760	Fire (2)	KCL540	203.5
39.500	Highway/C.D./Water/Dog	KUE518	

Hamilton
155.940	Police/Fire/Highway (5)	KCH523	127.3
156.000	Fire -F2- secondary	KCH523	127.3
156.180	Highway Department	WNNW364	
153.875R	No. Shore Emergency Net	KNAL776	127.3
154.570	Kinsley School -F1-	reported	

154.600	Kinsley School -F2-	reported	
461.8125	Gordon Conwell Seminary	KB79216	
461.275	Gordon Conwell Seminary	KNFB551	

Hampden
154.800	Police	(WEM)	KGW688	141.3
33.520	Fire	(11)	KCE779	CSQ
151.025	Highway Department		KNDL369	114.8

Hancock
154.740	Berkshire Cty. Police Net	KZF949	107.2
154.310	Fire/Berkshire Cty. Net	KNHG443	107.2

Jiminy Peak (KNIC960/WPCI829/WNIX737):
151.655, 151.745, 151.805, 151.865, 151.895, 151.925, 155.220, 155.235, 155.340

Hanover
482.5625	Police "Q1"	(PLC)	KZU621	203.5
33.960	Fire	(2)	KCH519	203.5
45.320	Highway Department		KBR216	162.2
45.320	Highway/Water Depts.		KNDW200-1	162.2
484.5625	Hanover Mall Security		WII295	203.5

Hanson
482.7875	Police "T1"	(PLC)	KZV267	203.5
33.800	Fire	(2/SE)	WNLY367	203.5
153.965	DPW/Water/Dog-Town Net		KXV523	
39.500	Municipal Services		KXV523	

Hardwick
39.100	Police/Ambulance	KKH283	85.4
154.650	Police -mobile repeater	KKH283	85.4
39.220	Police -area net/state tie	KTE739	CSQ
33.700	Fire/Mid-State Net	WQQ931	CSQ

Harvard
159.090R	Police/Ambulance	WQL932	107.2
154.785	Police -input to repeater	WQL932	107.2
37.100	Police -Bolton/Berlin tie	KB9831	CSQ
33.700	Fire/Mid-State Net	KCD523	CSQ
33.700	Fire/Mid-State Net	KFS979	CSQ
151.010	Highway Department	KUX251	CSQ

Harwich
155.520	Police "GEORGE"	(BAR)	KCA373	110.9
155.880	Police -F4-		WNHH855	110.9
33.960	Fire	(1)	KCD271	114.8
33.960	Fire -East Station		KCD271	114.8
37.940	Highway Department		KFD619	CSQ
155.880	Parks & Beaches		WNHH855	114.8

Hatfield

154.085	Police/Fire "15"	KJD424	127.3
154.370	Fire/Hampshire Cty. Net	KGD424	127.3
33.540	Fire/Tri-State Net tie		123.0

Haverhill

155.010	Police	KCA865	127.3
154.010	Fire (15)	KCA434	CSQ
154.445R	Fire -Lawrence tie	mobiles	100.0
154.385	Fire -Salem NH tie	mobiles	136.5
158.955R	Fire -Amesbury area tie	reported	203.5
151.085	Highway Department	KCG876	118.8
153.860	School Department	KVT798	151.4
154.600	High School	KA86805	
453.700	Merrimack Vlly. Trans-Buses	KNCP271	67.0
453.700	Merrimack Vlly. Trans-H/vans	KNCP271	114.8
158.940	Merrimack Transit	KNCP271	
469.775	Hale Hospital	KB70652	
158.760	No. Essex Community Coll.	WPAX830	
151.925	Bradford College	KEN955	
463.2125	Bradford College	KB77256	
154.515	Whittier Reg. Vocational	KCT728	

Hawley

39.160	Police (FRC)	KZU985	141.3
33.540	Fire/Tri-State Net (9)		123.0
154.370	Fire -Hampshire Cty. Net	WNVI267	127.3
154.025	Public Works Department	WNBV448	

Heath

39.160	Police "17" (FRC)	KZU986	141.3
39.080	Police -secondary/mobiles	WPAK259	141.3
453.4125	Police -mobile repeater	WPAK259	141.3
458.4125	Police -mobile repeater	WPAK259	141.3
33.540	Fire/Tri-State Net (9)	WRA389	123.0
154.010	Fire	WRA389	
156.120	Highway Department	WNBQ381	100.0

Hingham

484.4125	Police "R3" (PLC)	WIK257	203.5
482.9875	Police -area tie	KZV260	203.5
154.265	Fire -F1- ops. (SE)	KCA638	203.5
154.190	Fire -F2- area secondary	KCA638	203.5
153.830	Fire -F3- fireground	KCA638	203.5
37.260	Highway Department	KJB950	100.0
158.835	Sewer Department	KNCU926	100.0
155.025	School Department	KNGB989	
155.025	Emergency Management	WNMQ773	100.0
154.085	Emergency Management	WNMQ773	100.0
451.050	Hingham Water Dept.	KEP247	
48.340	Municipal Light Dept.	KCD443	
154.600	Notre Dame Academy	WNRR499	

Hinsdale
154.725	Police	(BER)	KUI587	107.2
154.070	Fire -operations		WNJM405	107.2
154.310	Fire/Berkshire Cty. Net		KNDV352	107.2
159.105	Public Works Department		WPBD247	

Holbrook
155.490	Police		KNCW960	156.7
46.360	Fire	(SE)	KCC742	131.8
46.140	Fire -F2- Avon/Stoughton		KCC742	136.5
465.2125	Fire -mobile repeater		reported	
155.040	Public Works Department		KDP274	156.7
155.100	School Department		WNAR996	

Holden
45.380	Police "H"	(WOR1)	KCD421	167.9
33.580	Fire	(8)	KCC705	CSQ
451.700	Fire -future use		WNSM406	
45.080	Highway Department		WQR283	CSQ

Holland
39.980	Police/Fire/Schools		KGW540	88.5
33.520	Fire/Ambulance	(11)	KOB459	CSQ
39.980	Highway Department		KGW540	91.5

Holliston
471.3375	Police	(SOM)	WIL394	123.0
39.420	Police -area regional		KCE221	123.0
46.460	Fire		KCE745	100.0
45.640	Highway Dept./Fire ch.2		WQZ701	CSQ
39.420	Ambulance		KCE221	136.5
153.875R	Emergency Management		WNGZ317	127.3
155.745	MEMA Area III Net		WNCD527	100.0

Holyoke
159.210R	Police	(WEM)	KCB264	114.8
155.970	Police -input to repeater		KCB264	114.8
158.970	Police -F2- records		KCB264	114.8
155.010	Police -future use		KCB264	
158.955	Police -future use		KCB264	
451.300	Police -repeater link		WDF819	114.8
451.075	Police -repeater link		WDF819	114.8
154.070	Fire	(11)	KGN525	123.0
153.950	Fire -fireground		KGN525	123.0
154.280	Fire -Springfield Area Net		KGN525	82.5
33.020	Highway Department		KON345	CSQ
158.895	School Department		KNDE221	114.8
158.205	Electric Light Department		WSY651	100.0
47.720	City Power Department		KBE285	162.2
37.780	Holyoke Water Power		KCA935	103.5
451.275	Holyoke Water Power		KNIC632	Data

153.470	Holyoke Gas & Electric	WNRM785	Data
153.650	Gas Department	KCB858	100.0
453.675	Housing Authority	WSB833	141.3
453.925	Housing Authority	WPEE498	
154.570	Board of Education	KB77677	
464.375	Mt. Holyoke College	WNQJ964	114.8
462.175	Community College	KWF204	141.3
155.400	Holyoke Hospital	WNLB854	141.3
453.1125	Holyoke Soldier's Home	KD38439	146.2
461.900	Providence Hospital	WNVG828	127.3
464.525	Ingleside Mall		110.9
461.1125	Holyoke Country Club		
155.220	Mt. Tom Ski Area	WNIX728	
155.295	Mt. Tom Ski Area	WNIX728	
155.340	Mt. Tom Ski Area	WNIX728	

Hopedale

45.900	Police	WNML996	123.0
155.790	Police -tie to Milford/Mendon	KAY980	123.0
45.600	Highway/Police secondary	KAY980	CSQ
46.220	Fire	WNXH758	123.0
46.460	Fire -regional net (7)	mobiles	
155.745	MEMA Area III Net	WNND783	100.0

Hopkinton

471.6125	Police (SOM/BAP)	WIJ890	123.0
471.6125M	Police -F2-	WIJ890	123.0
462.625	Police -F3-	KAD8036	141.3
39.42	Police -area tie	KJD275	123.0
46.46	Fire (7/14)	KCE204	136.5
72.48	Fire -fire alarm boxes	WNRB813	CSQ
465.5375	Fire -mobile repeater	WPCA361	203.5
453.050	Highway Department	KUN525	167.9
462.625	Civil Defense/Police	KAD8036	141.3
464.775	Public Schools -inactive	WNJM768	

Hubbardston

155.730	Police	WNNI770	192.8
155.790	Police -secondary	WNNI770	192.8
33.820	Fire (8)	KCB364	CSQ

Hudson

155.790	Police (SOM)	KCA952	136.5
155.475	Police -F2-	KCA952	136.5
46.420	Fire (14)	KNDV353	100.0
46.360	Fire -fireground/regional	KNCY353	100.0
37.940	Highway Department	KCE323	CSQ
48.380	Electric Light Company	WNDG649	CSQ
151.745	Council on Aging	KNBD886	
47.580	Community Ambulance	KJW731	114.8

Hull

482.9875	Police "R2" (PLC)	KZV259	203.5
154.265	Fire (2/4)	KNDD601	203.5
154.190	Fire -area secondary	KNDD601	203.5
153.830	Fire -fireground	KNDD601	203.5
155.760	Highway Department	KOB798	
155.865	Municipal Services	KNIY211	
453.375M	Municipal Services	KA78216	
158.760	Electric Light Department	KCI575	
464.000	Senior Citizen's Council	KNJF830	
153.845	Emergency Management	WNKC271	
155.055	Emergency Management	expired	
154.600	High School	KB84646	

Huntington

155.700	Police	KNFZ693	151.4
153.800	Fire (11)	WXF775	151.4
155.220	Lion's Club Ambulance	KNAG236	
150.790	Lion's Club Ambulance	KNAG236	

Ipswich

483.0625	Police (NES/BAP)	WIK328	131.8
486.0625	Police -car to car	WIK328	
482.7875	Police -Rowley tie	WIK328	146.2
158.880	Fire/Highway Depts. (5)	KCI421	131.8
153.830	Fire -fireground	WRS498	
159.390	Fire -future repeater		
460.5625	Fire -mobile repeater		131.8
155.235	R.T. Crane Reservation	WNFF974	
159.420R	R.T. Crane Reservation	WPDU730	
151.220	R.T. Crane Reservation	WPDU730	input
153.875R	No. Shore Emergency Net	KNFA314	127.3
461.225	Ipswich Country Club	WNMH674	

Kingston

482.4625	Police "O" (PLC)	KZU623	203.5
460.600	Fire -new channel(2/SE)	WPDG607	
33.480	Fire -old channel	KCB479	203.5
154.430	Fire -tie to Plymouth Fire	KCB479	173.8
45.600	Highway Dept./PD-FD tie	KCN212	131.8
45.480	County Mosquito Control	KWM744	
461.625	Independence Mall	WNQP910	CSQ

Lakeville

482.4875	Police "M1" (PLC)	KZU749	203.5
33.520	Fire (2)	KCF399	203.5
39.180	Highway Department	KXA265	162.2

Lancaster

37.100	Police/Ambulance	WPEM691	CSQ
453.0875	Police -mobile repeater	WPEM691	

33.700	Fire/Mid-State Net	KNFG737	CSQ
45.160	Highway Dept./Police -F5-	KAW391	114.8
45.460	Police -F7- old MCI tie	WPEM691	CSQ
151.775	Atlantic Union College	expired	
154.600	Perkins School	reported	CSQ

Lanesboro
155.865	Police/Highway (BEC)	KTI696	107.2
154.310	Fire/Berkshire Cty. Net	KNFQ444	107.2
464.375	Berkshire Mall		D-703

Lawrence
482.5625	Police (NEM)	KYR956	146.2
155.370	Police -housing/auxiliary	KNCT672	136.5
154.445R	Fire (15)	KAR981	100.0
159.075	Fire -repeater input	KAR981	100.0
153.830	Fire -fireground	reported	
154.025	Highway Department	KJG925	100.0
482.3125	Sewerage Treatment Plant	KNS537	
153.905	Lawrence Airport	KB68515	
155.265	Lawrence Hospital	KVD694	CSQ
464.775	School Police	WNMN233	
464.975	School Police	WNMN233	
47.660	Grtr. Lawrence Red Cross	WNGC971	
154.600	Alert 9 Radio	police assist	
155.160	EMT Corp	WNRV631	DPL
464.575	Downtown Parking	KB75895	

Lee
154.755	Police (BER)	KNBV320	107.2
154.310	Fire/Berkshire Cty. Net	KCD927	107.2
154.040	Public Works Department	KNIZ329	107.2
155.295	Lee Ambulance Squad	KNFM556	
155.925	Lee Ambulance Squad	KNFM556	
468.0125	Lee Amb. -mobile repeater	KNFM556	
468.1625	Lee Amb. -mobile repeater	KNFM556	

Leicester
45.420	Police "L" (WOR1)	WQM317	167.9
45.180	Police -backup/Spencer tie	WQM317	167.9
33.720	Fire -Comm. Center (7)	KCU288	131.8
33.720	Fire -Lake Ave. Station	KCD904	131.8
33.720	Fire -Stafford St. Station	WSY223	131.8
33.720	Fire -Main St. Station	WXR345	131.8
45.680	Highway Department	KLR355	167.9
155.745	MEMA Area III Net	WNGC981	100.0
154.600	Becker College	reported	

Lenox
158.835	Police	KLL719	CSQ
154.740	Police/Berkshire Cty. Net	KX4873	107.2

154.190	Fire -new channel	WNND471	
154.310	Fire/Berkshire Cty. Net	KNCZ361	107.2
161.400	Berkshire Railway-Museum		

Leominster
453.325	Police	KCA684	162.2
45.660	Police -auxiliary/C.D.	KCA684	100.0
33.600	Fire -operations (8)	KCB360	131.8
460.550	Fire -dispatch/officers	KUX394	151.4
460.6375	Fire -mobile repeaters	WPET483	131.8
156.000	Highway/Sewer Plant	KBF239	CSQ
151.085	Highway Department	WPDA276	
159.135	Highway Department	WPDA276	
151.865	Housing Authority	WRK552	
156.000	Civil Defense	KBF240	CSQ
462.0125	Searstown Mall -F1- Maint.	KB69234	CSQ
462.0875	Searstown Mall -F2- Sec.	KB69234	CSQ

Leverett
39.160	Police "21" (FRC)	WNIY701	141.3
460.3875	Police -mobile repeater	KD49677	141.3
465.3875	Police -mobile repeater	KD49677	141.3
33.540	Fire/Tri-State Net (9)	WNGY648	123.0
158.865	Highway Department	KR5689	CSQ

Lexington
471.1875	Police (BAPn)	KOB386	131.8
154.340	Fire (13)	KWI917	131.8
154.130	Fire -Belmont tie	KWI917	100.0
154.265	Fire -fireground	KWI917	CSQ
465.5875	Fire -mobile repeater	KWI917	136.5
155.280	Town Ambulance	KA60775	
155.340	Town Ambulance	KA60775	
158.820	Highway Department	KCH476	167.9
164.425	Minuteman National Park	KCA726-9	CSQ
155.760	Housing Authority	KD40239	
151.715	School Buses -F1-	reported	
151.955	School Buses -F2-	reported	
154.540	Minuteman VoTech	KNAV654	
151.775	Minuteman VoTech	KD42223	
461.900	M.I.T. Lincoln Labs	WPDC851	
464.775	M.I.T. Lincoln Labs	WPDD768	
464.975	M.I.T. Lincoln Labs	WPDE679	

Leyden
39.820	Police "22" (FRC)	KZU988	141.3
460.0625	Police -mobile repeater	KZU988	123.0
33.540	Fire/Tri-State Net	WNIV812	127.3
39.820	Highway Department	WNPM847	141.3

Lincoln

155.010R	Police	(SOM)	KUE603	107.2
156.150	Police -input to repeater		KUE603	107.2
155.820	Police -F2- secondary		KAQ230	107.2
155.475	Police -F4- regional		KUE603	107.2
154.145	Fire		WNNW206	107.2
155.820	Fire paging/Public Works		KAQ230	CSQ
464.325	Hartwell Elementary Schl.		WPEQ366	
154.540	Mass. Audubon Society		WNIE358	

Littleton

155.850	Police -F2- primary		WNDZ399	151.4
153.815	Police -F1- Boxboro PD		KDB450	*151.4
155.475	Police -F6- regional		WNDZ399	151.4
153.815	Fire -primary/Highway/PD		KDB450	CSQ
33.760	Fire -secondary		KB33494	
33.660	Fire -pagers	(6)	KDG722	CSQ
33.400	School Department		WPBN210	
48.380	Town Power		KAS282	*85.4
151.625	Mass. Youth Camp		WNZY426	
154.570	Minuteman Campground		KB29275	

* base only, mobiles CSQ

Longmeadow

460.425	Police	(WEM)	KNDR617	173.8
154.325	Fire	(11)	WQE936	179.9
153.830	Fire -fireground		WQE936	179.9
154.025	Highway Department		KNJV236	179.9
461.200	Bay Path Jr. College		KLE369	123.0
151.775	Longmeadow Transport		KNHA226	141.3

Lowell

482.4125	Police	(NEM)	KYR958-9	146.2
154.205	Fire	(6)	KNDV866	186.2
154.010	Fire -secondary		KNDV866	186.2
154.235	Fire -Pelham NH tie		mobiles	146.2
154.400	Fire -Dracut tie		mobiles	146.2
154.445R	Fire -Lawrence tie		mobiles	100.0
158.925	Highway Department		KLY751	107.2
453.9625	Housing Authority		WNVG266	110.9
453.575	Regional Transit		WRU769	162.2
453.100	Water Treatment Plant		WQK334	100.0
156.000	Parking Garage portables		KB78042	
464.525	Lowell High School		WQK908	CSQ
151.775	James F. Daley School		WNWZ850	
154.600	James F. Daley School		WNWZ850	
453.400	University of Lowell -F1-		KIG568	141.3
453.400M	University of Lowell -F2-		KIG568	141.3
458.900	University of Lowell -F3-		KIG568	
453.8375	University of Lowell		KD50821	151.4
461.900	University of Lowell WJUL		WNQE724	

155.205	Roadrunner Elderly Svc.		reported	131.8
861-5.2375	Frontline Ambulance		Trunked	
861-5.2375	Trinity EMS		Trunked	
155.160	Trinity EMS		WPAF755	D-125
472.6125	St. John's Hospital		WIH340	136.5
464.475	St. Joseph's Hospital		WQX277	127.3
154.570	Lowell General Hospital		KB85286	
155.235	St. Johns Hospital		WNIY788	
453.2375	Solomon Mental Health		WNZF592	141.3
155.265	Solomon Mental Health		KA77877	
155.340	City Hospitals		varies	CSQ
166.950R	Lowell National Park		KAC798	CSQ
153.710	Colonial/Lowell Gas		KCB706	CSQ
464.300	Lowell Cemetery		WNYD767	
173.375	Lowell Sun		KCF858	103.5

Ludlow

453.250	Police	(WEM)	KNFU334	173.8
853.5625	Police -mobile data		reported	Data
154.250R	Fire -primary	(11)	KNAK469	100.0
159.315	Fire -repeater input		KNAK469	100.0
154.205	Fire -fireground		KNAK469	100.0
154.280	Fire -Springfield Area Net		WNND402	82.5
155.340	Ambulance to Ludlow Hos.		KNIE861	CSQ
155.280	Ambulance to Ludlow Hos.		KNIE861	CSQ
464.475	Ludlow Hospital		WNRO716	
155.820	Highway Department		KDQ354	173.8
159.315	Forestry Department		WNNO49	
151.460R	Hampden Cty. Jail -F1-		KZF950	D-423
155.580	Hampden Cty. Jail -input		KZF950	D-423
158.730R	Hampden Cty. Jail -F2-		KZF950	D-662
155.430	Hampden Cty. Jail -input		KZF950	D-662
151.715	Ludlow Country Club		WNMB524	

Lunenburg

155.670R	Police -F2- operations		KUB805	100.0
154.770	Police -input to repeater		KUB805	100.0
155.760	Police -F1- Fire/DPW tie		KUB805	100.0
155.670M	Police -F3- simplex ops.		KUB805	100.0
155.535	Police -F4- Shirley tie		reported	131.8
155.760	Fire/Highways	(8)	KCH343	100.0
154.515	Whalom Park		KNFC818	100.0
154.570	Whalom Park		KNFC818	100.0

Lynn

472.4125	Police	(BAPn)	WYN677	131.8
475.4125M	Police -"side door"		WYN677	131.8
154.415	Fire	(5/13)	KCC886	131.8
153.830	Fire -fireground		KCC886	131.8
462.200	Fire -General Electric Plant		WYQ300	
155.025	Highway Department		KJU861	192.8

483.8375	Senior Services		KGA635	
159.165	Water & Sewer Comm.		WNNL795	192.8
453.050	Parking Department		WNDQ939	136.5
47.500	Red Cross -area ops.		WQS879	
464.375	Red Cross -transport		WQU919	
153.875R	No. Shore Emergency Net		KNBY541	127.3
155.280	Lynn Hospital		KXQ868	
155.340	Lynn Hospital		KXQ868	
155.340	North Shore EMS		KXQ703/Med 1-10	

Lynnfield

471.0875	Police	(BAPn)	WII354	131.8
154.935	Police -secondary		reported	
46.060	Fire	(5)	KNCR640	77.0
46.460	Fire -fireground/maint.		KNCR640	100.0
153.830	Fire -fireground/Lynn tie		KNCR640	131.8
465.6125	Fire -vehicular repeater		KNCR640	131.8
154.980	Public Works Department		WNDK988	136.5
453.3375	Water District		& 458.3375	CSQ

Malden

470.7625	Police	(BAPn)	KZP616	131.8
154.250	Fire -F1-		WNNO475	179.9
154.220	Fire -F2- District 13		WNNO475	CSQ
153.830	Fire -F3- fireground		WNNO475	131.8
154.265	Fire -F4- adm./fireground		WNNO475	179.9
158.985	Fire -inactive		WNNO475	179.9
154.965	Fire -proposed repeater in		KNHX636	179.9
461.575	Emergency Ctr. -F1-		reported	82.5
461.575M	Emergency Ctr. -F2-		reported	82.5
462.8375	Emergency Ctr. -F3- fgrnd.		reported	82.5
155.220	Emergency Ctr. -rescue		WXP335	114.8
154.515	Emergency Ctr. -pumping		KNGS369	
151.115	Highway Department		KAY988	151.4
153.875R	No. Shore Emergency Net		KNHD462	127.3
154.600	High School		KB65406	
155.265	Malden Hospital -security		KCP475	131.8
151.625	Malden YMCA		KB89645	

Manchester-by-the-Sea

472.2375	Police	(BAPn)	WIG751	131.8
158.760	Fire/Highway	(5)	KNCH500	136.5
151.955	Essex Country Club		KD27047	

Mansfield

856.4875	Police/Fire (trunked)	WNSM987	CSQ
857.4875	Police/Fire (trunked)	WNSM987	CSQ
858.4875	Police/Fire (trunked)	WNSM987	CSQ
859.4875	Police/Fire (trunked)	WNSM987	CSQ
39.540	Police -regional tie	KCA888	CSQ
33.460	Fire	KCA328	CSQ
33.460	Fire -Elm St. Station	KTR654	CSQ

33.500	Fire -secondary (4)	KCA328	CSQ
33.500	Fire -secondary (4)	KTR654	CSQ
46.580	Highway Department	KDG355	CSQ
158.235	Municipal Electric	WQG538	186.2
154.085R	MEMA Area II Net	WNYZ966	210.7
155.235	School Department	KNAB947	
464.475	Canoe River Campground	KNFT522	D-712

Great Woods Performing Arts Center

151.655	Security		107.2
151.805	Operations	WNGC866	107.2
151.835	Parking	WNGI570	107.2
151.625	Concessions		107.2
464.550	Capron Lighting & Sound	462.GMRS	123.0

Marblehead

472.3375	Police (BAPn)	WIG791	131.8
156.330	Police -marine patrol	KCA728	CSQ
154.370	Fire (5)	KCH550	107.2
155.835	Highway/Tree Department	KQO302	CSQ
153.605	Water/Sewer Department	WPCH414	
153.665	Municipal Light Dept.	KCC809	
463.700	Council on Aging	KNDS544	
153.875R	No. Shore Emergency Net	WQU838	127.3

Marion

483.1125	Police "S" (PLC)	WBR962	203.5
482.5375	Police -regional tie	WBR962	203.5
33.520	Fire (2)	KCE421	203.5
33.640	Fire -Bourne tie	KCE421	114.8
33.700	Fire -Barnstable Cty. tie	KCE421	114.8
45.440	Public Works Department	KCG437	
463.3375	Tabor Academy	KB62009	

Marlboro

856.4625	Police -dispatch	WNSM905	D-023
857.4625	Police -detectives	WNSM905	D-023
39.38	Police -area network	KCB300	127.3
858.4625	Fire -dispatch (14)	WNSM905	D-023
859.4625	Fire -secondary	WNSM905	D-023
46.420	Fire -old channel	KCD619	100.0
46.360	Fire -District 14 fireground	KCD619	100.0
72.760	Fire -fire alarm boxes		CSQ
151.115	Highway Department	KCH521	131.8
151.925	School Department	KJZ976	
155.745	MEMA Area III Net	reported	100.0
463.000	Marlboro Hosp.-Amb. base	KXZ792	167.9
468.000	Marlboro Hosp.-Amb. mob.	KXZ792	167.9
464.475	Marlboro Hospital -security	KNBH476	162.2
151.685	Assabet Valley Vo-Tech	WRE964	

(Note: Police and Fire may use frequencies in simplex mode on-scene.)

Marshfield

482.5625	Police "Q2" (PLC)	KZU620	203.5
458.050	Police -portables	KP2285	
33.920	Fire (2/SE)	KCF246	203.5
33.920	Fire -Outside Station	KCC359	203.5
154.190	Fire -Scituate tie	KCF246	203.5
72.680	Fire -Fire alarm boxes	WBE349	
45.400	Highway Dept./Landfill	KCG570	
154.4637	Water Pumping Stations	various	Data
173.3125	Water Pumping Station	WGJ860-2	Data

Martha's Vineyard (all communities on island)

158.850	Dukes Cty. Sheriff -F1-	KCB860	91.5
158.940	Vineyard Haven PD -F2-	KQG404	91.5
158.955	Dukes Cty. Sheriff -F3-	KQG404	91.5
158.865	Edgartown Police -F4-	KQG404	91.5
158.790	Oak Bluffs Police -F1-	WPEH314	
158.940	Oak Bluffs/Tisbury PD -F2-	WPED879	
159.150	Chilmark Police	WNNK740	91.5
155.565	Barnstable PD Net "Union"	KCB860	
33.760	Fire (1)	KSZ862	173.8
33.760	Fire -county dispatch	KNBH905	173.8
33.420	Fire -Oak Bluffs	WNYI547	
154.325	Fire -rescue/ambulance	KNBH905	CSQ
158.985	Edgartown Public Works	WVY996	
159.045	Oak Bluffs Public Works	WPDZ473	
156.015	Oak Bluffs Municipal Svc.	WPFC349	
155.205	Vineyard School District	WNUC922	
158.250	Oak Bluffs Water District	WPBB474	
153.845	Water Pollution Control	KNFM416	
158.745	Highway/Water Depts.	expired	118.8
159.180	Tisbury Highway Dept.	WNLK695	
158.820	Tisbury Municipal Svcs.	WNSA289	
453.3625	Water Pollution Control	WNRM771	
159.465	Trustees of Reservation	WNUZ802	
159.375	Wompanoag Tribal Council	WPEF342	

Mashpee

851.3125	Police "TANGO" (BRC)	WNGU851	D-445
855.3875	Police -F5- car to car	KZV322	D-445
155.835	Police -old channel	KZV322	
33.780	Fire (1)	KCF574	114.8
151.130	Highway Department	KEG436	

Mattapoisett

482.8125	Police (BRC)	KZM464	203.5
482.5375	Police -regional tie	WBR960	203.5
45.080	Fire (2)	KCG397	203.5
33.520	Fire -secondary/Marion tie	KNJA762	203.5
45.080	DPW/Senior Bus/Water	KCG397	

Maynard

155.010	Police -F1-	(SOM)	WNVN480	107.2
156.150	Police -mobile repeater		WNVN480	114.8
154.755	Police -F2- car to car		WNVN480	107.2
153.965	Police -F3- Highway tie		KLI990	141.3
154.815R	Police -F4- Acton tie		reported	173.8
155.595	Police -F5- Stow tie		reported	123.0
46.500	Fire	(14)	KCD309	100.0
46.400	Fire -F2- fireground		KCD309	100.0
153.965	Fire -F3- officers/Hgwy.		KLI990	141.3
153.965R	Highway Department		KLI990	141.3
158.985	Highway Department -input		KLI990	141.3

Medfield

471.5875	Police	(BAPs)	WII968	131.8
39.420	Police -regional tie		KCD812	CSQ
39.980	Police -regional tie		KCD812	CSQ
33.500	Fire	(4)	KCV350	CSQ
33.540	Fire -regional tie		KCV350	CSQ
159.195	Highway Department		KXF641	151.4
153.800	Emerg. Mngmt. -local		WNHW569	127.3
151.625	Emerg. Mngmt. -local		unlicensed	
153.875R	Emerg. Mngmt. -regional		WNCG784	127.3
154.085R	Emerg. Mngmt. -state tie		WNHW569	210.7
463.2125	School Department		KB93012	
463.6375	School Department		KB93012	
158.865	Medfield State Hospital		WNHV625	162.2

Medford

470.5875	Police	(BAPn)	KZR403	131.8
153.890	Fire	(13)	KNBS854	131.8
46.260	Fire -old frequency		KNBS854	
158.895	Highway Department		KXK369	
45.720	Public Works Department		WPEN776	
464.925	School Department		KRG246	
463.325	Tufts Campus Police		KRY217	192.8
462.675	Tufts Emergency Medical		KAE0439	
462.075	Tufts Emergency Medical		WNRC497	
464.875	Tufts Maintenance		WRO574	
464.575	Tufts Services		WPEW301	
464.725	Lawrence Mem. Hospital		WNQO879	
464.775	Lawrence Mem. Hospital		WNQO879	
461.0875	Meadow Glenn Mall		KB61661	162.2

Medway

39.420	Police "K"		KNGG512	136.5
39.260	Police -secondary		KNGG512	136.5
453.0875	Police -special operations		reported	
852.2375	Police -planned/not used		WNUG978	
33.540	Fire	(4)	KDX459	CSQ
159.195	Highway Department		KUX410	136.5

Melrose
471.0375	Police (BAPn)	KTS622	131.8
159.405	Fire (13)	WNQG977	127.3
46.060	Fire -Wakefield tie	KDD961	CSQ
153.830	Fire -fireground	WNQG977	
158.835	Highway Department	KFT459	131.8
155.175	School Dept. Transport	KNJL471	
155.385	Melrose Wakefield Hosp.	KAW431	

Mendon
155.520	Police	KCH317	114.8
155.790	Police -regional net	KCH317	123.0
33.620	Fire/So. Worcester Net	KCE448	131.8
39.900	Highway Department	KKQ704	136.5

Merrimac
482.8375	Police -F1- (NES)	WQG365	146.2
482.8375M	Police -F2- car to car	WQG365	146.2
482.3625	Police -F3- W. Newbury tie	WQG365	146.2
482.3625M	Police -F4- W. Newbury tie	WQG365	146.2
483.0125	Police -F5- Nwby./Nwbypt.	WQG365	146.2
483.0125M	Police -F6- Nwby./Nwbypt.	WQG365	146.2
483.1375	Police -F7- Regional	WQG365	146.2
483.7375	Police -F8- Salisbury tie	WQG365	146.2
158.955R	Fire -regional tie (15)	WNEC688	203.5
156.165	Fire -input to repeater	WNEC688	114.8
154.010	Fire -regional tie	KBX936	CSQ
154.190	Fire -Southeast NH tie	KBX936	CSQ
154.145	Fire -Southeast NH tie	KBX936	CSQ
47.720	Light & Water Depts.	KXM568	
173.3625	Municipal Light Company	KNES952	Data
153.965R	MEMA Area I Net		203.5

Methuen
482.4625	Police (NEM)	KYR955	146.2
155.490	Police -backup/aux./detec.	expired	136.5
155.475	Police -southern NH tie	WZY234	136.5
156.015	Police -Salem NH tie	WZM817	136.5
154.010	Fire (15)	KCI237	136.5
154.190	Fire -Southeast NH tie	KE6396	CSQ
154.445	Fire -Lawrence tie	KE6396	100.0
46.520	Highway/Civil Defense	KNCP292-3	136.5
46.520	Police/Highway/Water tie	KNCP291	136.5
484.7625	School Department	WIL779	
155.175	Bon Secours Hospital	KUU537	D-054
464.6875	Methuen Mall Security	KB76583	
154.570	Hickory Hill Golf Course	KD34140	
154.600	Hickory Hill Golf Course	KD34140	

Middleboro

482.4875	Police "M" (PLC)	KZU619	203.5
33.720	Fire (2/SE)	KCA633	203.5
33.980	Fire -Bridgewater area tie	KCA633	203.5
460.6375	Fire -mobile repeater	KCA633	203.5
465.6375	Fire -mobile repeater	KCA633	203.5
46.540	Highway/Water Depts.	KNDL459	
46.580	Highway/Water Depts.	KNDL459	
47.940	Gas & Light Department	KCB525	203.5
48.260	Gas & Light Department	WNJS464	203.5
153.740	Emergency Management	KD36806	

Middlefield

45.540	Police/Fire/DPW (10/12)	KNIW645	167.9
153.830	Fire -fireground	KNGE720	

Middleton

471.6125	Police (BAPn)	KNT432	131.8
46.060	Fire (5)	KNFL959	71.9
46.120	Fire -F2- inactive	KNFL959	71.9
460.575	Fire -46.06 rptr./future primary	WNUL599	131.8
460.5125	Fire -46.06 mobile repeater	KNFL959	
460.6125	Fire -fireground/F.A. const.	KNFL959	
155.280	Town Ambulance	KNFM429	
155.340	Town Ambulance	KNFM429	
MED 1-10	Town Ambulance	KNFM429	
45.720	Highway Department	KNFU626	71.9
158.175	Town Power	KCC418	
470.3375	Essex County Jail	WIK922	123.0
482.9125	Essex County Jail	KGC458-9	123.0
453.750	Essex Cty. Jail/DOC tie	WIK922	151.4
153.875R	No. Shore Emergency Net	KNBV916	127.3
164.750R	Department of Energy	KCI788	114.8

Milford

155.790	Police "M"	KNBA863	123.0
46.460	Fire (14)	KCE417	123.0
37.940	Highway Department	KCE263	107.2
153.875R	Town Adm./Emerg. Mgmt.	WNHP964	127.3
155.745	MEMA Area III Net	WNFN829	100.0
151.685	Sheraton Milford Hotel	WNDK602	
464.375	Milford-Whitinsville Hosp.	KNIM970	

Millbury

45.220	Police "M" (WOR2)	KSZ385	167.9
46.540	Fire/Highway (7)	KBC422	167.9
45.560	Sewer Department	WNGP566	
158.925	Housing Authority	WNJS604	
37.640	Mass.-American Water	KQW727	127.3
153.905	Water Treatment Plant	KD9158	
151.865	Senior Citizen's Council	KNGN361	

Millis
39.420	Police	KCD727	CSQ
39.980	Police -regional net	KCD797	CSQ
33.540	Fire (4)	KNDN904	CSQ
33.500	Fire -regional tie	KNDN904	CSQ
37.920	Highway Department	KUI646	CSQ
153.920	Civil Defense/Town Adm.	WZZ292	
155.160	School Buses	WPBI888	

Millville
39.680	Police	KCG654	100.0
39.980	Police -regional	KCG654	CSQ
33.620	Fire/So. Worcester Net	KGR326	131.8
158.880	Fire -F2- /Civil Defense	WNAX207	CSQ
154.190	Fire -tie to Northern R.I.	mobiles	CSQ
155.745	MEMA Area III Net	WNCD528	100.0

Milton
470.4625	Police (BAPs)	KZR405	131.8
483.5125	Fire -shared w/Braintree	WIJ842	131.8
153.950	Fire -old /Dedham tie (13)	KCB747	CSQ
48.100	Highway Department	reported	
45.500	Public Works (old)	KVF589	
471.9375	School Department	KEX338	
151.475R	Blue Hills Reservation "PK"	WNBQ331	71.9
151.475R	Friends of Blue Hills "BH"	WNBQ331	71.9
154.600	Blue Hills Ski Area	KB65261	
154.600	Wollaston Golf Club	WNVP916	
154.600	Curry College -F1-	KT7516	D-754
151.805	Curry College -F2-	WNYB848	D-664
464.500	Milton Academy	reported	
464.775	Milton Hospital	KNIU894	

Monroe
39.160	Police "24" (FRC)	KZU989	141.3
33.540	Fire/Tri-State Net (9)	KNGV886	123.0
33.780	Fire -fireground	KNGV886	
151.070	Highway Department	KNJX301	127.3
151.130	Highway Department	KNJX301	127.3

Monson
45.260	Police (WEM)	WBC459	127.3
45.940	Police -mobiles	WBC459	127.3
33.460	Fire/Hampden Net (11)	KCB981	CSQ
33.060	Highway/Ambulances	KSB837	CSQ
154.965	Development Center	KNEU787	
155.895	Senior Citizen's Center	KNIT320	

Montague
39.160	Police "25" (FRC)	KNDA348	141.3
33.540	Fire/Tri-State Net (9)	KCE562	123.0
33.640	Fire -Millers Falls "22"	KUZ895	123.0

33.460	Fire -Millers Falls "22"	KUZ895	123.0
33.480	Fire -County backup	KCE562	123.0
33.540	Fire -Turners Falls (9)	KCE570	123.0
33.640	Fire -Turners Falls "36"	KCE570	123.0
33.540	Fire -Montague Ctr. "25"	KCE562	123.0
158.925	Turners Falls Water Dept.	KTE596	
155.775	Highway Department	KUV569	114.8
158.760	Municipal Services	KNDA350	107.2
153.740	Treatment Plant	WQN759	
462.650	Franklin Co. School Dist.	KAC9701	

Monterey
154.740	Police/Berkshire Net	KDP353	107.2
154.310	Fire/Berkshire Cty. Net	KNAK279	107.2
151.055	Highway Department	WNFS588	131.8
156.015	Municipal Services	WPFE671	

Montgomery
45.700	Police	WNPU644	151.4
33.520	Hampden County Fire Net	WQK939	CSQ
33.100	Highway Department	WNJZ614	107.2

Mount Washington
154.740	Police/Berkshire Cty. Net		107.2
154.310	Fire/Berkshire Cty. Net	mobiles	107.2

Nahant
472.7125	Police (BAPn)	WII933	131.8
154.370	Fire (5)	KJF873	107.2
153.875R	No. Shore Emergency Net	KNAL777	127.3

Nantucket
159.090	Police "VICTOR"	WNCM720	114.8
158.850	Police -tie to Dukes Cty.	KCA367	91.5
854.2375	Police -future	WPAJ872	
854.4375	Police -future	WPAJ872	
855.9625	Police -future	WPAJ872	
154.430	Fire -operations	KCF907	141.3
154.145	Fire -secondary	KCF907	141.3
153.830	Fire -fireground	KCF907	141.3
155.280	Ambulance-Cottage Hosp.	WNGR717	
155.340	Ambulance-Cottage Hosp.	KJW483	
158.760	Highway Department	KSL460	192.8
158.835	Municipal Services	KSL460	114.8
154.040	Shellfish Warden	reported	131.8
453.150	School Department	WNGN652	131.8
451.225	Water Department	WNWN605	
461.825	Conservation Foundation	WRT978	
151.775	Elder Services	WQG548	
155.340	Ambulance-Hospital	KJW483	179.9
153.530	Nantucket Electric	KRH760	
153.605	Nantucket Electric	KRH760	
154.515	Island Tours	KUD671	

Natick

472.7375	Police (BAPw/SOM)	WIF495	131.8
154.205R	Fire (14)	KCB768	107.2
156.045	Fire -input to repeater	KCB768	107.2
153.830	Fire -fireground/mob rptr.*	KCB768	107.2
155.160	Fire -ambulance		107.2
33.980	Fire -District 14 (east)	WNIV955	127.3
46.360	Fire -District 14 (west)	WNIV955	100.0
483.7125	Fire -future regional net	WIK817	203.5
45.560	Highway/Water Depts.	KNBC430	123.0
153.845	Elderly Transport	WNHP844	123.0
39.960	C.D./Phone patches -base	KNBC430	123.0
39.180	C.D./Phone patches -mob.	KNDV398	123.0
39.320	Standby Town Emergency	KNBC430	123.0
154.515	MetroWest Medical Ctr.	KNDL340	107.2
464.1625	MetroWest Medical Ctr.	WNYZ953	
464.2625	MetroWest Medical Ctr.	WNYZ953	
463.5125	Natick Mall -primary	WPCF831	123.0
461.9125	Natick Mall -secondary	WPCF831	D-023
464.775	Natick Mall -Filenes Ops.	WPBY606	
154.570	Wilson Middle School	KD41777	
146.490	Natick Emerg. Radio Net	(MonPM)	

Natick Army Research Lab

150.775	Security/Fire -F1- primary	CSQ
150.450	Security/Fire -F2- emergency	CSQ
412.825R	Maintenance	CSQ
407.300R	Maintenance	192.8
413.500	Maintenance (repeater in)	192.8
150.600	Motor Pool	CSQ

*Will allow deputy to talk out on UHF district repeater

Needham

470.3625	Police (BAPw)	KZR401	131.8
153.950R	Fire (13)	KCH520	131.8
154.430	Fire -repeater input	KCH520	131.8
154.265	Fire -fireground	KCH520	
155.715	Civil Defense	KRZ259	146.2
155.715	School Buses	KSJ421	146.2
155.145	Town Admin./Events/C.D.	KB65503	
151.100	Public Works	KNBS896	107.2
453.3125	Public Works (& 458.3125)	WPCP836	
453.4125	Public Works (& 458.4125)	WPCP836	
155.280	Glover Memorial Hospital	KJJ850	
155.340	Glover Memorial Hospital	KJJ850	
464.475	Living Care Village	KNJU501	
461.275	Sheraton Needham	WNHV549	

New Ashford

154.740	Police/Berkshire Cty. Net		107.2
154.310	Fire/Berkshire Cty. Net	KNDZ332	107.2

Brodie Mtn. Ski Area
154.515, 154.540, 155.220, 155.295, 155.340

New Bedford

482.5875	Police -F1- (BRC)	KVX916	203.5
482.9125	Police -F2- secondary/aux.	KVX916	203.5
482.5125	Police -F3- Bristol Cty. Net	KVX916	203.5
39.640	Police -airport	KJB255	136.5
154.130	Fire -F1- (3)	KCA802	136.5
154.340	Fire -F2-	KCA802	136.5
460.575	Fire -Hazmat	WNLJ894	203.5
460.6125	Fire -fireground	WNLJ894	203.5
460.6375	Fire -mobile repeater	WNLJ894	203.5
151.010	Highway Department	KBP770	CSQ
151.115	Waste Collection	KBP770	CSQ
155.145	Water Department	KEY886	136.5
153.920	Mayor's Office/Events	KCH731	136.5
39.460	Civil Defense (limited use)	KJB255	136.5
47.660	School Department	KYU855	141.3
47.580	City Transport	WNQD296	
44.460	Regional Transit	KKD354	136.5/186.2
482.7625	Bristol County D.A.	WIG918	203.5
853.7625	Bristol County Jail -Sec.	WNQC503	DPL
39.340	Bristol County Jail -Maint.	KUE567	
154.085R	MEMA Area II Net	WNLC387	210.7
461.025	New Bedford High	KNAH977	
151.805	Grtr. New Bedford VoTech	KBD841	
43.000	Regional VoTech School	KNBM712	
151.715	County Constables Svc.	WNJH841	
155.325	Parkwood Hospital	KNBZ626	
35.700	Animal Rescue League	WPDT450	
155.400	St. Lukes Hospital	KQT882	
173.375	New Bedford Standard Times	KCA575	156.7

New Braintree

45.120	Police/Fire/Highway	KUS451-2	100.0
33.700	Mid-State Fire Net (8)	KW6821	CSQ
33.620	So. Worcester Net (7)	KW6821	131.8

Newbury

482.4625	Police -new frequency		146.2
158.850	Police -operations (NES)	KRV243	CSQ
42.340	Police -State Police tie	KA62485	141.3
483.1375	Police -Nespern regional	WIH730	146.2
483.0125	Police -Newburyport tie	WIH730	146.2
483.7375	Police -Salisbury tie	WIH730	146.2
482.7875	Police -Rowley tie	WIH730	146.2
482.8375	Police -Amesbury/Merrimac	WIH730	146.2
482.3625	Police -W. Newbury tie	WIH730	146.2
482.8625	Police -Possible future use	WIH730	146.2
154.010	Fire -Haverhill Dispatch	KNCC594	CSQ
154.145	Fire (15)	KNCC595	CSQ
154.145	Fire -Byfield Station	KCCC594	CSQ
158.955	Fire -regional tie	WNEC692	203.5
154.280	Fire -F5- NE seacoast	KNCC595	CSQ

Newburyport

Freq	Use	Call	Tone
483.0125	Police (NES)	KCA570	146.2
482.3625	Police -West Newbury tie	KCA570	146.2
482.7875	Police -Rowley tie	KCA570	146.2
482.8375	Police -Amesbury/Merrimac	KCA570	146.2
482.7375	Police -Salisbury tie	KCA470	146.2
154.145	Fire (15)	KNFX444	CSQ
158.955R	Fire -operations	WNEC684	203.5
151.100	Highway Department	WYK637	CSQ 203.5
462.625	Emergency Management	KAD2190	162.2
153.755	Emergency Management	KNJZ452	
155.100	Emergency Management	WNYF830	
153.875R	No. Shore Emergency Net	KNJZ452	127.3
155.340	Anna Jacques Hospital	KNHX256	CSQ
151.895	Anna Jacques Hospital	KB43765	
464.575	Anna Jacques Hospital	KB75491	

New Marlboro

Freq	Use	Call	Tone
155.775	Police -Gt. Barrington Disp.	WNPS474	107.2
155.940	Police/Fire backup/DPW/CD	WQU492	CSQ
154.310	Fire -First Responders (12)	KCH518	107.2
154.310	Fire -Southfield Station	KNCG834	107.2
155.760	Fire -Gt. Barrington backup	reported	
155.160	Town Ambulance	WNEB630	

New Salem

Freq	Use	Call	Tone
39.220	Police "26" (FRC)	KTA956	141.3
33.540	Fire/Tri-State Net (9)	KJW531	123.0
155.940	Highway Department	reported	CSQ

Newton

Freq	Use	Call	Tone
470.8375	Police (BAPw)	KZA726	131.8
470.3875	Police -F5- Traffic/backup	KZA726	131.8
483.4625	Fire (13)	KYD496	131.8
37.900	Highway Department	KCE618	151.4
45.760	Building Department	WYK348-9	
45.080	Engineering Department	WPBN886	141.3
45.440	School Department	WPBN886	
464.525	School Department	WYS399	206.5
47.620	Red Cross -Newton Base	KNFC841	
155.295	Newton Wellesley Hospital	KSQ476	
154.515	Newton Cemetery Corp.	KNDV563	CSQ
154.600	LaSalle Junior College	KB26386	
464.2625	LaSalle Junior College	KB91653	
151.805	Mt. Ida Jr. College	WQF806	
464.650	Mt. Ida Jr. College	WPAD234	
154.600	Fesenden School	KD52270	
151.685	Chestnut Hill Mall		71.9
461.675	Bloomingdales	WNDF984	
461.2625	The Atrium	KD50242	
464.425	The Atrium -security		114.8
464.5375	The Atrium -maintenance	KD20275	CSQ

464.425	Newton Marriott Hotel	WXM776	
464.675	Sheraton Tara Hotel	WNJC250	
151.775	Brae Burn Country Club	WNML868	
151.895	Brae Burn Country Club	WNML868	
467.8875	Charles River Country Club	WPCW755	
467.9125	Charles River Country Club	WPCW755	

Boston College
472.1375	Campus Police	KTX468	127.3
471.8125	Campus Services		
464.575	Campus Services	KNEG380	
483.8375	Network Services		
469.2625	Athletics Department	KB89921	
472.2625	Dining Services	WIJ874	127.3
483.0375	Maintenance Services	WIJ785	

Norfolk
851.3875	Police	WNVT402	D-251
39.420	Police -regional "N"	KCD475	CSQ
39.980	Police -regional	KCD475	CSQ
33.540	Fire (4)	KNDR721	CSQ
33.500	Fire -regional net	KNDR721	CSQ
39.580	Highway Department	WNYD320	CSQ

North Adams
156.210	Police (BER)	KNGE762	107.2
154.710	Police -Florida PD tie	KNGE762	107.2
156.000	Police -auxiliary units	KNGE762	
153.950	Fire (12)	WRG560	107.2
155.220	No. Adams Ambulance	WXK700	
460.5375	No. Adams Amb. -mo. rptr.	WXK700	
156.135	Highway Department	KNAS384	
152.300	No. Adams State College	KNGZ608	107.2
151.835	No. Adams State College	KUT695	CSQ
151.655	No. Adams Hospital	WQU239	

Northampton
155.685R	Police (WEM)	KCC212	131.8
158.745	Police -input to repeater	KCC212	131.8
159.150	Police -F2-	KCC212	131.8
155.835	Police -Look Park	KUN426	141.3
168.525	Veterans Hospital security	KUN426	100.0
154.220	Fire -primary	WSY543	127.3
154.370	Fire -Hampshire Cty. Net	WSY543	127.3
155.235	Municipal Ambulance	WNSI462	107.2
154.980R	Highway Department	KNFS352	167.9
159.015	Highway Dept. -rptr. input	KNFS352	167.9
158.805	Municipal Services	WNLR338	
45.280	Municipal Services	WNLR545	118.8
463.0125	Northampton Amb. Svc.	WNSJ462	
158.850	Hampshire County Jail	KNEZ569	131.8
453.550	Hampshire County Jail	WNCE391	141.3
453.1125	Northampton Dist. Court	KD42438	131.8

453.6375	Northampton Dist. Court	KD52726	114.8
151.775	Colley Dickinson Hospital	KNBG730	CSQ
153.755	State Hospital	KSZ310	CSQ
461.575	Smith College	WNUA688	127.3
461.725	Smith College	KNFS352	127.3
464.6375	Hotel Northampton	KD53316	

North Andover

484.7875	Police (NEM)	WIK335	146.2
462.6125	Police -Andover tie	WIK335	146.2
867.600	Fire	WPDG970	131.8
33.540	Fire -backup	KCB542	146.2
460.5875	Fire -mobile extenders	KCB542	
153.920	Public Works Department	KJW605	CSQ
482.3125	Grtr. Lawrence Sanitary	KNS537	
151.685	Brooks School	WNYJ899	
151.685	Merrimack College	WPAA319	
151.775	Merrimack College	WNKC843	
154.570	Merrimack College	WPAA319	
464.375	Merrimack College	KNBG436	
463.7625	North Andover Resco	KB65102	

North Attleboro

39.540	Police	KCA838	CSQ
46.440	Fire (4)	KCD918	CSQ
154.280	Fire -tie to Rhode Island	KCD918	CSQ
453.550	Dept. of Public Works	KOE270	
47.700	Town Power	KCC903	88.5
48.200	Town Power	KCC903	88.5
37.520	North Attleboro Gas Co.	WPEZ265	
154.600	Junior High School	KB62759	
461.725	Emerald Square Mall	WNPK918	CSQ

Northboro

155.970	Police -F1- ops. (WOR2)	KCD548	167.9
155.100	Police -F2- backup	KCJ958	167.9
155.700	Police -Shrewsbury tie	reported	131.8
154.755	Police -data terminals	WNWZ647	CSQ
39.380	Police -So. Middlesex Net	KCD548	123.0
453.0625	Police -mobile repeater	KD40247	167.9
453.0875	Police -mobile repeater	KD40247	167.9
453.1625	Police -mobile repeater	KD40247	167.9
453.2125	Police -mobile repeater	KD40247	167.9
453.5625	Police -mobile repeater	KD40247	167.9
154.445	Fire -F1- dispatch (7/8/14)	WNHP739	167.9
155.100	Highway/CD/PD/FD -F2-	KCJ958	167.9
155.745	MEMA Area III Net	WNHG551	100.0
158.925	Housing Authority	WNRD804	D-712
154.600	School Athletics	reported	100.0
470.4125	Cen. Ma. Mosquito Control	WIB846	167.9
154.600	Juniper Hill Golf Course	WPDF251	91.5
154.570	Juniper Hill Golf Course	WPDF251	91.5

Northbridge

39.860	Police	KCA918	162.2
39.980	Police -regional net	KCA918	CSQ
39.980	Police -emerg. mngmt. tie	KVA533	CSQ
453.1875	Police -mobile repeaters	KCA918	
472.3375	So. Worc. Cty. Investigators	WIK994	151.4/DVP
154.950	So. Worc. Cty. Investigators	reported	
33.680	Fire (7)	KBQ744	162.2
33.680	Fire	KCF897	162.2
45.840	Fire -DPW/town tie	KNDK588	167.9
45.840	Civil Defense	KTZ504	167.9
45.840	Highway Department	KLG577	167.9
45.840	Sewer Department	KNDM566	167.9
155.745	MEMA Area III Net	WPES846	100.0
46.560	Water Department	KUI582	CSQ
151.925	Elderly Services	WNPA813	

North Brookfield

45.660	Police (WOR)	WNVU936	192.8
45.520	Police/Fire/Highway	KQS853	CSQ
33.620	Fire/So. Worcester Net	KCW697	131.8

Northfield

39.160	Police "28" (FRC)	KRG723	141.3
453.4375	Police -mobile repeater	WNVM374	141.3
33.540	Fire/Tri-State Net (9)	KCE565	123.0
46.520	Highway Department	KNIT474	114.8
463.0875	Ambulance -repeater	WNVL624	123.0
157.620	Mt. Hermon School	KNFN971	CSQ
461.450	Mt. Hermon School -sec.	WNDG756	179.9
469.1375M	Mt. Hermon School -maint.	WNDG75	CSQ
151.715	Mt. Hermon School	KCL592	
451.9125	Mt. Hermon School	KCL592	
451.9875	Mt. Hermon School	KD29562	
155.175	National Ski Patrol	WNIX704	
155.220	National Ski Patrol	WNIX704	
155.340	National Ski Patrol	WNIX704	

North Reading

482.7375	Police "973" (NEM)	WBB973	146.2
453.950	Fire -F1- operations	WPCS289	136.5
453.950M	Fire -F2- fireground	WPCS289	136.5
458.950M	Fire -F3- fireground	WPCS289	136.5
460.575	Fire -secondary incident	WNUL600	136.5
465.575	Fire -fireground secondary	WNUL600	136.5
33.660	Fire/No. Middlesex Net	KNDH495	71.9
33.600	Fire -fireground (unused)	KNDH495	
460.5375	Fire -extenders/future use	KNDH495	(& 465)
460.5625	Fire -extenders/future use	KNDH495	(& 465)
154.340	Fire -Wilmington tie	WNBZ892	CSQ
155.340	Town Ambulance	WNBH397	
156.120	Highway Department	KJU229	

Norton

39.540	Police	KCD897	CSQ
46.180	Fire -dispatch	KNFU372	CSQ
46.180	Fire -Bristol Cnty. Control	KNFU372	CSQ
46.120	Fire -F2- backup/maint.	KNFU372	CSQ
46.120	Fire -S. Worcester St. Sta.	KNFS337	CSQ
46.120	Fire -Station 4/Bay Rd.	KNFU373	CSQ
33.980	Fire -Taunton/Raynham tie	KNFU570	
33.500	Fire -Mansfield/Easton tie	KNFU570CSQ/203.5	
33.980	Fire -Taunton/Raynham tie	KNFU570CSQ/203.5	
158.745R	Highway/Schools/C.D.	KNDL304	114.8
153.785	Highway -repeater input	KNDL304	114.8
151.925	Public Schools	WNYG317	
464.825	Wheaton College -security	KNIP440	D-116
151.685	Wheaton College -plant	WNCK437	

Norwell

482.5625	Police "Q" (PLC)	KZU622	203.5
33.940	Fire (2)	KCG933	203.5
154.190	Fire -Regional Net	KCG933	203.5
154.265	Fire -Regional tie	KCG933	203.5
458.8875	Fire -mobile repeater		203.5
453.3625	Municipal Services	WPCT508	
45.520	Water/Health/Animal/Tree	KDT275	

Norwood

472.0875	Police (BAPs)	KZR429	131.8
483.7875	Police -detectives	reported	131.8
470.4375	Police -Westwood tie	KZR429	131.8
453.850	Fire (4/SE)	WPJB404	131.8
155.340	Norwood Hospital	KUI669	
45.240	Highway Department	KDQ732	CSQ
453.975	Municipal Services	WPCY438	
453.4875	Municipal Services	WPEZ464	
45.040	Norfolk Mosquito Control	KB75901	
45.480	Norfolk Mosquito Control	KB75900	
151.685	Neponset Valley Health	WPAS920	
155.295	Neponset Valley Health	KNEJ678	110.9

Oakham

39.180	Police/Fire/Municipal	KJE304	131.8
453.2875	Police/Fire mobile extender	KJE304	131.8
33.700	Fire/Mid-State Net	KKR443	CSQ

Orange

39.220	Police "29" (FRC)	KNCA358	141.3
453.0375	Police -mobile repeater	WNYW367	141.3
33.540	Fire/Tri-State Net (9)	KNDB817	123.0
33.780	Fire -Southwest NH tie	KNDB817	123.0
33.700	Fire -Mid-State Fire Net tie	KNDB817	CSQ
37.960	Highway & Sewer Depts.	WNFV870	141.3

Orleans
155.640	Police	"MIKE" (BAR)	KCB709	110.9
33.660	Fire	(1)	KCD556	114.8
37.940	Highway Department		KCP537	CSQ
47.740	Water Department		KLF756	CSQ
154.040	Parks Department		WNZL776	

Otis
153.965	Police	(BER)	KNEM488	107.2
42.460	Police -State PD Coverage		KR9796	141.3
44.740	Police -State PD Coverage		KR9796	CSQ
154.310	Fire/Berkshire Cty. Net		KNID483	107.2
156.105	Highway Department		KJV232	107.2
155.220	Otis Rescue Squad		KUI556	
154.600	Otis Ridge Ski Area		KB42391	

Oxford
45.740	Police	"O" (WOR2)	KAG535	167.9
46.240	Fire		KTB236	71.9
33.620	Fire/So. Worcester Net		KTB236	131.8
45.240	Police/Fire/DPW/Amb.		KTK601	71.9
151.655	School Department		WNVD434	

Palmer
155.670R	Police	(WEM)	KNDP584	118.8
156.090	Police -input to repeater		KNDP584	118.8
33.600	Fire -new frequency		WPFG739	
33.520	Fire	(11)	KCF798	CSQ
33.520	Fire -Bondsville	(11)	KFR552	CSQ
33.520	Fire -3 Rivers	(11)	KFG510	CSQ
460.6125	Fire -mobile repeater		KCF798	
465.6125	Fire -mobile repeater		KCF798	
154.995	Highways/Elderly Svc.		WZU592	118.8
153.725	Fire -Water District 1		KNIG321	
154.600	Pathfinder Vo-Tech		KB75182	
154.515	Wing Memorial Hospital		WNCT927	192.8
155.280	Wing Memorial Hospital		WQI380	CSQ
155.340	Wing Memorial Hospital		WQI380	CSQ
155.325	Monson Development Ctr.		KNDU692	103.5
154.965	State Hospital/School		KNEU787	

Paxton
45.380	Police	"P" (WOR1)	KNGL848	167.9
33.440	Fire	(8)	KNGG788	131.8
33.700	Fire/Mid-State Net		KNGG788	CSQ
154.980	Highway/Amb./Power		KNGS32	179.9

Peabody
471.5125	Police	(BAPn)	KNM910	131.8
484.6625	Fire		WIH990	203.5
483.3375	Fire -tie to Danvers		WIH990	131.8
453.475	Highway/Tree/Park/Water		KTR797	141.3

156.120	DPW./PD Surv./C.D.	KFY993	127.3
158.865	Elder Vans	KJU221	173.8
48.460	City Water	KCC664	
151.625	School Dept. Maintenance	KB68970	
153.875R	N. Shore Emergency Net	WQS280	127.3
461.150	N. Shore Shopping Plaza	KTL895	123.0
155.280	Josiah Thomas Hospital	KNCW677	
155.340	Josiah Thomas Hospital	KNCW677	
155.220	Higgins School	WNHE813	
151.715	Salem Country Club	KB61072	

Pelham

159.000R	Police (WEM)	WNRE389	127.3
153.935	Police -repeater input	WNRE389	127.3
154.370	Fire/Hampshire Cty. Net	KUY514	127.3
159.000	Highway Dept./Police tie	KXO860	162.2

Pembroke

482.7875	Police "T" (NEM)	KZV265	203.5
33.680	Fire (2/SE)	KAS874	203.5
33.680	Fire -North Station	KDW282	203.5
33.680	Fire -Bryantville Station	KDW283	203.5
39.500	Fire -Admin./Highway tie	KJB951	
39.500	Water Department	KNDN597	
39.500	Highway Department	KNDN598	
153.800	Municipal Services	WNBL998	

Pepperell

453.550R	Police/Amb. -F1- "9"	KNAG309	136.5
453.550M	Police -F2- simplex	KNAG309	136.5
458.550M	Police -F3- mobiles only	KNAG309	136.5
39.420	Police -area base net	KDZ480	CSQ
155.475	Police -regional system	KDZ480	136.5
33.520	Fire	KNAB761	141.3
33.660	Fire/No. Middlesex Net	KNAB761	CSQ*
154.325	Fire -Nashua tie (chief only)	reported	103.5
45.520	Highway Dept./Ambulance	KNAL532	141.3

* base and chief have PL 141.3

Peru

155.640	Police	WNVB340	
154.740	Police/Berkshire PD Net	KX4876	107.2
154.310	Fire (12)	KDU371	107.2
154.130	Fire -fireground	KDU371	107.2
154.055	Public Works Department	KNCU927	

Petersham

39.220	Police "G-23/P" (FRC)	KVP433	100.0
39.160	Police -County Net	KVP433	141.3
453.7375	Police -mobile repeater	WPEC517	
33.700	Fire/Mid-State Net (9)	KGP720	CSQ
33.540	Fire/Tri-State Net tie	KGP720	123.0
151.040	Highway Department	KNED288	CSQ

Phillipston
39.220	Police	KCC491	CSQ
33.700	Fire/Mid-State Net (9)	WNHT223	CSQ
37.900	Highway Department	KB88737	

Pittsfield
155.070	Police -Tac 1	KCA876	107.2
154.800	Police -ambulance -Tac 2	KTL673	107.2
153.965	Berkshire Cty. Sheriff	KRO333	107.2
154.740	Berkshire PD Net -Tac 3	KCA876	107.2
154.340	Police -Fire tie	KTL674	107.2
154.340	Fire (12)	KNCG444	107.2
153.830	Fire -fireground	KNCG444	107.2
154.160	Fire -county fireground	WPBG767	107.2
154.310	Fire -Berkshire County Net	KCH470	107.2
154.310	Fire -G.E. Plant tie	WZX991	107.2
153.785	School Department	KVF638	
37.940	Highway Department	WPEX798	107.2
37.760	Water & Power Dept.	WPEZ485	179.9
45.400	Health Department	KGL378	
453.275	Public Buildings Dept.	KXH256	114.8
453.375	Municipal Services	KXH256	114.8
453.150	Municipal Services	KGL378	
453.0875	Public Works Department	KD40077	107.2
154.980	Emergency Management	KGL395	
155.340	Berkshire County EMS	WNCM664-8	
155.385	Berkshire County EMS	WNCM664	123.0
151.685	School Buses -mobiles	WPCY459	
151.775	School Buses -base	WPCY459	
154.770	Corrections Dept. -portables	KA62488	107.2
453.050	Regional Transit Authority	KNJT287	131.8
151.805	Berkshire Elder Services	WNSI579	91.5
151.955	Berkshire Elder Services	KNHH285	D-346
155.160	Berkshire Ambulance Svc.	KYU480	107.2
155.280	County Ambulance Svc.	KNFG805	
155.340	County Ambulance Svc.	KNFG805	
461.650	Berkshire Medical Center	KKF892	123.0
155.340	Pittsfield Hospitals	varies	
153.935	Berkshire College	KNBU623	
155.880	Berkshire College	KNBU623	107.2
151.925	Boys Club of Pittsfield	KNIL338	162.2
151.955	Community Action Council	WNFC409	D-343
154.570	Country Club of Pittsfield	KB93756	
154.600	Country Club of Pittsfield	KB93756	
464.775	Lakeside Christian Camp	KNJW712	
154.600	IUE Local 255	KB93941	
155.175	National Ski Patrol	KNEA840	
155.220	National Ski Patrol	KNEA840	
155.340	National Ski Patrol	KNEA840	
155.205	Brodie Mtn. Ski Area	WNXJ539	
154.570	Bousquet Ski School	KB66693	

173.225	Berkshire Eagle	KNBM699	D-114
47.700	Berkshire Gas	KCD711	127.3

Plainfield
154.995	Police/Fire/Highway (11)	WXY415	141.3
154.770	Police -F2- secondary	WSL566	114.8
154.995	Highway/Police	WXY402	141.3
154.370	Fire/Hampshire Cty. Net	WXT895	127.3

Plainville
39.540	Police	KNBB206	CSQ
39.240	Police -secondary	KNBB206	CSQ
39.420	Police -regional net	KNBB206	CSQ
46.440	Fire (3/4)	KNFL943	CSQ
33.540	Fire -regional tie	KNFL943	CSQ
151.070	Highway Department	KBM941	
453.800	Area Elder Vans	KNJT291	114.8

Plymouth
482.6625	Police "D" (PLC)	WBT736	203.5
155.565	Police -Barnstable Cty. tie	KNDJ393	110.9
154.430	Fire -Operations (2/SE)	WNJL433	173.8
154.430	Fire -Sta. 1 -Sandwich St.	KCA585	173.8
154.430	Fire -Sta. 2 -Samoset St.	KXG958	173.8
154.430	Fire -Sta. 4 -Bourne Rd.	KGU247	173.8
154.430	Fire -Sta. 5 -State Rd.	KAT541	173.8
154.430	Fire -Sta. 6 -Cedarville	WNBH267	173.8
154.430	Fire -Sta. 7 -Standish Ave.	KXE576	173.8
154.430	Fire -Operations	WNQA827	173.8
154.310	Fire -fireground	WNKT379	203.5
33.900	Fire -county fireground	KCA585	203.5
33.900	Fire -Plymouth Airport	KCH429	203.5
154.190	Fire -Regional tie	WNKT379	203.5
154.265	Fire -Hingham area tie	WNKT379	203.5
33.700	Fire -Barnstable Cty. tie	WNKT379	114.8
45.160	Highway & Civil Defense	KBX385	
Trunked	Town Svcs./Schools/Hsng.	Business SMR	
458.9625	Municipal Services	WNSH275	
151.805	Council on Aging	KNHK527	
472.0375	Plimoth Plantation	WIH272	
461.1125	Plimoth Plantation	KD29504	203.5
154.600	Plymouth Schools	KB75758	
154.600	South River School	WPEC885	
153.500	Pilgrim Nuclear Plant	KNGA850	156.7
451.625	Pilgrim Nuclear Plant	WNMB625	
461.850	Pilgrim Nuclear Plant	reported	131.8
154.085R	MEMA Area II Net	WNKK990	210.7
155.955	MEMA input	WNKK990	210.7
45.360	MEMA State Net	WNKQ573	162.2
44.740	Power Plant-State PD	reported	
464.6125	Jordan Hospital	WNYH822	

Plympton
482.4625	Police "O2" (PLC)	KZU625	203.5
33.440	Fire (2)	KCA974	203.5
39.500	Highway Department	KNJB866	

Princeton
154.710	Police	WNMJ738	167.9
33.880	Fire -dispatch	KCN575	167.9
33.700	Fire -Mid-State Net	KCN575	CSQ
156.060	Fire -ch.B- Chief	WNLY760	167.9
156.060	Highway Department	WNLY760	167.9
48.380	Town Power	KCF702	103.5
464.575	Wachusett Mt. Ski Patrol	KNFU506	
464.375	Wachusett Mt. Ski Area	KNJK458	
464.975	Wachusett Mt. Ski Area	WNAN723	131.8

Provincetown
155.700	Police "ABLE/A" (BAR)	KCA371	110.9
33.460	Fire -headquarters (1)	WXT893	114.8
33.460	Fire -backup	KNBC936	114.8
33.460	Fire -dispatch	KCD697	114.8
33.460	Fire -Johnson St. Station	KNBA962	114.8
33.700	Barnstable Cty. Fire Net	KCD697	114.8
156.180	Highway Department	KNHU625	103.5
155.940	Building Inspectors	KNEX897	103.5
171.725R	Cape Cod Seashore	KCB738	CSQ
171.725R	Cape Cod Seashore	KCB743	CSQ
158.025	Dolphin Whale Watchers	scrambled	CSQ
154.515	Coastal Acres Tours	WRW361	141.3
154.570	Cape Pilgrim Memorial	KCB715	CSQ
154.570	Holiday Inn Cape Cod	KB79021	CSQ
154.570	Best Western Hotel		79.7
154.570	Chateau Motel		179.9
154.570	Tide Hotel		179.9
154.570	Dunes Edge Campground		

Quincy
453.250	Police -alternating main	KSL347	192.8
453.225	Police -alternating main	KSL347	192.8
453.275	Police -detectives/misc.	KSL347	192.8
470.3375	Police -local/county detec.	KEF7151	131.8
159.150	Police -aux/dog/CD/rescue	KNDD885	123.0
483.5375	Fire -F1- operations (13)	KNFC533	131.8
483.5375M	Fire -F2- simplex	KNFC533	131.8
483.3375	Fire -F3/4- rptr./simplex	KNFC533	131.8
483.3125	Fire -F5/6- rptr./simplex	KNFC533	131.8
483.1625	Fire -F7- Boston ch.1 tie	reported	118.8
483.1875	Fire -F8- Boston ch.2 tie	reported	118.8
153.890	Fire -Boston Fire tie	KNFC533	
154.265	Fire -Hingham area tie	KNFC533	203.5
153.785	Fire/Municipal Svcs./DPW	KSU423	CSQ
33.020	Highway Department	KNHH320	CSQ

453.7875	Housing Authority		KD44008	110.9
151.745	School Department			71.9
464.375	School Department		KSA608	71.9
484.9625	Council on Aging		KNR212	131.8
469.525	Quincy City Hospital		reported	186.2
Trunked	Elder Vans		Business SMR	
159.150	Emerg. Mngmnt. -primary		KNDD885	123.0
153.815	Emerg. Mngmnt. -F1-		WNCL907	123.0
153.905	Emerg. Mngmnt. -F2-		WNCL907	123.0
153.875R	No. Shore Emergency Net		WNCC672	127.3
155.220	No. Shore Emergency Net		WNAV485	127.3
154.085R	State Emerg. Management		WNDK461	210.7
154.085	State Education Dept.		WNHQ211	

Randolph

471.4375	Police	(BAPs)	KCZ956	131.8
45.500	Police -old ch./renewed		KCE482	
483.6625	Fire	(13/SE)	WIJ204	103.5
154.295	Southeast Fire Net		KCB474	203.5
46.140	Fire -area tie		KCB474	136.5
46.240	Fire -Avon tie		KCB474	136.5
45.680	Highway Department		KTP825	
155.160	Town Ambulance		KA34300	
155.280	Town Ambulance		KA34300	
155.340	Town Ambulance		KA34300	

Raynham

483.0625	Police	(BRC)	KZM469	203.5
33.980	Fire	(3)	KCD371	CSQ
72.620	Fire -Fire Alarm boxes		WNQH963	CSQ
37.960	Highway/Water Depts.		WQU999	CSQ

Raynham Dog Track
Park Operations Channels: 464.0625, 464.5875, 464.8875

151.805	Massasoit Greyhound Assoc.	reported	
154.570	Massasoit Greyhound Assoc.	KB83641	
464.500	Rezendes Racing	KB69001	

Reading

483.6625	Police	(NEM)	KYL897	146.2
482.7375	Police -No. Reading tie		KYL897	146.2
45.980	Police -old ch./renewed		KCA844	
46.340	Fire	(5/6/<u>13</u>)	KCF810	156.7
46.060	Fire -regional net		KNIB552	156.7
465.6375	Fire -mobile repeater		KB94620	156.7
151.025	Highway Department		KBH772	CSQ
155.880	Elderly Transport		WNPL341	131.8
47.780	Municipal Light Dept.		KCC900	110.9
48.260	Municipal Light Dept.		KCC900	110.9
451.0375	Municipal Light Dept.		KCC900	
39.900	Mass. Army Nat'l Guard		WNGM564	

Rehoboth

155.670R	Police	KCD885	100.0
154.740	Police -repeater input	KCD885	100.0
154.100R	Fire (3)	KAZ443	100.0
155.025	Fire -repeater input	KAZ443	100.0
156.120	Highway Department	WNNY515	

Revere

470.8625	Police (BAPn)	KCZ967	131.8
473.8625	Police -"side door"	KCZ967	
471.8375	Police -F2- /Highway	WIL358	127.3
154.175R	Fire (13)	KDR728	123.0
159.060	Fire -repeater input	KDR728	123.0
154.205	Fire -secondary	KDR728	123.0
154.265	Fire -fireground/training	KDR728	
153.830	Fire -fireground	KDR728	123.0
471.3375	Highway Department	WIL358	127.3
482.3375	Municipal Svc./PD backup	reported	146.2
453.9625	Municipal Services	WPEH761	
155.745	Public Schools	KWR453	
464.375	Wonderland Park	KNAL762	

Richmond

154.740	Berkshire County PD Net	KX4877	107.2
154.310	Fire/Berkshire County Net	KNEY879	107.2
154.100	Highway Department	KNGN544	

Rochester

482.5375	Police "S2" (PLC)	KZU628	203.5
33.520	Fire -operations	KJE934	203.5
33.900	Fire/Plymouth County Net	KJE934	203.5
45.480	Public Works Department	KUG798	
155.145	New Bedford Water Dept.	KEY886	136.5
154.600	Old Colony Vo-Tech High	KB67648	

Rockland

483.0125	Police "X" (PLC)	KZV257	203.5
158.895	Police -tie to town services	WYF295	
33.800	Fire (2/SE)	KCD427	203.5
158.895	Water Dept./Civil Defense	KIK694/WQQ345	
158.895	High School	KKD969	
158.895	Public Works Department	WYE430	100.0
153.935	Town Schools/Town Svcs.	WYE430	
158.955	Town Schools/buses	KIK994	
153.875R	Civil Defense Network	WNHI781	
154.085	MEMA Area II Net	WNHI781	127.3

Rockport

154.785	Police	KCA872	127.3
482.9625	Police -detectives	WIL550	
470.xxx	Police -future BAPERN	repoted	

155.145	Fire (4)	KDT268	127.3
156.105	Highway Department	KWV643	127.3
158.775	Town Ambulance	WNZC282	127.3
153.875R	No. Shore Emergency Net	KNAL780	127.3
154.600	Seaward Inn	KD35451	
461.1375	Thatcher Island Assn.	WNWG782	

Rowe
39.160	Police "30" (FRC)	KZU990	141.3
33.540	Fire/Shelburne Disp. (9)	KVS268	123.0
155.820	Public Works Department	KCI282	CSQ

Rowley
482.7875	Police "410" (NES)	WNAX410	146.2
482.7625	Police -secondary	WIJ497	146.2
154.145	Fire -Rowley Vol. (15)	KDC289	CSQ
154.430	Fire -Rowley Vol	WPCD779	
151.055	Highway Department	KNJN833	136.5
153.620	Municipal Light	WQT273	
470.4125	Mosquito Control	WCD284	203.5
153.875R	No. Shore Emergency Net	KNJN397	127.3

Royalston
39.220	Police	KYQ492	141.3
33.700	Fire/Mid-State Net (8)	KXZ508	CSQ
154.100	Highway Department	KA77627	

Russell
46.560	Police/Fire/Highway	KBV985	141.3
42.460	Police -State PD coverage	KB27844	141.3
33.520	Fire/Hampden Cty. Net	KTZ275	CSQ

Rutland
37.220	Police	KCF353	141.3
37.400	Police -car to car	reported	
33.560	Fire -dispatch (8)	KCH585	131.8
158.805	Highway Department	KJD228	127.3
154.600	Town Services	KD52317	
154.600	Pout & Trout Campground	KA80495	

Salem
471.6375	Police (BAPn)	WXW959	131.8
483.4625	Fire -F1- (5)	WIJ983	146.2
483.6375	Fire -F2- portables	WIJ983	146.2
151.040	Highway Department	KBT464	
158.775	Municipal Services	WNDL449	
153.875R	No. Shore Emergency Net	KNAL781	127.3
453.925	S. Essex Cty. Sewer Dist.	KUP427	
484.2125	Salem Elder Vans	reported	
417.775	Salem Maritime Historic Site	reported	
464.925	Salem Hospital -security	KZL995	
155.340	Salem Hospital -transport	KSL319	

472.6125	Salem State College Sec.	WIK378	CSQ
464.475	Salem State College	WNJP857	
464.425	Salem State College	WNMN255	
155.160	Salem High School	WNQG627	
154.600	Peabody Museum	KB66989	
173.325	Salem Evening News	KQU729	
151.715	Salem Country Club	KB61072	

Salisbury
483.7375	Police -F1-	(NES)	KCA571	146.2
486.7375	Police -F2-		KCA571	146.2
158.955R	Fire	(15)	KDO241	203.5
156.135	Fire -input to repeater		KDO241	114.8
154.145	Fire -F2- area tie		KDO241	CSQ
154.190	Fire -New Hampshire tie		KDO241	
154.280	Fire -New Hampshire tie		KDO241	
151.055	Highway/Civil Defense		WQS830	

Sandisfield
154.740	Berkshire County PD Net	reported	107.2
154.310	Fire/Berkshire Cty. Net	KLV939	107.2

Sandwich
851.3875	Police	"HENRY" (BAR)	KNFU755	D-445
33.600	Fire	(1)	KCD498	114.8
460.6375	Fire -mobile repeaters		KCD498	114.8
465.6375	Fire -mobile repeaters		KCD498	
453.100	Water District		WNCD435	100.0
159.075	Highway Department		KYJ243	156.7
154.540	School Department		KCG791	
151.925	Peters Pond Park		WQY721	
151.775	Peters Pond Park		KD27262	
464.9125	South Shore YMCA		WPAK481	

Saugus
471.3875	Police	(BAPn)	WIE467	131.8
154.370	Fire	(5/13)	KDN542	131.8
151.070	Highway Department		KGW565	131.8
155.775	Municipal Services		WPAC852	
154.515	Housing Authority		reported	
154.540	Hilltop Steak House		KQJ312	
463.575	Days Inn		WNZZ535	
464.525	Square One Mall			D-116

Savoy
154.740	Police	(BEC)	reported
154.205	Fire -operations	(12)	WNGS750
151.685	Shady Pines Campground		KNGV791

Scituate
482.5875	Police	"R1" (PLC)	KZV261	118.8
482.9875	Police -regional tie		KZV261	203.5

154.265	Fire	(2/SE)	KNDE629	203.5
154.190	Fire -secondary/regional		KNDE629	203.5
153.830	Fire -fireground		KNDE629	203.5
37.100	Highway Department		KJB952	
37.900	Public Schools		WNPG816	

Seekonk

155.010R	Police		WNXS933	CSQ
158.790	Police -repeater input		WNXS933	CSQ
155.940	Police -secondary		KDS668	
154.220	Fire	(3)	KCD606	
154.280	Fire -tie to Rhode Island		KCD606	CSQ
155.340	Town Ambulance		KA4026	
151.745	Esquire Motel		KB83833	
154.600	Ledgemont Country Club		KB54391	

Sharon

483.1375	Police	(BAPs)	KYF647	141.3
483.3375	Fire	(4/SE)	WIK794	141.3
33.500	Fire -regional net/pagers		KCF980	107.2
33.540	Fire -tone alert		KCF980	107.2
483.0875	Highway/Civil Defense		WAX900-3	141.3
155.145	School Department		WPEM305	88.5
453.8125	Municipal Services		WPEY590	
464.850	Spring Valley Country Club		KB95793	

Sheffield

155.775	Police -Gt. Barrington Disp.	WXM323	107.2
154.740	Berkshire County PD Net	KA91702	107.2
154.310	Fire/Berkshire County Net	KNBU763	107.2
155.955	Highway Dept./Amb.	WNAN683	107.2
154.600	Berkshire School	KD20336	

Shelburne

39.160	Police "31/32"	(FRC)	KNEJ961	141.3
39.080	Police -F3		KNEJ961	141.3
453.3125	Police -mobile repeater		KD23940	141.3
42.460	Police -State PD coverage		KF7716	141.3
33.540	Fire -Shelburne Vol.	(9)	KCE786	123.0
33.480	Fire -Shelburne Falls	(9)	KIT866	123.0
460.6125	Fire -mobile repeater		WNRW517	141.3
453.350	Highway Department		WNUJ603	127.3
462.650	Municipal Operations		reported	

Sherborn

471.6375	Police	(BAPw)	WIK565	114.8
39.680	Police -old ch.	(SOM)	KBM662	123.0
39.420	Police -area tie		KBM662	123.0
483.0875	Fire	(14)	WIK580	114.8
39.500	Fire -pagers		WNKK777	151.4
39.500	DPW/Ambulance/C.D.		KWL481	151.4

Shirley

155.535	Police/Ambulance "2"	KNCI322	131.8
155.580	Police -F2- Groton tie		151.4
155.760	Police -F3- Lunenberg		100.0
155.475	Police -F4- area regional	KNCI322	131.8
39.420	Police -area base network	KCF350	CSQ
46.140	Fire -operations (8)	KNCE969	CSQ
46.540	Highway & Water Depts.	KNIA328	CSQ
155.775	Fire -mobile repeater		131.8
155.340	Town Ambulance	KC7341	CSQ
46.540	Highway & Water/FD ch.2	WYE613-5	CSQ
155.895	Highway -mobile repeater		131.8

Shrewsbury

155.700	Police "S" (WOR2)	WNKU888	131.8
155.970	Police -Northboro tie	reported	167.9
155.745	Police -F3- car to car	WNSV366	100.0
154.235	Fire (7)	WNWZ902	131.8
155.880	Highway Dept./Fire Pagers	KAU742	131.8
155.880	Town Light/Cable TV	KAU743	131.8
154.600	Shrewsbury Middle School	KB85370	
453.450	Galvin Mental Health Ctr.	WRE497	141.3
461.1375	Water Department -data	WPEY301	CSQ
155.745	MEMA Area III Net	WNSV366	100.0
463.2625R	Spag's Supply	WNUB557	D-051
463.8125	Spag's Supply	WNUB557	D-051
464.475	Worcester Biology Fndtn.	WNZX765	
464.8125	Southgate at Shrewsbury	WNYK990	
151.625	Ward Hill Ski Area	WPEH367	
151.685	Ward Hill Ski Area	WPEH367	

Shutesbury

155.745R	Police/DPW "33" (FRC)	KVN719	146.2
158.940	Police -input to repeater	KVN719	146.2
39.160	Police -county tie	KZU992	141.3
33.540	Fire/Tri-State Net (9)	KCH469	123.0
154.370	Fire -Hampshire Cty. tie	KCH469	127.3
155.085R	MEMA Area IV Net		100.0

Somerset

482.3375	Police (BRC)	KZM465	203.5
482.7625	Police -mobiles	KX2835	
453.100	Fire (3)	WPDA669	203.5
153.950	Fire -regional tie	KCC849	CSQ
154.995	Public Works Department	KAV455	114.8
45.700	Public Works Department	WPEK833	
153.860R	Emergency Mgmnt./Fire	KNJN710	
153.755	Emergency Mgmnt. -input	KNJN710	
155.715R	Emergency Mgmnt.	KNJN710	
155.955	MEMA -repeater input	KNJN710	
154.085R	MEMA -state tie	KNJN710	210.7
45.360	MEMA -state tie	KWO557	162.2

151.685	School Department	WZY981	
45.240	Council on Aging	WNIY645	

Somerville

470.5375	Police (BAPn)	KVP492	131.8
483.3875	Fire -F1- ops. (13)	WIF775	131.8
483.2625	Fire -F2- Metrofire hazmat	WIF775	131.8
483.3125	Fire -F3- Metrofire firgrnd.	WIF775	131.8
483.2875	Fire -F4- Metrofire bases	WIF775	131.8
483.4125	Fire -F5- arson squad	WIF775	131.8
33.860	Fire -training/backup	KDR298	
453.500	Highway Department	KWJ238	141.3
453.550	Highway Department	WNPQ639	141.3
453.625	Housing Auth./Traffic Dept.	WNQV680	141.3
453.5375	Municipal Services	WPEP744	
453.8625	Municipal Serivces	WNQV680	
453.400	Municipal Services	WNXD932	
464.4875	Assembly Square Mall	KB50942	136.5
462.075	Community Action Agency	WNRH754	

Southampton

460.025	Police (WEM)	WDT397	173.8
154.370	Fire/Hampshire Cty. Net	KNBC411	127.3
153.785	Fire	KNBC411	103.5
159.060	Highway Department	KXQ795	146.2

Southboro

39.100	Police (SOM)	KBR639	123.0
46.420	Fire (14)	KCE864	100.0
46.380	Fire -Dist. 14 fireground	KCE864	CSQ
155.955	Highway/Civil Defense	KFI555	CSQ
47.940	Water Department	KCE928	123.0
154.600	St. Marks School	KB25236	

Southbridge

158.850R	Police	KCA348	167.9
155.640	Police -repeater input	KCA348	167.9
154.145	Fire -primary (7)	KBG787	123.0
154.415	Fire -command channel	KBG787	173.8
460.6375	Fire -mobile repeater	KBG787	
465.6375	Fire -mobile repeater	KBG787	
156.135	Highway Department	KNAY899	127.3
153.680	Water Department	KCZ420	
464.925	Harrington Memorial	KNAU667	
461.175	Harrington Memorial	WPEZ867	
43.820	Worcester Rgnl. Transport	WNSL433	79.7

South Hadley

460.250	Police (WEM)	KCC396	173.8
853.5625	Police -mobile data	WNZB260	Data
853.4875	Police -future system	WPDU934	
854.4375	Police -future system	WPDU934	

154.370	Fire/Hampshire Cty. Net	KCH735	141.3
154.445	Fire -District 1	KCE703	141.3
151.175	Fire -District 2	KCE735	141.3
153.890	Fire -F2- fireground	KCH735	141.3
154.280	Fire -area intercity	KCE703	82.5
159.510	Highway Department	WQN913	103.5
155.115	Public Works/Wastewater	KB66312	103.5
153.410	South Hadley Water Dist.1	WNNA846	141.3
153.620	South Hadley Water Dist.2	KBX443	192.8
153.500	South Hadley City Power	KCC710	131.8
463.325	South Hadley Housing	WNWM824	
464.375	Mt. Holyoke College -sec.	WNQJ964	114.8
154.540	Mt. Holyoke College	KAQ978	
461.150	Mt. Holyoke College	WPCH637	
461.250	Mt. Holyoke College	WPDF589	

Southwick

154.815R	Police (WEM)	KGT550	114.8
155.850	Police -input to repeater	KGT550	114.8
465.3375	Police -mobile repeater	WNIT551	114.8
159.195R	Fire -operations (11)	KCF769	D-503
151.400	Fire -input to repeater	KCF769	D-503
154.235	Fire -secondary	KCF769	
154.340	Fire -fireground	KCF769	D-503
154.280	Fire -area intercity	KCF769	82.5
46.560	Highway Department	KGT550	167.9

Spencer

45.180	Police	KRZ253	167.9
154.950	Police -investigations	WPCP381	
33.640	Fire -primary (7/8)	WXB983	131.8
45.240	Highway Department	WXP514	100.0
33.080	Rescue Squad	KUP303	131.8
152.885	Spencer Water District	WNFK820	
155.745	MEMA Area III Net	WNLZ765	100.0
151.445	Jr. Conservation Camp	WNJN342	

Springfield

460.100	Police -F1- operations	KGR699	156.7
460.450	Police -F2- records/license	KRG699	156.7
460.500	Police -F3- detectives	KRG699	156.7
460.300	Police -F6- DVP/talkaround	KRG699	156.7
154.770	Police -mobiles/inactive	KA67798	
460.225	Police -WEMLEC Network	WBC465	173.8
460.475	Police -WEMLEC Network	WBC465	173.8
154.400	Fire -F1- dispatch/adm.	KDU448	82.5
154.175R	Fire -F2- operations/disp.	KDU448	82.5
158.880	Fire -F3- repeater input	KDU448	82.5
154.280	Fire -F4- area intercity	WNND402	82.5
153.830	Fire -F6- tactical/dispatch	KDU448	82.5
154.585	Fire -Hazmat Intercity	reported	82.5
155.625	Fire -fireground	KLX949	179.9
33.520	Hampden County Fire Net	KDU448	CSQ

Frequency	Description	Call Sign	Tone
451.700R	Fire -Hampden Cty. Link	WOV76	131.8
MED 1-10	City Ambulance Services	KNEN660	151.4
156.195R	Highway Department	KEM702	179.9
159.075	Highway Dept.-repeater in	KEM702	179.9
158.985	Highway Dept.-simplex	KD37271	179.9
156.000	Public Works Dept. -mobs.	KAU437	179.9
158.820	Municipal Services	KAU437	
453.6125	Civic Center	KB69037	141.3
453.3625	Civic Center	reported	
453.4875	High School	KB87243	
161.430	Civil Preparedness Net	KCE714	179.9
453.875	Forestry & Parks Dept.	KRG627	179.9
453.825	School Department	KNGU723	179.9
453.150	Housing Authority	WRB572	100.0
453.975	Public Bldgs./Radio Techs	WQU338	179.9
155.025	Dial-A-Van/Library/Escort	KYU959	82.5
158.940	Sewer Department	KA60767	179.9
155.865	Treatment Plant	KFU263	179.9
37.520	City Power Department	KEN712	179.9
37.820	Water Department	KEN712	179.9
173.210	Water Department -data	WNZS750	CSQ
173.3125	Water Department -data	WGZ849	CSQ
453.2875	Communications Division	WNWK425	127.3
458.2375	Communications Division	WNWK425	127.3
466.5125	Library & Museums Assoc.	KNIY558	
464.5625	Parking Enforcement HT's	KD26270	114.8
453.900	Western MA Youth Center	WNGL272	
154.725	Alcohol Treatment Ctr. -sec.	WNFF977	107.2
154.725	Alcohol Treatment Ctr. -mnt.	WNFF977	162.2
464.475	BayState Medical Center	WQC940	
464.875	BayState Medical Center	WQC940	100.0
453.7125	Municipal Hospital	KB72799	
452.650	Pioneer Valley Transport	WDF915	173.8
452.750	Pioneer Valley Transport	WDF915	123.0
452.800	Pioneer Valley Transport	WDF915	CSQ
452.725	Peter Pan Buses -base	WNKT456	100.0
452.725	Peter Pan Buses -mobiles	KNKT456	114.8
461.150	American Int'l College	KLC314	71.9
154.540	Springfield College	KCU889	D-134
464.325	Springfield College	WNVK233	88.5
155.160	Springfield College	WPDX869	91.5
464.925	Springfield College	WNZR764	D-134
464.975	Springfield College -Maint.	WSX829	
469.9125	Springfield College	KD45445	
464.375	Springfield Tech College	WNAN935	162.2
151.715	Springfield Tech College	WNDA871	
461.1625	West N.E. College -sec.	WNUF628	91.5
464.475	West N.E. College -sec.	KNDX556	192.8
461.2375	West N.E. College -maint.	WNRM591	91.5
462.8875	West N.E. College	WPDS389	241.8
154.570	West N.E. College	KB82311	

417.200	General Services Adm.	KPA505	
162.225	US Postal -production	KWN207	CSQ
172.300	US Postal -marshalling	KWN204	114.8
170.125	US Postal -maintenance	KWN206	CSQ
166.200	US Postal -operations	KVO724	114.8
171.2625	US Postal -operations	KWN205	CSQ
461.6875	Winchester Sq. Citizens	KD47536	
461.8125	Hampden Probate Security	WNYJ798	D-245
464.675	Eastfield Mall	KTF428	131.8
469.9125	Eastfield Mall	KD36877	141.3
461.600	Springfield Marriott	KNEM406	131.8
463.8125	Springfield Marriott	WNXH299	
463.300	Sheraton Springfield	WNJV328	
464.0375	Sheraton Springfield	WPBF868	
461.025	Holiday Inn	KD22764	123.0
464.750	Allendale Management	WNQQ724	218.1
464.425	Beacon Management	WPBK393	D-606
461.150	Chestnut Park	KNDJ606	CSQ
463.400	Forge Development Corp.	KB95347	218.1
463.475	Forge Development Corp.	KB95347	218.1
173.375	Springfield Republic	WNFW237	107.2

Sterling
37.100	Police	KJW623	118.8
37.140	Police -portables	KJW623	118.8
33.760	Fire (8)	KCE537	100.0
155.235	Fire Ambulance	WNYJ549	100.0
45.720	Highway Department	KLH940	CSQ
48.380	Town Power	KCE725	CSQ

Stockbridge
154.740	Berkshire County PD Net	KX4880	107.2
154.310	Fire/Berkshire Cty. Net	KDR721	107.2
153.845	Highway Department	KUE566	

Stoneham
482.5375	Police (NEM)	KYL890	146.2
46.060	Fire	KBZ954	CSQ
483.1125	Highway Department	KNM203	146.2
151.655	School Department	KJZ578	
153.875R	No. Shore Civil Defense	WNHF212	127.3
154.540	New England Memorial	KNAK971	
155.295	New England Memorial	WNBY437	
484.2375	New England Memorial	WNJV328	

Stoughton
471.6625	Police (BAPs)	WXW961	131.8
155.730	Police -area regional	KCA214	
46.140	Fire (4/SE)	KCA629	136.5
460.6125	Fire -mobile repeater	WNVJ850	
460.6375	Fire -mobile repeater	WNVJ850	
151.025	Highway Department	KCG335	CSQ

155.865	School Department	KNHR818	
462.650	South Shore REACT	KAD0591	
155.280	New England Sinai Hosp.	WZM676	
464.575	New England Sinai Hosp.	KB80360	
155.160	Goddard Memorial Hosp.	KXH201	
155.340	Goddard Memorial Hosp.	varies	
463.6125	Goddard Memorial Hosp.	WNVG470	

Stow
155.595	Police (SOM)	KJN740	123.0
155.790	Police -F2- Hudson area	KJN740	136.5
155.010	Police -F3- Maynard area	KJN740	107.2
155.475	Police -F8- regional	reported	136.5
154.935	Police -F10- mobiles	reported	123.0
46.500	Fire	KLI225	100.0
46.420	Fire -secondary/regional	KLI225	100.0
159.060	Highway Dept./PD ch. 7	WZY455	127.3

Sturbridge
155.415	Police	KNER808	110.9
155.940	Fire/Ambulance (7)	KCN235	CSQ
33.460	Fire -Hampden County tie	KCG653	CSQ
155.745	MEMA Area III Net	WNUS542	100.0
33.080	Tantasqua School District	KXL286	
464.375	Old Sturbridge Village	KUD481	D-205
462.775	Old Sturbridge Village	KNFQ958	
462.750	Public House -paging	WQE273	

Sudbury
867.9125	Police (SOM)	WNVP202	D-023
33.740	Fire -F1-	KCA583	127.3
33.980	Fire -F2- S. Middlesex Net	KCA583	127.3
154.115	Parks & Recreation	KBI879	114.8
156.195R	Highway Department	WNJZ617	100.0
154.600	Lincoln Sudbury High	KB74665	
156.075	Carroll School	WNQH233	CSQ
461.4375	Camp Sewataro	WPCF769	
463.4375	Camp Sewataro	WPCF769	

Sunderland
39.160	Police "35" (FRC)	KJZ924	141.3
42.460	Police -State PD coverage	KJZ924	141.3
33.540	Fire/Tri-State Net (9)	KCN366	123.0
37.960	Highway Department	WNCK527	146.2

Sutton
39.660	Police	KDS617	114.8
39.980	Police -regional net	KDS617	CSQ
45.220	Police -F2- Millbury tie	KDS617	167.9
33.620	Fire/So. Worcester Net	KDF582	131.8
46.520	Highway Department	KLR442	123.0
155.745	MEMA -Area III Net	WPEY676	100.0

464.475	Pleasant Valley C.C.		KNBC478	
154.570	Pleasant Valley C.C.		KD45729	

Swampscott
472.3375	Police	(BAPn)	KCA973	131.8
154.370	Fire	(5)	KNBQ200	107.2
151.010	Highway Department		KSQ844-5	
153.875R	No. Shore Emergency Net		KNAL782	127.3

Swansea
482.3375	Police	(BRC)	KZM471	203.5
153.950	Fire	(3)	KCB615	CSQ
460.5875	Fire -mobile repeater		KCB615	
156.105	Highway Department		KDD918	
154.025	Water Department		KLY268	
45.360	Mosquito Control		KZQ563	
154.085	MEMA Area II Net		KNDG607	210.7
461.450	Council on Aging		KNFD287	

Taunton
483.0625	Police	(BRC)	KZM466	203.5
33.980	Fire	(2/3)	KNGJ819	203.5
75.660	Fire -Fire Alarm boxes		WNMF670	CSQ
460.5875	Fire -mobile extender		KNGJ819	
465.5875	Fire -mobile extender		KNGJ819	
460.6125	Fire -mobile extender		KD38646	
33.060	Highway Department		KNBT575	100.0
33.100	Parks & Recreation		KNIV647	100.0
154.055	Housing Authority		KNAS383	
48.400	Water Department		KNHT486	
158.130	Taunton Municipal Light		KCA983	162.2
453.400	Attleboro-Taunton Transit		KNJT995	110.9
45.040	County Mosquito Control		KBV956	
154.570	High School		KW2785	
154.600	High School		KW2785	
158.775	State Hospital		KNIT373	141.3
453.800	State Hospital		KNHM918	162.2
155.175	Visiting Nurse Assn.		WNKB692	
154.515	Morton Hospital		WSB221	CSQ
156.000	Paul Dever School		KNBB765	
463.8125	Silver City Galleria Mall		reported	D-065
464.325	Taunton Regency Hotel		WNKR897	
152.480	Bristol Plymouth Voc.		KNFH320	

Templeton
155.940	Police/Fire/DPW	KAX598	CSQ
155.760	Police -secondary	WNNQ934	192.8
33.700	Fire/Mid-State Net	KRJ877	CSQ
48.380	Municipal Light Dept.	KNHQ626	
451.075	Municipal Light Dept.	WNQV731	
151.895	W E Fernald School	KNCB625	

Tewksbury

482.6625	Police (NEM)	KYR961	146.2
483.7125	Fire -F1-	WIL204	100.0
483.6375	Fire -F2-	WIL204	100.0
484.3875	Fire -F3- Fireground	WIL204	100.0
33.660	Fire/No. Middlesex Net	KCF307	CSQ
33.480	Fire -reserve	KCF307	
453.2125	Fire -mobile repeater		146.2
458.2125	Fire -mobile repeater		146.2
158.820	Civil Defense	KUL830	
151.100	Highway/Forestry	KGL516	146.2
45.200	Water Department	KTV836	
453.150	State Hospital -security	WQA886	123.0
453.6375	State Hospital -maint.	KD34226	
154.570	State Hospital -admin.	KO21309	
465.000	State Hospital -paging	WNMT455	
463.725	Tewksbury Hospital	WNYS779	
151.685	Trull Brook Golf Course	WNUY905	

Tolland

155.985	Police/Fireground/Highway	KNCZ364	114.8
33.460	Fire/Hampden Net (11)	KBM367	CSQ

Topsfield

154.100	Police & Fire Departments	KEL403	107.2
154.710	Police -Wenham tie	KLU331	107.2
154.845	Police -area tie/backup	KLU331	
151.460	Fire -secondary	WNPL239	107.2
154.445	Fire (unused)	KJL701	
154.070	Fire -Essex County Net	WNPL239	
154.540	Mass. Audubon Society	KA81490	
151.625	Topsfield Fair		
154.600	Topsfield Fair		

Townsend

39.080	Police "4"	KSQ823	114.8
39.420	Police -regional base net	KWQ823	CSQ
45.280	Fire (6/8)	KBR231	CSQ
33.900	Fire -southern NH fire tie	mobiles	CSQ
45.280	Public Works/Water Dept.	KDV432	CSQ
153.755	Ambulance -mobile rptr.	WNZL634	100.0
158.865	Ambulance -mobile rptr.	WNZL634	100.0

Truro

155.520	Police "BAKER" (BAR)	KCA700	110.9
155.700	Police -regional tie	KCA700	CSQ
156.195	Police -surveillance	reported	
155.505	Police -F3- car to car	reported	110.9
33.660	Fire (1)	KCF264	114.8
37.180	Public Works Department	KNGA976	173.8
165.0125	USAF -Disaster Network		

171.725R	Cape Cod Nat'l Seashore	KCB740	CSQ
151.655	North Truro Camping Area	WNFL782	D-445
461.1125	Hortons Park Inc.	KB82718	D-026

Tyngsboro
852.2875	Police -voice disp. (temp.)		100.0
155.130	Police -data	KFF222	CSQ
482.5125	Police -NEMLEC tie	KYR950	146.2
33.660	Fire/No. Middlesex Net	KCF314	123.0
154.295	Fire -mobile repeater	KCF314	
156.135R	Highway Department	WNPL340	167.9
155.880	Highway Dept. -repeater in	WNPL340	167.9
154.600	Grtr. Lowell Rgnl. School	KA65065	
464.975	Grtr. Lowell Rgnl. School	KSF615	

Tyringham
154.740	Police/Berkshire Cty. Net		107.2
154.310	Fire/Berkshire Cty. Net	KDP422	107.2
156.195	Highway Department	WNJR471	107.2

Upton
155.685	Police	WNWA752	123.0
155.790	Police -regional tie	KCF855	CSQ
155.040	Fire/Amb./DPW/PD backup	KDS601	123.0/CSQ
33.620	Fire -South Worcester Net	KEM634	131.8
156.120	Highway Department	WNSC748	

Uxbridge
39.780	Police	KCC462	100.0
39.980	Police -regional net	KCC462	CSQ
45.800	Police -F3-/Highway Dept.	KNBF426	CSQ
33.840	Fire (7)	KCF918	131.8
45.800	Highway Dept./PD -F3-	KNIE803	CSQ

Wakefield
471.7875	Police (BAPn/NEM)	WIG752	131.8
46.060	Fire (13)	KCC215	CSQ
460.5375	Fire -mobile repeater	KD24444	CSQ
155.865	Highway Department	KGT603	97.4
37.500	Town Power	KCD721	
464.550	Mass. Special Olympics	WNJT986	
463.7875	Colonial Hilton	KD53645	

Wales
39.080	Police	reported	123.0
45.460	Police/DPW/Fire	KCQ767	123.0
33.460	Fire -New Braintree Disp.		131.8

Walpole
471.5875	Police (BAPs)	WIG663	131.8
33.500	Fire (4/SE)	KCF375	*CSQ
33.540	Fire -Norfolk Cty. secondary	KCF375	CSQ

33.540	Fire -Norfolk Cty. secondary	KCF375	CSQ
33.840	Fire -F3- fireground	KCF375	107.2
37.260	Fire Alarm Maintenance	KCF375	
151.085	Highway Department	KNFE790	CSQ
156.180	Highway Department	KNFE790	
154.100	Municipal Services	WNKP452	
461.525	Michael J. Connolly Buses		186.2

*Walpole Fire is considering switching to UHF in the future.

Waltham

470.5125	Police (BAPw)	KZR402	131.8
154.400	Fire -F1- primary	KCD489	123.0
154.130	Fire -F2- Belmont tie	KCD589	100.0
154.220	Fire -F3- Metrofire	KCD489	CSQ
154.265	Fire -F4- alt./fireground	KCD489	
153.830	Fire -fireground	WNUA363	
153.860	Fire -fire alarm maint.	WNDY357	123.0
37.940	Highway Department	KCD589	CSQ
159.375	Parks & Recreation	KNJC575	114.8
153.875R	Civil Defense/N. Shore Net	KRC905	127.3
156.015	Cemetery Department	WXK232	
153.860	Council on Aging	WNDY357	114.8
159.000	Wires Department	WNNK482	
464.375	Waltham High School	KD50705	
464.275	Brandeis -campus police	KNAT408	127.3
464.825	Brandeis -escort service	KNFW839	127.3
464.775	Bentley College	KQQ244	107.2
464.075	Bentley College -security	KQQ244	107.2
467.775	Bentley College	WNRZ808	
154.845	Fernald School -security	WNQZ844	127.3
154.085	Fernald School -maint.	WNQU632	127.3
151.685	Fernald School	KD53059	
151.805	Fernald School -maint.	reported	156.7
155.325	Metropolitan State Hosp.	KNHZ862	
470.4125	Waltham-Weston Hospital	simplex	
171.525	USDA Inspection Service	KQC316	
453.375	Middlesex County Hosp.	WNGG337	
464.775	Vista International Hotel	WNPY755	
154.570	Best Western/TLC Hotel	KB82044	
464.325	Prospect Hill Exec. Park	WNMI711	131.8

Ware

154.845R	Police (WEM)	WNLY684	141.3
155.850	Police -input to repeater	WNLY684	141.3
153.920	Fire (10)	KNAQ859	CSQ
451.025	Highway/Water/Forestry	KBL738	B-103.5
451.025	Highway/Water/Forestry	KBL738	M-141.3
154.600	Ware Middle School	KB80575	
155.895	Elderly Transport	WNQU408	D-051
155.340	Mary Lane Hospital	WZT852	
461.750	Mary Lane Hospital	WNFU839	

Wareham

482.5375	Police "S3" (PLC)	KZW222	203.5
155.565	Police -Barnstable Cty. tie	KCG227	110.9
33.880	Fire -Wareham Fire (1/2)	KCD915	203.5
33.880	Fire -West Wareham Sta.	KLX742	203.5
33.920	Fire -Onset Fire Dist.	KCA410	203.5
33.080	Fire -ambulance	WNWD433	203.5
154.400	Fire -unknown use	KCD915	
154.235	Fire -Onset Fire District	KCA410	
173.210	Fire -Onset Fire District	KWB885	Data
45.560	Police/Fire/DPW/Water tie	many	131.8
45.240	Aging Council/Assesors	WSQ950	203.5
463.400	Friends of the Elderly	WRR836	
154.980R	School Buses	WNDU629	100.0
158.925	School Buses -repeater in	WNDU629	100.0
155.220	Tobey Hospital	KTE550	

Warren

45.480	Police	WNAH634	74.4
154.770	Police -mobiles	WPAJ684	
154.130	Fire (7)	KNDU318-20	CSQ
154.130	Fire -West Warren Station	KNEU319	CSQ
45.280	Public Works Department	WNKU407	74.4
37.180	Municipal Services	WNGA882	

Warwick

39.160	Police "37" (FRC)	KSS205	141.3
39.220	Police -Orange/Royalston	KSS205	141.3
33.540	Fire/Tri-State Net (9)	KWV807	123.0
33.060	Highway Department	KNGP421	

Washington

154.740	Police/Berkshire County	107.2
153.965	Police/Berkshire County	107.2
154.310	Fire/Berkshire County	107.2
154.115	Highway Department	

Watertown

470.7125	Police (BAPw)	KXG909	131.8
483.7125	Fire (13)	KCY613	131.8
156.135R	Highway Department	KEX227	131.8
159.015	Highway Dept -repeater in	KEX227	131.8
155.955R	Municipal Services	WQU340	
158.925	Municipal Services -input	WQU340	

Wayland

484.4375	Police (BAPw/SOM)	WIH972	131.8
39.360	Police -old channel	KCE471	
483.4125	Fire (14)	WII891	203.5
156.180	Highway Department	KXJ371	CSQ
153.410	Water Department	KCF930	151.4

Webster

156.210	Police	KNCT689	71.9
153.860	Fire/Highway (7)	KAR464	100.0
155.745	MEMA Area III Net		100.0
43.820	Worc. Regional Tranport	WNSL433	79.7

Wellesley

471.4875	Police (BAPw/SOM)	KOB384	131.8
39.140	Police -F14- old channel	KCB455	
46.100	Fire (13/14)	KCE403	136.5
154.040	Highway/Sewer/Water	KAP961	123.0
158.940	Electric Light Department	KAP961	123.0
462.700	Auxiliary Police/C.D.	KAD4034	
462.075	Babson College -security	WSF406	167.9
464.925	Babson College -maint.	KNBG404	131.8
464.375	Babson College	WSF406	
471.4625	Dana Hall -security	WIJ439	203.5
463.600	Wellesley College	KZD798	107.2
151.745	Wellesley College B & G	KCJ343	162.2
464.975	Wellesley College Sci. Ctr.	WZV935	
464.425	Wellesley College	WPDW912	
151.865	MA Bay Cmmnty. College	KJN315	
154.540	Wellesley Office Park	KTH220	
464.625	Wellesley Office Park	KNIN390	
464.875	Wellesley Inn	WNDC591	

Wellfleet

155.700	Police "CHARLIE" (BAR)	KCA370	110.9
155.760	Police -F4- /Beaches	KBF878	110.9
33.540	Fire -operations (1)	KCD500	114.8
33.660	Fire -Truro tie	KCD500	114.8
33.520	Fire -inactive	KCD500	114.8
155.760	Public Works Department	KBF878	CSQ
171.725R	Cape Cod Nat'l Seashore	KCB742	CSQ
151.805	Spring Brook Center	KNCG588	

Wendell

39.160	Police (9) (FRC)	KWM784	141.3
39.220	Police -area net	KWM784	
33.540	Fire/Tri-State Net (9)	KTZ304	123.0
158.955	Highway Department	KB20504	

Wenham

471.1375	Police (BAPn)	WIJ787	131.8
155.940	Police/Fire/Highway (5)	KES711	127.3
155.370	Police -secondary	KB36883	127.3
154.710	Police -Topsfield tie	KB36883	107.2
153.770	Fire -F2-	WNUK819	127.3
156.180	Highway Department	WNNW365	127.3
153.875R	No. Shore Emergency Net	KNBW698	127.3
154.540	Gordon College	KP2237	
154.600	Gordon College	KP2237	

Westboro

Freq	Description	Call	Tone
39.420	Police (SOM)	KBD924	123.0
46.080	Fire	WNPL242	114.8
465.6125	Fire -mobile repeaters	WNPL242	114.8
45.200	Highway Department	KBD924	*114.8
155.355	Westboro State Hospital	WNDD478	146.2
464.475	Mass Technology Park	KD40092	
464.525	Westboro Marriott	KNJV898	
464.825	Willows Retirement Home	WNVB896	D-464

* Tone on base only; mobiles are CSQ.

West Boylston

Freq	Description	Call	Tone
45.620	Police "WB" (WOR1)	KAG534	167.9
45.320	Police -F2- secondary	reported	
39.720	Police -F3- car to car	reported	CSQ
33.920	Fire (8)	KCH239	CSQ
45.440	Highway Department	KCI273	100.0
48.380	Town Power	KCB565	
154.025	Regional Education Ctr.	KNHC278	
453.7125R	Worcester County Jail	WNRQ384	D-364
460.3625R	Worcester County Jail	KB78749	D-023
460.4375R	Worcester County Jail	KB78749	D-023
37.200	County Prisoner Transport	KSN242	192.8
37.360	County Prisoner Transport	KSN242	

West Bridgewater

Freq	Description	Call	Tone
482.6125	Police "J2" (PLC)	KZV263	203.5
155.730	Police -regional network	KCD819	
33.720	Fire (2/4/SE)	KNCB532	203.5
154.310	Fire -Brockton tie	KCD820	203.5
460.6375	Fire -mobile repeater	KNCB532	203.5
156.225	Highway Department	KNEJ673	
154.085R	MEMA Area II Net	WNAS290	210.7

West Brookfield

Freq	Description	Call	Tone
39.840	Police	KUI536	85.4
154.890	Police -future mobile rptr.	reported	
33.620	Fire/So. Worcester Net	KBK403	131.8
153.785	Highway/Water Depts.	WNJV364	179.9

Westfield

Freq	Description	Call	Tone
155.190R	Police (WEM)	KCB394	114.8
155.910	Police -input to repeater	KCB394	114.8
154.430R	Fire -primary (11)	KNAG577	82.5
153.770	Fire -input to repeater	KNAG577	82.5
153.830	Fire -fireground	KNAG577	82.5
46.060	Fire -new channel	KNAG577	
154.280	Fire -area intercity	WNDD402	82.5
72.820	Fire -fire alarm boxes	WFN249	CSQ
151.100	Highway Department	KNEF678	141.3
155.880R	Parks/Water Departments	KCW411	141.3

153.860	Parks/Water Depts. -input	KCW411	141.3
48.140	Municipal Light Dept.	KCC952	103.5
45.320	Civil Defense/State tie	WXM704	162.2
45.360	Civil Defense/State tie	WXM704	162.2
148.455	Barnes Airfield -Security		CSQ
153.920	Barnes Airfield -Adm./Amb.	WNCX656	141.3
151.685	Housing Authority	KMH882	
155.265	Public Schools Transport	WYC870	82.5
154.965	Westfield State College	WPDZ942	141.3
151.775	Westfield State College	WNRR207	
154.570	Western Mass. Hospital	KA43348	
154.570	Noble Hospital	WNVJ451	
155.385	Noble Hospital	WNAZ510	

Westford

482.5125	Police (NEM)	WBF973	146.2
154.785	Police -amb./backup	KCE644	
33.660	Fire/North Middlesex Net	KCF315	CSQ
33.760	Fire -F2- fireground/Rgnl.		CSQ
46.140	Fire/MIT Emergency tie	KDJ595	CSQ
155.925	Highway Department	KFZ784	118.8
155.160	School Buses	WNQH991	
464.775	Westford Regency Inn	WNBG330	151.4
464.825	Westford Regency Inn	WNBR576	
151.715	Nashoba Valley Ski Area	KNBU500	97.4
151.745	Nashoba Valley Ski Area	KNBU500	97.4
461.325	Nashoba Valley Ski Area	KNBU500	

Westhampton

460.325	Police -F1- operations	KNFJ246	173.8
465.325M	Police -F2- repeater input	KNFJ246	173.8
460.225	Police -F3- WEMLEC	KNFJ246	173.8
460.025	Police -F4- Easthampton	KNFJ246	173.8
154.370	Fire/Hampshire Cty. Net	KWQ578	127.3
154.250	Fire -fireground	KWQ578	127.3
153.830	Fire -fireground -F3-	KWQ578	127.3
152.360	Hampshire Reg. Schools	WPDC826	

Westminster

155.730	Police	KCG832	192.8
155.790	Police -F2-	KCG832	192.8
155.805	Police -MCI Gardner tie	KNCP300	192.8
33.960	Fire (8)	KCD658	CSQ
33.820	Fire -Ashburnham tie	KCD658	118.8
33.520	Fire -inactive	KCD658	
33.020	Highway Department	KCC842	CSQ

West Newbury

482.3625	Police "570" (NES)	WII289	146.2
482.7875	Police -Rowley tie		146.2
482.8375	Police -Amesbury/Merrimac	WII289	146.2
483.0125	Police -Nwby./Nwbyprt.	WII289	146.2

483.7375	Police -Salisbury tie	WII289	146.2
483.1375	Police -Nespern Regional	WII289	146.2
39.820	Police -old re-licensed ch.	KTG611	
154.710	Police -Groveland tie	KTG611	131.8
154.010	Fire (15)	KNFX445	CSQ
154.010	Fire -Haverhill Dispatch	KCA434	CSQ
158.955R	Fire -regional tie	KNFX445	203.5
154.280	Fire -Seacoast Net tie	KNFX445	CSQ
156.195	Highway Department	WNYU879	127.3
155.100	Civil Defense	KNBS866	127.3
153.875R	No. Shore Emergency Net	KNGS866	127.3

Weston
472.2375	Police (BAPw/SOM)	KCA857	203.5
154.160	Fire (13/14)	KRN846	123.0
154.265	Fire -secondary	KRN846	
45.160	Fire -Public Works tie	KCI424	CSQ
45.160	Highway Department	WXY504	CSQ
154.600	Regis College	KB60392	
463.800	Regis College	WNVK844	D-423
464.325	Regis College	WPEB698	
151.715	Henderson House Center	WPDU614	
151.745	Henderson House Center	WPDU614	

Westport
155.370	Police	KCB305	203.5
155.595	Police "slide channel 4"	reported	
46.180	Fire -Main St. Station (3)	KNFQ483	CSQ
46.180	Fire -Briggs Rd. Station	KNFQ482	CSQ
46.180	Fire -Reed Rd. Station	KNFQ484	CSQ
45.640	Highway Department	KWM646	203.5

West Springfield
155.520R	Police	KCB305	167.9
155.130	Police -input to repeater	KCC712	167.9
154.710	Police -Eastern States Expo	KD31797	141.3
452.200	Police -link	KCC712	131.8
452.500	Police -link	KCC712	131.8
460.1375	Police	KCC712	136.5
465.1375	Police	KCC712	136.5
155.100	Fire/Highway (11)	KBP899	167.9
154.145R	Fire -F1- primary	KUB744	167.9
154.145M	Fire -F2- direct	KUB744	167.9
159.360	Fire -repeater input	KUB744	167.9
154.445	Fire -fireground	KUB744	167.9
154.280	Fire -area intercity	KUB744	82.5
453.925	School Department	WNKY288	127.3
Trunked	Municipal Services	Business SMR	
462.700	Eastern States Esposition		71.9
154.600	Eastern States Exposition	KB67352	
461.8125	Eastern States Exposition	WNVR385	

West Stockbridge
154.740	Berkshire Cty. Police Net	KX4881	107.2
154.310	Fire/Berkshire Cty. Net	KCD558	107.2
153.995	Highway Department	WZT891	

Westwood
470.4375	Police (BAPs)	KZR404	131.8
39.980	Police -regional tie	KNEH240	
460.625	Fire	WNWS304	156.7
460.5875	Fire -mobiles	WNWS304	
465.5875	Fire -mobiles	WNWS304	
33.500	Fire -regional net (4/SE)	KCR898	CSQ
453.875	Highway Department	KEL989	156.7
451.200	Westwood Water Dept.	WNZI268	118.8

Weymouth
470.9375	Police (BAPs)	KCA985	131.8
154.235R	Fire -F1- primary (13/SE)	KCA302	136.5
156.075	Fire -F1- repeater input	KCA302	136.5
154.190	Fire -F2- Hingham/Hull	KCA302	203.5
154.295	Fire -F3- Southeast Net	KCA302	203.5
154.220	Fire -F4- Metrofire	KCA302	CSQ
154.265	Fire -tie to Hingham/Hull		203.5
151.055	Highway Department	KCH583	
39.900	Civil Defense/Park Police	KNCC342	
153.875R	No. Shore Emergency Net	KNCC342	127.3
464.575	School Department	WNAD631	
154.600	South Shore Hospital	KD47688	
155.265	South Shore Hospital	KTR574	
461.100	South Shore Hospital	WNUA415	
463.6625	South Shore Hospital	WPAT363	

South Weymouth Naval Air Station
140.475	Security	"Sierra Base"
140.010	Security -internal	secondary
140.700	Security	
140.425	Security	
140.060	Security -F2-	secondary
138.750	Medical Network	"White Base"
140.950	Crash/Fire/Rescue -F1-	"Red Base"
140.100	Crash/Fire/Rescue -F2-	internal
154.235R	Crash/Fire/Rescue	Weymouth FD tie
140.525	Public Works	
140.040	Administration	
140.580	Runway Control	
154.295	Regional Fire Network tie	

Whately
39.160	Police "39" (FRC)	KZU993	141.3
33.540	Fire/Tri-State Net (9)	KLM647	123.0
463.0375	Ambulance -mobile rprtr.	WNVH988	
155.025	Highway Department	WNHP645	100.0
452.100	Link channel	WNJJ228	

Whitman

482.3125	Police "X2" (PLC)	WII702	203.5
159.120	Highway/PD/Fire/Amb. tie	reported	
33.800	Fire (2/SE)	KCB715	203.5
155.895R	Municiapl Svcs./Police	KJV849	156.7
153.995	Municipal Services -input	KW9203	156.7
155.295	Whitman-Hanson School	WNVE892	

Wilbraham

854.5375	Police (WEM)	WNXR889	100.0
45.300	Police -old channel	KNGS317	107.2
46.100	Fire (11)	KCE264	107.2
46.280	Fire -secondary	KCE264	107.2
154.280	Fire -area intercity	KCE264	82.5
150.775	Ambulance -mobile rptr.	WPAK660	
45.640	Highway Department	KAR674	100.0
462.600	Middle School	KAE4343	
453.3625	Public Works Department	KD51418	
855.5875	Regional Schools	WNVJ702	D-043
154.600	Regional Schools	KB46143	

Williamsburg

154.040	Police -F1- ops. (WEM)	KNBF392	127.3
154.115	Police -F2- Goshen tie	KNBF392	127.3
154.370	Police -F3- Fire/Hamp. Cty.	KSV765	127.3
154.190	Police -F4- Goshen Amb.	KSV765	127.3
153.890	Police -F5- Cty. Fireground		127.3
154.995	Police -F6- Plainfield tie	KNBF392	141.3
154.845	Police -F7- Cummington tie	KNBF392	127.3
154.085	Police -F8- Hatfield tie	KNBF392	127.3
155.415	Police -F9- Hadley tie		123.0
159.150	Police -F10- Northampton		131.8
458.850	Police -mobile repeater	KB61622	127.3
154.370	Fire/Hampshire Cty. tie	KSV765	127.3
154.040	Highway Department	KNBF392	91.5

Williamstown

155.250	Police (BEC)	KNAK468	107.2
156.210	Police -North Adams tie	KNAK468	107.2
154.130	Fire -F2- (12)	KNEX803	107.2
154.310	Fire -F1- Berkshire Cty.	KNEX803	107.2
154.235	Fire -Hazmat Team	WNUA283	107.2
156.165	Highway & Sewer Depts.	KNDN772	
37.180	Highway Department	KQV605	
153.740	Haz-Mat response	KD29801	
453.675	Hoosac Water Quality Dist.	WNVQ881	
155.220	Village Ambulance	KNDD859	
151.805	Council on Aging	WNNL824	
151.955	Williams College -security	KB80543	146.2
464.550	Williams College -security	KQY579	146.2
461.775	Williams College -maint.	KQY579	146.2
464.475	Williams College -maint.	KQY579	146.2

464.875	Williams College	KQY579	
155.160	Mt. Greylock Rgnl. School	WNQT250	
461.700	Clark Art Institute	WNNL734	D-734

Wilmington
482.3125	Police (NEM)	WIL431	146.2
485.3875	Police -Tac 5	WIL431	
155.130	Police -Auxiliary/Portables	KCC421	CSQ
154.340	Fire (6)	KBR364	CSQ
154.965	Public Works Department	KEY847	118.8
155.340	Regional Health Center	WXP455	

Winchendon
39.220	Police	KCA677	173.8
155.730	Police -area tie	KCA677	192.8
33.780	Fire -operations (8)	KCN857	123.0
154.430	Fire -S.W. NH Fire tie	KNCE417	136.5
154.100	Highway Department	WNFZ470	CSQ

Winchester
471.3625	Police (BAPn/NEM)	WIE464	131.8
482.8125	Police -Woburn tie	KYL887	146.2
483.6875	Fire (13)	WII700	131.8
46.200	Fire -old channel	KFE606	
45.120	Public Works Department	WQN842	CSQ
461.5875	Winchester Hospital	WPAB231	
151.955	Winchester Country Club	WPEX920	
154.515	Winchester Country Club	WPEX920	

Windsor
155.715R	Police/Fire/Highway	WXY514	107.2
158.745	Police/Fire/Highway -input	WXY514	107.2

Winthrop
471.7375	Police (BAPn)	KAA931	131.8
474.7375M	Police -car to car	KAA931	131.8
155.580	Police -auxiliary	WXK752	
483.6375	Fire (13)	KYD496	131.8
154.055	Public Works Department	KUN410	CSQ
153.875R	No. Shore Emergency Net	KNBX709	127.3

Woburn
482.8125	Police (NEM)	KYL899	146.2
471.7625	Police -possible future use	reported	
483.6125	Fire (13)	WII507	146.2
46.380	Fire -old channel	KCH684	
72.820	Fire -Fire Alarm boxes	WGW25	CSQ
46.560	Civil Defense	KNIK971	
482.7625	Highway/Water Depts	WIG720	146.2
464.4875	Woburn Mall	KB32904	146.2
154.570	New England Trade Center	reported	
154.600	New England Trade Center	reported	

Worcester

Frequency	Service	Call Sign	Tone
TRUNKED	New Police/Fire/City Svcs.	See Below	
460.050	Police -F1- east operations	KRJ698	131.8
460.150	Police -F2- west operations	KRJ698	131.8
460.250	Police -F3- detectives -DVP	KRJ698	131.8
460.025	Police -F4- special ops.	KRJ698	131.8
460.325	Police -detectives -link	KRJ698	131.8
45.100	Police -Airport Security	WXP418	192.8
45.540	Police -regional net "W"	KRJ698	167.9
460.525	Fire -Citywide	KSM207	*179.9
460.575	Fire -dispatch/paging	KTO305	179.9
33.860	Fire -prevention/maint.	KCA706	167.9
33.700	Fire -Mid-State Net (8)	WYE395	CSQ
33.620	Fire -So. Worc. Net (7)	WYE395	131.8
37.980	Highway/Water Depts.	KNAN808	CSQ
45.000	Parks Department	KSI310	CSQ
46.580	Traffic Department	KFV884	100.0
46.580	Health Department		100.0
46.580	Housing Authority Maint.	KUS473	114.8
453.925	Housing Authority	KNGJ540	151.4
45.320	Emergency Mgmt.-State tie	WXT813	162.2
464.575	Municipal Services	WNME872	
464.350	Laidlaw School Bus Trans	WNUG725	D-612
154.600	Doherty High School		91.5
154.600	Forest Grove Middle School		103.5
462.950	Worcester City Ambulance	WXP693	186.2
220.22105	Worcester-Himmer Amb.	ACSB	
464.475	Hahnemann Hospital	KNBM477	
464.925	Memorial Hospital	WNDM831	186.2
461.150	St. Vincent Hospital	KWW620	162.2
467.8125	Worcester City Hosp. Link	U.MA Med	D-503
154.540	Worcester State Hospital	WRY636	79.7
154.570	Worcester State Hospital	WRY636	79.7
155.160	Med Flight Helicopters	KNFB453	118.8
854.4375	WRTA -elder vans	KNHQ788	141.3
854.4375	WRTA -elder vans	KNHQ788	131.8
856.2625	WRTA -buses	KNHQ788	CSQ
857.2625	WRTA -vans	KNHQ788	110.9
151.685	Assumption College	KRD952	123.0
464.525	Assumption College	WNXW248	
464.4875	Becker Jr. College	KB92721	DPL
151.805	Clark University -escorts	KLQ285	151.4
151.865	Clark University -maint.	KZR990	151.4
464.425	Clark University -security	WMCW890	D-032
151.715	Holy Cross College -maint.	WPEJ542	85.4
464.475	Holy Cross College -sec.	KNDA667	D-662
151.895	Holy Cross College	WPEN701	
453.475	Quinsigamond College	WNCS958	123.0
463.850	U MA Med School -sec.	WXL551	D-503
464.775	U MA Med School -maint.	KNBK684	D-032
151.895	Worcester Poly -maint.	KJA620	186.2
464.375	Worcester Poly -security	KNGL724	D-043

464.875	Worcester Poly -media svc.	WPAQ774	
154.570	Worcester Poly -ROTC	reported	
151.625	Worcester Poly -activities	reported	
453.675	Worcester State -security	WNIW486	
464.575	Worcester State -maint.	WXK827	DPL
464.4625	Worcester State	WPFC511	
464.3125	Worcester State	KB80121	
461.800	Worcester Common Mall	reported	DPL
464.5375	Greendale Mall Security	KD20275	D-032
464.8125	Worcester Marriott	KNAY595	
464.425	Worcester Marriott		D-244
151.955	Worcester Art Museum	WNRX250	
461.100	Worcester Flea Market	WPBH413	
151.835	Worcester Country Club	151.865 also	

*New Police, Fire, DPW Trunked System: 855.4875 (FD Tests), WNQJ840: 855.7125, 855.7375, 855.9625, 855.9875 ; WPAR399: 851.4625 data, 851.9125, 852.0375, 852.3625, 854.2125

Worcester Centrum
458.900	Centrum (police) security	KA92878	179.9

Worcester First Night
467.8625	Security	
464.550	Food Vendors	
151.625	Food Vendors	

Worthington
155.310	Police	WQJ357	110.9
154.370	Fire/Hampshire Cty. Net	KO6423	127.3
154.965	Highway Department	KNAN806	97.4
151.895	Hickory Hill Touring Ctr.	WNKP941	

Wrentham
39.420	Police "W"	KCD546	CSQ
39.540	Police -area tie	KCD546	CSQ
33.540	Fire (4/SE)	KCH794	CSQ
33.500	Fire -secondary	KCH794	CSQ
467.950	Ambulance -mobile rptr.	KD37070	
467.975	Ambulance -mobile rptr.	KD37070	
158.865	Highway Department	KNIE524	167.9
158.955	Wrentham State School	KQR540	141.3

Yarmouth
855.2375	Police "JOHN" (BAR)	WNPE241	D-244
810.2375	Police -car to car	WNPE241	D-244
155.055	Police -Marine Patrol	WPDU374	110.9
453.475	Police -inactive	KNDN559	
33.580	Fire -Headquarters (1)	KNCS289	114.8
33.580	Fire -Yarmouthport Station	KNCS288	114.8
33.580	Fire -West Yarmouth Sta.	KNCS290	114.8
460.6125	Fire -mobile extenders	KNCS289	114.8
465.6125	Fire -mobile extenders	KNCS289	114.8
453.550	Fire -HazMat operations	WNVZ651	
458.050	Fire -HazMat operations	WNVZ651	

151.055R	Highway Department	WNQV740	203.5
156.045	Highway Department -input	WNQV740	203.5
453.4625	Highway Department	WNVB862	
45.320	Mosquito Control	WNRS887	
154.115R	Municipal Services	WPDU374	
155.055	Municipal Services -input	WPDU374	
153.620	Town Administration	WNRZ748	
155.085	Town Administration	WNPU367	123.0
47.780	Water Department	KBM288	186.2
173.210	Water Department	WDA402	Data
151.445	Forestry Department	WNRW207	123.0
463.900	Dennis-Yarmouth Schools	WNBV862	179.9

Tone Codes

The numbers shown after the call sign are "PL (CTCSS) tone codes" which newer radios employ to discriminate between users. Some scanners are capable of accepting PL tones and this allows the user to monitor one licensee of a certain frequency while blocking other licensees who are operating with different, or no, tone code on that same frequency. "CSQ" indicates "carrier squelch" which indicates that there is no tone being used. A tone code with a "D" prefix indicates a digital tone which no scanners currently on the market can discriminate, however many two-way radios may be programmed with these tones.

Acronyms & Identifiers

Whenever you see a system acronym, e.g. (BAPn) or system district (7), refer to the regional police and fire sections. Thse acronyms and designators are indicating system affiliations such as the BAPERN system -north district; or the Fire District 7 network. These networks all have their own set of frequencies which, in an effort to save space, are not included with each community, but which are explained in the regional sections which follow.

Abbreviations

An "R" following a listing indicates that this is the output frequency of a repeaterized radio. Because just about all UHF (400 MHz & above) frequencies are repeaterized, only the output -the channel you want to listen to- is listed without the "R". If an agency goes "talkaround", then they will either use the repeater-out frequency sans repeater or they will use the repeater-input channel which is exactly 5MHz above the listed output frequency between 450 and 470MHz and exactly 3MHz above the listed channel from 470MHz to 512MHz. 800MHz systems are also repeaterized with inputs 45MHz below. An "M" following a listing indicates that the agency uses the channel with mobiles only.

STATE POLICE/Department of Public Safety

See Below for Metro Boston 800 MHz trunked frequencies.

		(42MHz PL tone: 141.3)
42.440	-F1-	STATEWIDE -Emergency/ Tactical/Escorts/Special Events
42.340	-F2-	TROOP "A" -eastern MA
		TROOP "A" -also uses 800 MHz
858.2375		TROOP "A" -northern area/HT's (temporary use; also 856.2375)
42.400	-F3-	TROOP "C" -central MA
856.2375		TROOP "C" -testing phase only
42.500	-F4-	TROOP "D" -southeast MA
42.540	-F5-	HQ & special units/command & detec.
42.460	-F6-	TROOP "B" -western MA
		TROOP "A" -car to car
42.420	-F7-	Detectives/Team "55" patrols
44.740	-F 8-	Admin./Small Town Patrol CSQ
		Paging/Helicopter/Command Staff
44.900	-F9-	Governor's Auto Theft Strike Force
		Turnpike car to car CSQ
155.475	-F10-	Turnpike car to car CSQ
159.030R		TROOP "E" -Pike Patrol
		(See below for more Pike details)
856-860.2625		TROOP "F" -Logan Airport Ops.
856-860.4375		TROOP "F" -Logan Airport Ops.
856-860.8125		TROOP "F" -Logan Airport Ops.
465.0125R		TROOP "D" link repeater
158.970		East New England Police Intercity
154.920	Portable	F1- repeats troop channel 141.3
154.920	Portable	F2- portable to portable
155.475	Portable	F3- intercity/tactical

Note: 42.460 is used as a car-to-car frequency in eastern MA as 42.340 is used out west & 42.540 in central areas.

<u>Radio Codes</u>

1. Emergency
2. Phone the station
3. Phone
4. Out of service
5. Back in service
6. Location
7. Return to station
8. Stopping suspicious vehicle
9. Registration request
10. Stolen status request
11. License status request
12. Message request
13. Radio check
14. Make & wants-person
15. Emergency request for assistance
16. Investigation
17. Clear from assignment
18. Request to clear

New State Police Radio System (former Metro System)

With the consolidation of the State Police, Metro Police, Capital and Registry Police Departments into a single State Police agency, the former Metro Police 800 MHz trunked radio system used in greater Boston is being gradually expanded across the state.

All units which had patrolled for the Metro Police use the 800 MHz system as before, while units from other areas and departments, notably State Police units between routes 128 and 495, have been using both the low-band system as well as the 800 MHz system (primarily with portables). State Police barracks across the eastern portion of the state have dispatch capabilities on 800 MHz.

This sophisticated 800 MHz system is trunked, meaning users hop about its 20 (and soon possibly more) channels using computer control so that many agencies may share the same frequencies without hearing one another.

The agencies on the system include:

State Police	MDC Central Services
(still using 42 MHz also)	MDC Parks & Recreation
Former Metro Police	Water Resources Authority
Former Registry Police	Convention Ctr. Authority
(still using low-band also)	Inspector General
Former Capital Police	State Medical Examiner
(still using 460 MHz)	Parole Board
Dept. of Public Safety units	
Auto Theft Strike Force	and many others
State Fire Marshal	

The following 20 channels are used in the trunked radio system. One or more of the channels listed below will be used for data and will rotate at certain intervals.

856.7125, 857.7125, 858.7125, 859.7125, 860.7125
856.7375, 857.7375, 858.7375, 859.7375, 860.7375
856.9625, 857.9625, 858.9625, 859.9625, 860.9625
856.9875, 857.9875, 858.9875, 859.9875, 860.9875

Frequencies to be implemented in the future:
854-860.2125, 856-860.2375, 856-860.2625, 852.2625,
856-860.4625, 857-860.7875, 853.0375, 852.3625
And some MassPort freqs. (Dukes County: 855.7375)

National Public Safety Frequencies
(Tactical, Station-to-Station, Foxboro Stadium use, etc.)
866.0125, 866.5125, 867.0125, 867.5125, 868.0125

Additional State Police Frequencies

853.8375	State Police (formerly Metro) at Central MA Reservoirs	146.2
854.0375	State Police (formerly Metro) at Quabbin Reservoir	146.2
158.970	Eastern New England Intercity Police	CSQ
470.7875	BAPERN Intercity Network -F3-	131.8
470.5625	BAPERN Intercity Network -F4-	131.8
460.225	WEMLEC tie (also 460.475)	173.8
851.6375	Mobile Data Terminals	data
852.2375	Mobile Data Terminals	data

TROOP "A" -Station A- Framingham Headquarters
- A-1 Andover
- A-2 West Newbury
- A-3 Concord
- A-4 Foxboro
- A-5 Framingham patrol desk
- A-6 Salisbury (summer)
- A-7 Peabody
- A-9 State Police Radio Repair
- A-11 MEMA HQ (Framingham)

TROOP "B" -Station B- Northampton Headquarters
- B-1 Lee
- B-2 Shelburne Falls
- B-3 Springfield
- B-4 Cheshire
- B-5 Russell
- B-6 Northampton patrol desk

TROOP "C" -Station C- Holden Headquarters
- C-1 Athol
- C-2 Grafton
- C-3 Brookfield
- C-4 Leominster
- C-5 Sturbridge
- C-6 Holden patrol desk
- C-7 Quabbin Reservoir
- C-8 Wachusett Reservoir

TROOP "D" -Station D- Middleboro Headquarters
- D-1 Norwell
- D-2 Yarmouth
- D-3 North Dartmouth
- D-4 Middleboro
- D-5 Oak Bluffs
- D-6 Nantucket
- D-7 Bourne

TROOP "E" -Massachusetts Turnpike- Weston HQ
- E-1 Weston sub.
- E-2 Charlton
- E-3 Westfield
- E-4 Sumner/Callahan Tunnels

TROOP "F" -Logan Airport
STATION "G" -General Headquarters (Framingham)

TROOP "H" -Greater Boston/North (Former Metro)
- H-2 Revere
- H-3 Medford
- H-4 Boston/Lower Basin

TROOP "I" -Greater Boston/South (Former Metro)
- I-5 Brighton/Upper Basin
- I-6 So. Boston/Old Colony
- I-7 Milton
- I-8 Hull/Nantasket

STATIONS/UNITS J, N, R, X -Bureau of Investigative Services
STATION/UNITS T -Tango Base- Truck Team
STATION/UNITS V -Victor Base- Motorcycle Squad

Massachusetts Turnpike – State Police Patrol

159.030R	Operations (Western - m.m. 0-25)	131.8
159.165R	Operations (Central - m.m. 25-85)	88.5
159.030R	Operations (Eastern - m.m. 85-end)	162.2/110.9
159.030R	Tunnels	141.3
159.315R	Extension	110.9
156.030	Repeater input	varies
156.060	Car to Car	
156.075	Car to Car	162.2/186.2
155.475	Car to Car (Channel 10)	CSQ
44.900	Car to Car	CSQ
44.740	State Police Headquarters to Pike	CSQ

The Turnpike also has access to all 42 MHz SP freqs.
Link Frequencies: 453.1875, 453.3125, 453.3375.

Massachusetts Turnpike – Maintenance

159.105R	Lee	(m.m. 0-20)	110.9
159.240R	Blandford	(m.m. 20-41)	141.3
159.045R	Warren/Chicopee	(m.m. 41-83)	192.8
159.120R	Auburn	(m.m. 83-105)	123.0
159.240R	Weston	(m.m. 105-end)	167.9
159.105R	Newton to Boston Extension		136.5
156.240M	Unit to Unit		100.0
159.045R	Tunnels		114.8
159.180R	Administration (156.060 input)		94.8

Inputs are all 156.240 for maintenance unless noted.

Former Registry of Motor Vehicles Police -Station "R"

39.760	Channel 1 -Operations -statewide	110.9
39.800	Channel 2 -Operations -inside Rte 128	110.9
39.020	Channel 3 -Car to car	110.9
39.120	Channel 4 -Car to car	110.9
453.1875	Boston HQ -Building Security/Administration	

State/County Law Enforcement & Miscellaneous Agencies

471.5625	Massachusetts Attorney General (& 800 MHz)
483.2875	Bristol County District Attorney (& 800 MHz)
483.2375	Bristol County District Attorney (& 482.7625)
472.6875	Essex County District Attorney (& 482.9125)
453.125	Hampshire County District Attorney
471.5625	Middlesex/Norfolk Cty. D.A. (& 471.2875 Nflk)
470.3375	Norfolk County Task Force
483.7375	Plymouth County BCI/District Attorney
471.1125	Suffolk Cty. District Attorney -detectives/phone
470.9875	Suffolk Cty. District Attorney -simplex ops.
460.025	MA State House -Capitol PD
453.100	MA State House - Maintenance
471.7125	MA Criminal Justice Training Council
453.9375	MA Parole Board (Boston) (& 800 MHz)
154.025	MA Fire Training Academy (& 153.905) 71.9
159.435	MA State Lottery Commission 203.5

STATE DEPT. OF CORRECTIONS (UHF PL 151.4)

453.500R -F1- WALPOLE "A" System -operations at:
Walpole/Norfolk Pre-release/Shirley/Warwick/Plymouth
453.650R -F2- NORFOLK "B" System -operations at:
Norfolk/Bay State Med Ctr./Concord/North East Correctional
453.450R -F3- BRIDGEWATER "C" Sys. -operations at:
Bridgewater/Southeast Correctional/Framingham Women's

453.975M	-F4-	Car to Car/Emergency
453.750R	-F5-8-	Statewide Prisoner Transport
453.850M	-F9-	Tactical Operations
453.6125R	-F10-	Walpole Maint. (Bridgewater Ops.)
453.7125R	-F11-	Norfolk Maintenance
453.675M	-F12-	Administration/Special Operations
153.935R		Prisoner Products Delivery (203.5)

COUNTY SHERIFFS/COUNTY JAILS

155.535	Barnstable	173.8
453.700	Barnstable -maint.	114.8
153.965	Berkshire	107.2
39.340	Bristol -jail maint.	
853.7625	Bristol -jail sec.	DPL
Trunked	Bristol (855.4875, 855.9875, 859.4875, 860.4875 + SP 800)	
482.5875	Essex	123.0
470.3375	Essex	123.0
482.9125	Essex (F-2)	123.0
39.160	Franklin	141.3
39.240	Franklin	141.3
453.400	Franklin	141.3
458.5875	Franklin	141.3
151.460R	Hampden (int. ops.)	D-423
155.580	Hampden (input)	D-423
158.730R	Hampden (patrols)	D-662
155.430	Hampden (input)	D-662
158.850	Hampshire	
453.550	Hampshire	141.3
453.1125	Hampshire -Court	146.2
458.1125	Hampshire -Court	146.2
45.940	Middlesex	CSQ
46.020	Middlesex	
45.780	Middlesex -new	
158.730	Middlesex -Camb. Court	
855.4625	Norfolk (& SP 800 MHz)	
483.7375	Plymouth (K9/Trans)	203.5
483.0375	Plymouth (BCI)	203.5
453.1375	Plymouth (Jail) F-1	203.5
453.4625	Plymouth (Jail) Adm	D-606
453.8375	Plymouth (Jail) Ops	110.9
453.2875	Plymouth (453.6375, .9875)	
471.6875	Suffolk	131.8
471.1125	Suffolk	131.8
854.9875	Suffolk ch. #1	
800.MHz	Suffolk ch. #2	
453.300	Suffolk -sheriff's in Bos.	
37.200	Worc. Sheriff (F-1)	192.8
37.360	Worc. Sheriff (F-2)	
460.3625	Worc. W. Boyl. Jail	D-023
453.7125	Worc. W. Boyl. Jail	D-364
460.4375	Worc. W. Boyl. Jail	D-023

Possible Future Hampden County
System: 866.650, 866.900,
867.3125, 867.2875, 867.400,
867.7125, 867.7375, 867.9875,
868.325, 868.400, 868.900

STATE HOSPITALS/SPECIAL NEEDS SCHOOLS

156.075	Mass. Mental Health Center
158.745	Mass. Mental Health Center
155.145	Belchertown State School (also 153.965)
158.865	Medfield State Hospital
158.775	Paul Dever School (Taunton)
156.000	Paul Dever School (Taunton) Maintenance
453.6875	Solomon Carter Fuller Mental Health (Boston)
453.8375	Solomon Carter Mental Health Ctr. (Lowell)
453.800	Taunton State School
453.150	Tewksbury State Hospital
453.6375	Tewksbury State Hospital (& 458.6375)
155.355	Westboro State Hospital
158.955	Wrentham State School

STATE EMERGENCY MANAGEMENT AGENCY (MEMA)

45.360	Statewide Civil Defense	162.2
45.320	Mobiles to area HQ/Area sectors	162.2
155.955	Statewide Admin./Repeater input	varies
153.965R	Area I net (Boston area & nor'east MA)	203.5
154.085R	Area II net (southeastern MA)	210.7
156.135	Area II net repeater input	210.7
155.745	Area III net (central MA)	100.0
155.085R	Area IV net (western MA)	136.5/162.2

Note: MEMA also uses the State 800 MHz trunked system.

Additional Emergency Management Networks

153.875R	North Shore Civil Defense	127.3
155.985	North Shore Civil Defense -repeater in	127.3
155.220	North Shore Civil Defense -backup	127.3
143.600R	Federal Emergency Management	118.8
45.320	NIAT -Nuclear Response Teams- base	162.2
45.360	NIAT -Nuclear Response Teams- mob.	162.2

Amateur Radio (HAM) Emergency -RACES- repeaters

53.310	Wachusett	146.895	Walpole	147.315	Wareham
53.230	Greylock	146.910	Greylock	147.375	Foxboro
145.210	Greylock	146.910	Malden	147.390	Beverly
145.230	Red Cross	146.910	Brockton	224.320	Walpole
145.250	Pittsfield	147.030	Peru	224.520	Andover
		147.075	Wakefield	448.825	Lowell
145.490	Fairhaven	147.135	Taunton	449.575	Wilmington
146.835	Andover	147.195	Attleboro	448.625	Wachusett-
146.880	Salem	147.210	Dedham		New England-wide

MASS HIGHWAY (47 MHz PL: 141.3)

47.280	Statewide Channel
47.260	District #1 Operations (Berkshire County)
47.260	District #2 Operations (Franklin/Hampshire)
47.360	District #3 Operations (Worcester County)
47.360	District #4 Operations (Middlesex)
47.140	District #4 Operations (Essex County)
47.140	District #4 Operations (Boston)
47.360	District #5 Operations (Norfolk/Bristol Cty.)
47.140	District #5 Operations (Plymouth/Barnstable)
453.2375	Bridge Inspection Divers
151.040	Central Artery/Northern Artery Repair (also 151.505 through 151.565)

NOAA CONTINUOUS WEATHER BROADCASTS

162.475	Boston	162.400	Concord, NH
162.550	Hyannis	162.400	Providence, RI
162.550	Worcester	162.475	Hartford, CT

ENVIRONMENTAL MANAGEMENT

151.205	-F1-	Statewide Administration	71.9
151.145R	-F2-	Statewide Repeater	71.9
		Future Statewide Fire Intercity	
151.415	-F2-	Input to repeater	varies
151.235	-F3-	Fire Towers/Ground Support	71.9
151.310	-F4-	Fire Towers/Ground Support	71.9
151.370	-F5-	State Parks & Recreation	71.9

Regional Operations by Channel

151.310	Barnstable/Dukes/Plymouth/Bristol/Norfolk/ Franklin/Hampshire/Hampden Counties	
151.235	Essex/Middlesex/Worcester/Berkshire	
151.475R	Metro Parks	71.9

FISHERIES, WILDLIFE & ENVIRONMENTAL LAW

31.460	-F1-	Car to Car/Base to Car	131.8
		(Car to Base on Cape Cod)	131.8
31.500	-F2-	Car to Base (except Cape)	131.8
31.420	-F3-	Inactive	

ENVIRONMENTAL PROTECTION (DEP)

| 453.750 | Western and Southeastern Mass. | 179.9 |
| 453.950 | Central and Northeastern Mass. (inactive) | |

FEDERAL ENVIRONMENTAL AGENCIES

163.225	National Marine Fisheries Services	
34.810	U.S. Fish & Wildlife Service	
34.830	U.S. Fish & Wildlife Service	
171.725R	Cape Cod National Seashore	CSQ

UNITED STATES COAST GUARD

156.450	-ch. #09-	Boston Area Hailing
156.600	-ch. #12-	Port Navigation
156.650	-ch. #13-	Navigational
156.800	-ch. #16-	Distress/Calling
157.050	-ch. #21-	Woods Hole/Brant Point/ Provincetown/Cape Cod Canal
157.100	-ch. #22-	Working/Main Operations/NOTAMS
157.150	-ch. #23-	Occasional Use
157.075	-ch. #81-	Boston/Gloucester/Merrimack/Hull
157.175	-ch. #83-	Coast Guard Auxiliary
157.125		Gloucester secondary
166.225		Cape Cod Air Rescue -Primary
164.550		Cape Cod Air Rescue -Secondary
381.700		Cape Cod Air Rescue -(& 381.800)
162.125		LANT 30 (DVP/100.0)
162.325		LANT 32 (DVP/100.0)

MISCELLANEOUS MILITARY/FEDERAL CHANNELS

142.350R	Army National Guard -repeater	110.9
142.975	Army National Guard -secondary	110.9
49.690R	Army National Guard (F-1) Boston area	110.9
49.930R	Army National Guard (F-2) So. Shore	110.9
49.710R	Army National Guard (F-3) W. MA	110.9
49.790R	Army National Guard (F-4) C./W. MA	110.9
40.600	Army National Guard -emergencies	
34.400	Army National Guard -armories (34.70 also)	
39.900	Army National Guard -armories -backup net	
38.700	Army National Guard -copters (38.75 also)	
34.150	Air National Guard -copters (34.35/34.55)	
168.325R	US Corps Army Eng. -main channel	CSQ
168.125R	US Corps Army Eng. -western MA	CSQ
163.4125	US Corps Army Eng. -Cape Cod Canal	173.8
417.200R	GSA -Federal Protective Svc. -bldg. sec.	192.8
148.150R	Civil Air Patrol (149.925R also)	
418.050R	National Transportation Safety Board	
172.950R	Federal Aviation Administration	136.5
148.150R	Civil Air Patrol (Waltham/Springfield)	100.0
148.925R	Civil Air Patrol (Bourne, Mt. Greylock, Worc.)	
138.050	Air National Guard	
138.250	Air National Guard	
140.075R	United States Navy Operations (Boston)	173.8

Barnes (Westfield)

148.455	Security Network	CSQ
148.215	Fire/Crash Network	CSQ
149.525	Maintenance (148.095 also)	CSQ
148.475	Barnes Disaster Preparedness Net	CSQ
149.300	Weapons Landing	
118.900	CTAF/Tower	
127.100	ATIS	
121.700	Ground Contro/Clearance Delivery	
121.050	Approach/Departure Control	
122.950	UNICOM	
153.920	Airport Security/Administration	141.3

Devens (Ayer area - deactivating- mainly CSQ)

142.950R	Security -channel 1(DVP) (142.075 input)
142.575	Security -channel 2
142.600	ISD Security -channel 1
142.325	CID Security
34.330	Fire
38.500	Range Control
165.0875	Utility/Common (all agencies)
150.600	Motor Pool
142.375	Cutler Hospital (hospital-ambulance)
49.80	EOD units
38.45	ISD Operations
163.4375	Military Contractors
119.350	Moore Airfield Tower
143.990R	MARS Repeater

Hanscom (Bedford) (see Air section for frequencies)

163.4625	Security Network	CSQ
173.5875	Fire/Crash Network	136.5
165.1625	Taxi Network	CSQ
173.5125	Medical Network	136.5
149.325	Air Force Security	CSQ
138.165	OSI Operations (& 138.025, 138.175)	
149.205	Engineers Network	
149.220	Civil Engineers	
149.175	Instrument Network (149.475 also)	
164.700	Commanders Network	CSQ
155.820	Foam pick-up truck	
453.875	Massport Authority (see Logan for 800MHz)	
855.2375	Hanscom Fire	D-365

Otis Air Force Base/Edwards Marine Base (Sandwich)

163.5875R	Air Base Security (163.1375 input)	131.8
173.5875	Air Base Fire/Crash Network	
165.5375	Air Base Munitions Network	
165.1125	Air Base Taxi/Civil Engineers Net (& 163.5125)	
150.195	Air Base Maintenance Net	
165.0375	Pave Paws Security	
173.5625	Pave Paws Fire Net	
150.165	Air National Guard Security	
150.225	Air National Guard Ramp Control	
36.600	Air National Guard Aircraft	
149.205	Air National Guard Operations	
148.515	Aircrew Alert Network (413.450 also)	
419.215	Coast Guard Public Works Net	
171.3375	Coast Guard Utility Network	
30.450	Edwards -Marine Training	
38.750	Edwards -Range Control	
121.000	Tower	
121.600	Ground Control	
126.300	Approach Control -south (118.20 also)	
118.100	Approach Control -north (118.75 also)	

Westover Air Force Base (Chicopee)

165.1875	Security (& 165.5875, 164.3875)	CSQ
163.4875	Security	100.0
138.175	OSI Security	
173.4125	Fire/Crash Network (33.520 County)	
173.5625	Medical Network	
165.0375	Maintenance Network (165.1375 also)	
173.5375	Civil Engineers (413.200/413.300 also)	
149.550	Commanders Net -base (149.565 also)	
148.050	Commanders Net -mobile (148.065 also)	
138.900	USAF Air-to-Air Command	
413.450	USAF Tactical Aircrew Alert	
40.170	USAF Intelligence (40.190 also)	
138.075	USAF Radio Net (138.165 also)	
163.4875	Air Show Security	100.0
469.550	Air Show Flight Coordinators	82.5
464.550	Air Show Operations	D-134
154.570	Air Show Operations	179.9

154.570	Air Show Concessions		94.8
34.150	Military Refueling		
30.450	US Marine Corps (38.750 also)		
134.850	CTAF/Tower		
118.350	Ground Control		
125.350	Bradley Approach/Departure Control		
114.000	ATIS		
123.000	UNICOM		

MARINE CHANNEL PLAN

CH. #	SHIPS (TX)	COAST (RX)	TRAFFIC TYPE
06		156.300	Intership Safety
07	156.350	156.350	Commercial
08	156.400		Commercial
09	156.450	156.450	Commercial (marinas)
10	156.500	156.500	Commercial
11	156.550	156.550	Commercial
12	156.600	156.600	Port Operations/CG
13	156.650	156.650	Navigation/Bridges
14	156.700	156.700	Port Operations/CG
15	156.750		Environmental
16	156.800	156.800	Distress/Calling
17	156.850	156.850	State Control
18	156.900	156.900	Commercial
19	156.950	156.950	Commercial (fishing)
20	157.000	161.600	Port Operations
21	157.050	157.050	Coast Guard
22	157.100	157.100	Coast Guard
23	157.150	157.150	Coast Guard
24	157.200	161.800	Marine Telephone
25	157.250	161.850	Marine Telephone
26	157.300	161.900	Marine Telephone
27	157.350	161.950	Marine Telephone
28	157.400	162.000	Marine Telephone
65	156.275	156.275	Port Operations
66	156.325	156.325	Port Operations
67	156.375		Commercial
68	156.425	156.425	Non-commercial
69	156.475	156.475	Non-commercial
70	156.525		Non-commercial
71	156.575	156.575	Non-commercial
72	156.625		Non-commercial
77	156.675	156.675	Port Operations
78	156.925	156.925	Non-commercial
79	156.975	156.975	Commercial
80	157.025	157.025	Commercial
83	157.175	157.175	Coast Guard Aux.
84	157.225	161.825	Marine Telephone
85	157.275	161.875	Marine Telephone
86	157.325	161.925	Marine Telephone
87	157.375	161.975	Marine Telephone
88	157.425		Commercial

REGIONAL POLICE NETWORKS
Note: These nets are not listed in alphabetical order.

Network Abbreviations Used in Community Section

BAP	=	BAPERN	NEM =	NEMLEC Network
BAR	=	Barnstable Cty.	NES =	NESPERN Network
BRC	=	Bristol County Net	PLC =	Plymouth County
BEC	=	Berkshire County	SOM =	South Middlesex
FRC	=	Franklin County	WEM =	WEMLEC Network
			WOR =	Worcester Area Net

Intercity (or Interstate) 158.970 (CSQ)

158.970 was the most widely used intercity police radio channel in eastern New England. Because so many police departments maintain a base station on the frequency, it is not listed in the Community Section. State, Metro, local police and others report major police incidents on 158.970.

National Law Enforcement 155.475 (PL: varies)

A nationwide intercity channel which is used throughout New Hampshire, the frequency is only now being employed in some Massachusetts police radio systems.

BAPERN (BAP n/w/s in the CommunitySection)(PL:131.8)

The Boston Area Police Emergency Radio Network is a large system including state, local, college, MBTA and even hospital police departments. Some towns are now experimenting with Mobile Data Terminals in their cruisers (cruisers with 800MHz antennas on their roof).

47x.---	BAPERN channel #1 -City Operations Freq.
470.---	BAPERN channel #2 -District Channel (n/w/s)*
470.7875	BAPERN channel #3 -Intercity/Tactical Ops.
470.5625	BAPERN channel #4 -Investigations/Intercity

*BAPERN CHANNEL #2 DISTRICT FREQUENCIES

470.4875	North District "BAPn" in the Community Section
470.7375	West District "BAPw" in the Community Section
470.9125	South District "BAPs" in the Community Section
471.7625	Northeast District (118.8)/ 473.4875 input (118.8)

Barnstable County Police Network - 155.565 (PL: 110.9)

155.565 is the Cape-wide intercity channel common among all communities in the county and in communities to the north and west, such as Plymouth. Cape police dispatchers ID with the three numerals in their call sign, such as 372 in Falmouth, along with a name for cruisers, such as "David" for Eastham patrol units. Many Cape communities have switched to 800 MHz, and there is talk of a capewide 800 MHz trunked system in the future.

COMMUNITY	CALL	ID	PRIMARY
Barnstable	374	EASY	855.2125
Bourne	375	YOKE	851.1625
Brewster	454	KING	155.955
Chatham	368	FOX	155.640
Dennis	951	ITEM	155.985
Eastham	710	DAVID	155.640
Falmouth	372	OSCAR	855.4625
F.B.I.*		LIMA	
Harwich	373	GEORGE	155.520
Martha's Vineyard	860/404	UNION	158.850
Mashpee	322	TANGO	851.3125
Mattapoisett*	685		
Nantucket	367	VICTOR	159.090
National Shore*	737-743		171.725
Orleans	709	MIKE	155.640
Otis Air Base	364	ZEBRA	163.5875
Provincetown	371	ABLE	155.700
Registry*		ROMEO	
Sandwich	702/755	HENRY	851.3875
Truro	700	BAKER	155.520
Wareham*	227		
Wellfleet	370	CHARLIE	155.700
Yarmouth	559	JOHN	855.2375
County Sheriff*	376	X-RAY/SUGAR	

* Not formally part of network, but have 155.565 to tie in.

Berkshire County Police Communications Net (PL:107.2)

153.965	County Dispatch (KRO333)
	County Sheriff (KZM798)/ Small town police
154.740	Interdepartment Communications
154.755	Operations (various towns)

State Police Small Town Patrol is also used: 42.46 & 44.74.

Bristol County Police Network (BRC) (PL: 203.5)

482.5125	Community Intercity Channel
482.3875	Comunity car-to-car simplex
483.2875	District Attorney
482.7625	DA/Special Operations

Franklin County Police Net (FRC) (PL: 141.3)

39.160	County Towns	- Main Operations
39.240	Channel #2	- Mobiles/Base-to-State PD

Note that many of the small towns in the county have State Police Small Town Patrol coverage on 44.740 and 42.460. Police departments in the county use their Franklin County Fire town ID, also; e.g., Shutesbury units are 33-1, etc.

Plymouth County Radio Network (PLC) (PL: 203.5)

48 -- .--	Channel 1	Community Operations
482.8875	Channel 2	REGIONAL #1/Sheriff
483.0375	Channel 3	REGIONAL #2/Sheriff
482.3875	Channel 4	Mobile/Portable Operations
483.7375		B.C.I./District Attorney

Note: Plymouth County will be changing their regional plan soon. One regional channel may be dropped as most towns now have programmed in mobile radios all adjacent towns to speak directly on neighbors' primary.

COMMUNITY	ID	UNITS	FREQUENCY
Brockton	B	601-700	482.7125
Brockton - backup	B	601-700	482.8625
Plymouth	D	1-20	482.6625
Carver	D1	21-2	483.3625
Bridgewater	J	241-260	484.7875
East Bridgewater	J1	201-220	482.6125
West Bridgewater	J2	221-240	"
MCI Bridgewater	J5		
Middleboro	M	30-55	482.4875
Lakeville	M1	161-170	"
Kingston	O	151-160	482.4625
Duxbury	O1	171-190	482.4125
Plympton	O2	111-120	482.4625
Norwell	Q	321-340	482.5625
Hanover	Q1	341-360	"
Marshfield	Q2	541-570	"
Scituate	R1	421-450	482.5875 118.8
Hull	R2	451-480	482.9875
Hingham	R3	391-420	484.4125
Cohasset	R4		482.9875
Marion	S	91-110	482.5375
Mattapoisett	S1		(Bristol) tie only
Rochester	S2	76-90	482.5375
Wareham	S3	55-75	"
Pembroke	T	121-140	482.7875
Hanson	T1	481-500	"
Halifax	T2	501-520	"
Rockland	X	261-280	483.0125
Abington	X1	281-300	"
Whitman	X2	301-320	482.3125
Sheriff Dept.	Z	810-850	483.7375/Reg.
County BCI/DA	Z2	670-681	"

South Middlesex "REGIONAL" (SOM) (PL: 123.0)

Including communities in both the southern area of Middlesex County, as well as towns in southeastern Worcester County, 39.380 is the "Regional" frequency. It is identified by "SOM" in the main section. There has been discussion of adding a west Middlesex regional BAPERN frequency.

NEMLEC (NEM) (PL: 146.2)

The North East Massachusetts Law Enforcement Council comprises northern Middlesex and western Essex communities. The State Police barracks in Andover has a NEMLEC radio and is frequently heard on channels 2 & 3. SWAT teams of the county also use channel two.

48 -.----	NEMLEC channel #1 -Community Ops. Freq.
482.6875	NEMLEC channel #2 -Regional Emergency
482.6375	NEMLEC channel #3 -Regional Adm./Detec.
482.3875	NEMLEC channel #4 -Mobile/Portable Ops.
485.3875	NEMLEC channel #5 -Tactical Portables

NESPERN (NES) UHF PL: 146.2)

The Northern Essex Police Emergency Radio Network is the newest of all systems. It was implemented as a result of the improved communications needs of towns within the ten-mile radius of the Seabrook Nuclear Plant. Note that channel plans differ among communities.

482.8375	-F1-	Amesbury Police/Merrimack Police
482.3625	-F3-	West Newbury Police
483.0125	-F5-	Newburyport PD/Newbury PD tie only
483.1375	-F7-	Mobile/portable operations
483.7375M	-F8-	Salisbury Police
482.7875	-F10-	Rowley Police
482.4625		Newbury Police

Note: Channels 2, 4, 6, 9 & 11 are non-repeaterized ops.

Western MA Law Enf. Council -WEMLEC (WEM) (PL: 173.8)

460.225	Channel 1 -Primary Intercity Operations
460.475	Channel 2 -Backup (at times out of service)

Utilized by Springfield and the surrounding communities, this network is often used to relay crime data as well as for chases between towns and detective operations.

Worcester Area Police Regional Net (WOR) (PL: 167.9)

45.540	Primary Regional -(may be called channel 3)
45.340	Sub-Regional #1
45.580	Sub-Regional #2

The following communities all use the primary regional channel as well as the sub-regional channel as indicated. In the Community Section of this book, either "WOR1" - indicating the additional capacity of sub-regional #1, or "WOR2" is shown beside the main police frequency.

FIRE NOTIFICATION/BUFF NETWORKS
(All frequencies are repeaterized unless otherwise noted.)

462.575	Amesbury Notification	79.7
472.1125	Boston Fire Radio	136.5
463.825	Central Radio System "C-1"	103.5
463.825M	Central Radio System "C-2"	103.5
462.575M	Central Radio System "C-3"	103.5
461.550	Central Radio System "C-4"	103.5
463.550	Citywide Boston	167.9
463.550M	Citywide Boston	167.9
463.550M	Citywide Boston (Dispatch)	91.5
461.375	Citywide North	203.5
464.100	Citywide Cape Cod	167.9
464.975	Citywide Hartford CT "1"	167.9
464.875	Citywide Hartford CT "2"	203.5
462.200	Citywide Hartford CT "3"	173.8
462.725	Citywide Hartford CT "4"	167.9
463.550	Citywide Hartford CT "5"	167.9
461.600	City News/Chelsea Notification	162.2
463.775	Citywide Providence RI	167.9
471.4625	Countywide Abington	103.5
464.725	Countywide Brockton	167.9
464.550	Countywide Hingham	167.9
461.700	Merrimack Valley "1"	110.9
461.700	Merrimack Valley "2"	71.9
462.025	Merrimack Valley "3"	82.5
464.700	Merrimack Valley Group	D-223
461.800	Merrimack Valley Group	D-223
461.575	Metcomm	167.9
463.450	Metro Radio Assn	186.2
462.725	Metro Radio System "1" Primary	167.9
462.725M	Metro Radio System "2"	167.9
462.650M	Metro Radio System "3"	167.9
463.425	Metro Radio System "4"	203.5
461.975	Metro Radio System "5"	167.9
461.625	Metro Radio System "6"	167.9
461.650	Metro Radio System "8"	167.9
462.575	Metro Radio System "A2"	77.0
462.650	Metro Radio System "A3"	77.0
461.775	Metro Radio System "A8"	100.0
464.300	Metro Radio System "CH1" North	203.5
464.950	Metro Radio System "CH2" North	94.8
462.725	Metro Radio System - Night Dispatch	77.0
462.650	Metro Radio System - South	123.0
463.425	Metro Radio System - West (future)	114.8
462.625	Metro South Brockton	110.9
462.625M	Metro South	77.0
461.250	Middlesex Notification	67.0
464.375	New Hampshire Notification "1"	77.0
464.900	New Hampshire Notification "2"	179.9
464.975	New Hampshire Notification "3"	156.7

Frequency	Name	Tone
463.400	New Hampshire Notification "4"	79.7
461.400	New Hampshire Statewide "1"	118.8
462.125	New Hampshire Statewide "2"	118.8
464.275	Newscomm Boston	91.5
463.550	Newscomm Boston	91.5
462.600	South Shore Sparks Clubs "Bundy"	107.2
461.025	South Shore Sparks Clubs "Crimson"	162.2
464.225	South Shore Sparks Clubs	
463.750	South Shore Sparks Clubs	D-743
464.300	South Shore Sparks Clubs	
464.550	South Shore Sparks Clubs	
462.625	South Worcester County	CSQ
464.850	Southern ME Notification "1"	173.8
463.775	Southern ME Notification "2"	118.8

(Some channels listed above are not officially sanctioned.)

REGIONAL FIRE NETWORKS

15 fire-fighting districts share resources during major fires. Each district has its own radio frequency/(ies) for mutual aid communications. In less populated regions, communities will use one or two frequencies for both local and mutual aid operations -for districts 4, 9 and 11 only one channel is listed beside the towns in the Community Section of this book. City and town district affiliation is indicated in the Community Section after the primary fire listing and in parenthesis, e.g., (9) or (6/13). Note that if the primary fire channel for a town is also the district fire frequency, then the district number is not repeated -no parenthesis listing. 151.145, the DEM statewide, may be used in the future as an inter-district net. New regional centers run by the State Police are operational and provide dispatching for many area towns in Western MA.

<u>Fire District Mutual Aid Systems</u>

DISTRICT	FREQUENCY	CONTROL	COUNTY/NAME
1	33.70B/33.68M	Yarmouth	Barnstable
2	154.295B/33.90M	Hanson	Plymouth
SE	154.295	Randolph	Southeastern
3	46.180	Norton	Bristol
4	33.50/33.54	Stoughton	Norfolk
5	154.070	Beverly	South Essex
6	33.660	Chelmsford	N. Middlesex
7	33.620	Southbridge	S. Worcester
8	33.700	Fitchburg	N. Wrc/Mid-State
9	33.54/33.48	Greenfield	Franklin/Tri-State
10	154.370	Amherst	Hampshire
11	33.52/33.46	Chicopee	Hampden
11	154.280	Chicopee	Springfield Area
12	154.310	Pittsfield	Berkshire
13	483.2875	Newton	Metrofire
14	33.980/483.7125	Natck	So. Middlesex
15	154.070	Haverhill	North Essex

District #1 -Barnstable County Net- 33.700 (PL: 114.8)
New mobile channel: 33.680 (PL:114.8)

- Barnstable Fire
- Bourne Fire
- Brewster Fire
- Chatham Fire
- Cotuit Fire
- Dennis Fire
- Eastham Fire
- Falmouth Fire
- Harwich Fire
- Hyannis Fire
- Martha's Vineyard Fire
- Mashpee Fire
- Orleans Fire
- Osterville Fire
- Otis Fire
- Plymouth Fire
- Plymouth County Fire
- Provincetown Fire
- Sandwich Fire
- Truro Fire
- Wareham Fire
- Wellfleet Fire
- West Barnstable Fire
- Yarmouth Fire

District #2 -Plymouth County Network- (Tone: 203.5)
154.295 Station to Station Intercity (shared w/SE)
 33.900 Mobile units -fireground intercity

The Plymouth County Emergency Communications Center in Hanson controls the 154.295 and 33.900 intercity fire radio channels for the county. While sharing some communications duties with Southeast Control on 154.295, Plymouth has, in effect, taken over for Plymouth County intercity fire dispatch. Not all towns in the county have 154.295. 33.900 was long used as the primary fire channel in the county, but now every town now has their own 33MHz channel for primary communications, leaving 33.900 as the county fireground. Note that in the ID list below, units below 100 may add a "0".

Plymouth County Network - Stations & Units

COMMUNITY	UNIT ID'S	CALL SIGN
Abington - Central	293-294	KTE698
Abington - North Dispatch	290-299	KCD823
Bridgewater	30-39	KCB281
Carver	20-29	KCA661
Duxbury		KCA351
Duxbury - Ashdod #2		KJZ993
East Bridgewater	250-259	KCC350
Halifax	50-59	KCL540
Hanover	100-109	KQG716
Hanover - Ctr. Station #4		KCH519
Hanson	60-69	KCD453
Hull/Hingham/Scituate	1-9/40-46/30-38	Thru SE
Kingston	70-79	KCB479
Lakeville	80-89	KCF399
Marion	120-129	KCE421
Marshfield	130-139	KZE660
Marshfield - Out Station	Cl, C2	KZE661

Mattapoisett	210-219	KCE397
Middleboro	90-96	KCA633
Middleboro - South Station	97-99	KCF907
Norwell - Central	110-119	KCG933
Norwell - Ridgehill #2	113-114	KSL396
Pembroke - HQ Station	150-159	KAS874
Pembroke - Station #3	153	KDW284
Plympton	180-189	KCA974
Plymouth - Apparatus	160-179	KCA585
Plymouth - State Rd.		KAT541
Plymouth - Bourne Rd.		KGU247
Plymouth - Samoset St.		KXG958
Plymouth - Plane/DEM	10/11-19	KE9550
Rochester	190-199	KJE934
Rockland		KCD427
Wareham - Fire District	360-379	KCA915
Wareham - Onset Alarm	140-149	KCA410
Wareham - West Station	220-229	KLX742
West Bridgewater	230-239	KNCB532
Whitman - Central	240-249	KCB715
Whitman - East Side	242	KSP269

District #3 - Bristol County Fire Network - 46.180 (CSQ)

This district utilizes 46.180 for fire intercity radio, but many towns also use the channel for local operations, The frequency generally only swings into mutual aid action when a task force of water tankers is required to help put out brush fires. Many towns in the county also have radio ties to Rhode Island on 154.280.

Acushnet	KNDN830
Attleboro - Headquarters	KCC341
Attleboro - Park Street Station	WZX843
Attleboro - Newport Avenue	WZX844
Attleboro - West Street Station	WZX845
Berkley	KFZ756
Dartmouth - Headquarters	KCC952
Dartmouth - North Station	KTV678
Dartmouth - District #1	KCC452
Dartmouth - District #2	KNFF850
Dartmouth - District #3	KCC922
Dighton - Communications Center	KNDU338
Dighton - Headquarters	KNDU339
Dighton - North Station	KNDU337
Fairhaven - Washington Street	KCB836
Fairhaven - Adams Street	KTK874
Fairhaven - East Fairhaven	KTY971
Fall River	KNFF610
Freetown	KCG726
Freetown - Assonet Station	KRZ246
New Bedford	KCA802

North Attleboro	KCD918
Norton - Communications Center	KNFU570
Norton - Communications Center	KNFU372
Norton - Bay Road Station	KNFU373
Plainville	KNFL943
Raynham	KCD371
Rehoboth	KWF931
Seekonk	KCD606
Somerset	KCC849
Swansea	KCB615
Taunton	KNGJ819
Wesport - Main Street Station	KNFQ423
Wesport - Briggs Road Station	KNFQ422
Wesport - Reed Road Station	KNFQ424

District #4 - Norfolk County Network - 33.50/33.54 (CSQ)

Within this district both 33.50 and 33.54 are used for local operations. There is no roll call on the system and both the channels must be monitored during any major fire activity for intercity operations. Generally, 33.50 is used in the northeast end of the county and 33.54 in the southwest. Note that, for the most part, only the numerals within the call sign are used.

COMMUNITY	UNIT ID'S	CALL SIGN
Bellingham		KEP595
Canton	50'S	WSZ316
Dover	70'S	KCA303
Easton - Station #1	10's/100's	KCA627
Easton - Station #2	10's/100's	KCG574
Foxboro	20's	KCF297
Franklin		KCY582
Mansfield	30's	KCA328
Medfield	80's	KCV350
Medway		KDX459
Millis		KNDN504
Norwood	NA1, NC1	KDG816
Norfolk		KNDR721
Plainville		KNFL943
Sharon	90's	KCP980
Walpole	400's	KCF375
Westwood	600's	KCR898
Wrentham		KCH794

Southeastern Control Mutual Aid - 154.295 (PL: 203.5)

This network comprises towns within districts #2 & #4. The communities below have radio capabilities for both their own district and the Southeastern network. Southeastern is used strictly a base-to-base intercity mutual aid system. Town names and not call signs are used. Much of the work has been taken over by Plymouth Cty. Control.

Abington	Hanover*	Randolph
Avon	Hanson	Rockland
Braintree	Hingham	Scituate
Bridgewater	Holbrook	Sharon
Brockton	Hull	So. Weymouth
Canton	Kingston	Naval Air
Cohasset	Marshfield	Stoughton
Duxbury	Middleboro	Walpole
East Bridgewater	Norwell*	W. Bridgewater
Easton	Norwood	Westwood
Foxboro	Pembroke	Weymouth
Halifax*	Plymouth	Whitman
(* Towns not now on the freq.)	Quincy Civil Def.	Wrentham

Districts 5 & 15 - Essex Cty. - 154.070 (131.8/CSQ)/153.830 FG

Beverly is the South District #5 control, covering the North Shore. North District #15, with Haverhill as its control, also operates on 154.070. 153.830 is used as a fireground channel. Many towns within ten miles of the Seabrook Nuclear Plant use 158.955R (203.5).

South District #5 Communities and their call signs (131.8):

TOWN	CALL SIGN	TOWN	CALL SIGN
Beverly	KAY259	Middleton	KNFL959
Danvers	KDN607	Nahant	KJF873
Essex	KZI325	No. Reading	KNIB495
Gloucester	KNCN367	Peabody	KCC847
Hamilton	KBI813	Rockport	KDT260
Ipswich	KBA346	Salem	KCH507
Lynn	KCC886	Saugus	not member
Lynnfield	KCF511	Swampscott	KNBQ200
Manchester	KCX594	Topsfield	KJL701
Marblehead	KCH550	Wenham	KBI813

North District #15 Communities and their call signs (CSQ):

Amesbury	KCV354	Merrimac	KBX936
Andover	KWII892	Methuen	KCI237
Boxford	KCH315	Newbury	KNCC595
Byfield	KNCC594	Newburyport	KNFX444
Georgetown	KCD690	No. Andover	KCB542
Groveland	KCF251	Rowley	KCD289
Haverhill	KCK562	Salisbury	KDO241
Lawrence	KAR981	W. Newbury	KNFX445

District #6 - North Middlesex County Net - 33.66 (CSQ)

A very unstructured district. Many of the towns active on 33.660 also have radios to tie into other area nets. Some communities still use 33.66 for primary operations. Some communities also use 33.760 as a fireground.

District #7 - S. Worcester Cty. Net -33.620 (131.8/CSQ)

Many of the communities in the district use the channel for both mutual aid and local operations.

STA.	COMMUNITY	STA.	COMMUNITY
#10	Leicester	#31	Northboro
#11	Spencer	#32	Westboro
#12	North Brookfield	#34	Millbury
#13	East Brookfield	#35	Grafton
#14	Brookfield	#36	Upton
#15	West Brookfield	#40	Sutton
#16	Warren	#41	Northbridge
#17	New Braintree	#42	Douglas
#20	Auburn	#43	Uxbridge
#21	Oxford	#44	Mendon
#22	Webster	#45	Blackstone
#23	Dudley	#46	Millville
#24	Charlton	#47	Hopedale
#25	Southbridge	#49	Milford
#26	Sturbridge	#50	Worcester
#30	Shrewsbury		Charlton Fire Tower

District #8 - N. Worcester Cty. /"Mid-State" - 33.700 (CSQ$)

On the Mid-State, or North Worcester County Fire Net, many communities conduct local and intercity operations. Station "calls" are used infrequently, never call signs, and each district piece of apparatus is numbered for easy identification. Thus, "10E4" indicates Fitchburg engine 4.

CALL	COMMUNITY	CALL	COMMUNITY
1	Acton*	20	New Braintree #
2	Ashburnham	21	Oakham
3	Athol	22	Paxton
4	Ashby	23	Petersham # *
5	Barre	24	Phillipston
6	Berlin	25	Princeton
7	Bolton	26	Royalston
8	Boylston	27	Rutland
9	Clinton	28	Sterling
10	Fitchburg	29	Templeton
11	Gardner	30	Townsend
12	Hardwick	31	West Boylston
13	Harvard	32	Westminster
14	Holden		Ft. Devens
15	Hubbardston		Orange
16	Hudson *	35	Shirley
17	Lancaster	39	Winchendon
18	Leominster	50	Worcester
19	Lunenburg	---	Northboro Fire
		---	Wachusett Tower #

$ = Some towns using 131.8; * = on net without 33.70 radio; # = not on roll

District #9 - Tri-State Network - 33.54/33.48 (Tone: 123.0)

The Tri-State Mutual Aid Fire Network operates on 33.54 for local as well as mutual aid operations throughout Franklin County. 33.48, frequency two, is used as a backup or fireground channel. The network is named "Tri-State", as New Hampshire and Vermont towns operate on 33.54, also. The following list includes towns in all three states. Communities are identified by the "call" along with alpha-numeric identifications for units. Thus, 4-R-1 is car 1 in the town of Bernardston.

The Police also use the town identification system.
KCE358 Tri-State Fire Mutual Aid Dispatch
KCH729 Amherst (District #10) Dispatch tie
"A" = Amb./ "R" = Car/ "M" = Mobile/ "P" = Portable

CALL	COMMUNITY	CALL	COMMUNITY
2	Ashfield	26	New Salem
3	Athol	28	Northfield
4	Bernardston	29	Orange
5	Brattleboro	G23	Petersham
7	Charlemont	30	Rowe
8	Colrain	31	Shelburne Vol.
9	Conway	32	Shelburne Falls
10	Deerfield	33	Shutesbury
11	Erving	34	South Deerfield
12	Gill	35	Sunderland
13	Greenfield	36	Turners Falls
13-R-1	Radio Super	37	Warwick
14	Hadley	38	Wendell
15	Hatfield	39	Whately
17	Heath	40	Winchester
18	Hinsdale	41	Vernon
20	Lake Pleasant	42	Guilford
21	Leverett	43	Swanzey - West
22	Leyden	44	Swanzey - East
23	Millers Falls	45	Swanzey - Center
24	Monroe		
25	Montague		

Hampshire County Fire Network - 154.370 (Tone: 127.3)

With Amherst as its control, The Hampshire County Fire Defense Association encompasses many towns which have ties to other systems, such as the Tri-State Net to the north and Berkshire County to the west. 153.890 is used as a firegound and training channel.
Stations ID by FCC call signs or by their town prefix.

UNIT TYPE IDENTIFIERS
"X" Chief officers and fireground commanders
"E" Engine companies "R" Rescue Sq.
"L" Ladder companies "A" Ambulances
"Tank" Tanker companies "Brush" Brush

KCH888   County Control
KCH729   Amherst small- town dispatch

PREFIX	COMMUNITY	CALL SIGN
51	Amherst	KCH729
52	Belchertown	KCW396
53	Chesterfield	KCH620
54	Cummington	WXT896
55	Easthampton	KCH431
56	Goshen	KQI374
57	Granby	WRE375
14	Hadley	KBF372
15	Hatfield	KGO424
58	Huntington	KZP998
59	Middlefield	KNGE720
60	Northampton	WSY543
61	Pelham	KUY514
62	Plainfield	WXT895
63	South Hadley District #1	KCE735*
64	South Hadley District #2	KCE703*
65	Southampton	KNBC411
66	Ware	KDB431
67	Westhampton	KWQ578
68	Williamsburg	KSV765
69	Worthington	KO6423

(South Hadley PL Tone: 141.3)

District #11 - Hampden County Fire Net - 33.52/33.46 (CSQ)

The Hampden County Fire Mutual Aid Association has control points in Chicopee and Springfield. 33.52 is primary, with 33.46 for hill towns. 451.70 repeats 33.52.

Hampden County	KCI426	Monson	KCB981
Agawam	KKR599	Montgomery	WQK939
Agawam - Feeding Hills	KNGN40	Palmer	KCF798
Blandford	KTZ395	Palmer - Bondsville	KFR552
Brimfield	KCF790	Palmer - Three Rivers	KFG510
Chester	KCH549	Russell	KTZ275
East Longmeadow	KUB896	Southwick	KCF769
Granville	KTZ509	Tolland	KRM367
Hampden	KCE779	Westfield	KNAG579
Holland	KOB459	West Springfield	KUB774
Holyoke	KCG775	Wilbraham	KCE264
Longmeadow	KTX662		

Springfield Area Intercity Fire Radio -154.280 (PL: 82.5)

Chicopee Control -WNDD402 County Call Sign

This new network covers communities in the greater Springfield area. Other frequencies available include 153.830, 153.890, 153.950 for fireground operations.

District #12 - Berkshire County Fire Net - 154.310 (107.2)

The Berkshire County Communications Center in Pittsfield dispatches police, fire and ambulance calls throughout nearly this entire western Mass. county.

All fire communications are handled on 154.310 - except in the cities, such as Pittsfield and North Adams, where separate frequencies are used - for both local and mutual aid operations. If a community fire station such as Becket were notified of a fire, they would call "470", the county comm. center, to have the dispatcher activate the tones and notify the rest of the county on 154.310.

153.830 is used as fireground channel in many towns.

Berkshire County Network Dispatch
KCH470   Pittsfield Communications Center

DEPARTMENT	CALL SIGN
Adams	KNHJ799
Alford	KJ5411
Becket	KNCH825
Cheshire	KNBU762
Clarksburg	KJU245
Dalton	KCD784
Egremont	KC9005
Florida	KNGW959
Great Barrington	KCB849
Hancock - Station #I/Station #2	KNHG443
Hinsdale	KNDV352
Housatonic	KCE664
Lanesboro	KNFQ444
Lee	KCD927
Lenox	KMCZ361
Middlefield	KNGE720
Monterey	KNA729
Mount Washington	CALL EGREMONT
New Ashford	KNDV332
New Marlboro	KCH518
North Adams	KCC377
Otis	KNID483
Peru	KDU371
Pittsfield	KNCG444
Richmond	KNEY879
Sandisfield	KLV939
Savoy	KGW957
Sheffield	KCC876
Stockbridge	KDR791

Community	Call Sign
Tyringham	KDP422
Washington	CALL BECKET
West Stockbridge	KCD558
Williamstown	KNEX803
Windsor	KG9156
General Electric Plant Protection	WZX991
Columbia County, New York	KEG594

District #13 - "Metrofire" - 154.220/483.2875R (PL 131.8)

Metrofire is the fire mutual aid association comprised of Boston, communities in the metropolitan area and Massport. Most of the communities transmit on either 154.220, which is re-transmitted on UHF, or directly on 483.2875. Newton is the control for the system, with Boston as its backup.

Frequency	Description
483.2875R	Base to base mutual aid operations
154.220	Simulcasted on UHF
483.3125R	"Fire Red" Fireground communications
483.2625	"Fire Blue" HazMat incident channel

METROFIRE COMMUNITIES

Arlington
Belmont
Boston
Braintree
Brookline
Burlington
Cambridge
Chelsea
Dedham
Everett
Lexington
LynnSomerville
Malden
Massport
Medford
Melrose
Milton
Needham
Newton
Quincy
Reading
Revere
Saugus
Stoneham
Wakefield
Waltham
Watertown
Wellesley
Weston
Weymouth
Winchester
Winthrop
Woburn

District #14 - Natick Area Net - 33.98 (46.36, 483.7125)

Some district 14 fire radio network stations are using a PL tone of 127.3 while many are still CSQ. Stations using this PL tone are shown with an *.

COMMUNITY	CALL SIGN	COMMUNITY	CALL SIGN
Ashland	KCF945	Natick	KCB768*
Concord	KNBP838*	Southboro	KCE864
Framingham	KCC457	Sudbury	KCA583*
Hudson	KNDV353	Wayland	KCE587
Lincoln	KAQ230*	Wellesley	KCE403
Marlboro	KCD619	Weston	KRN846
Maynard	KCD309*		

(Notes: In the near future, 33.98 and 46.36 will be inputs to a 483.7125 network fireground repeater. 46.36 with a PL of 100.0 repeats 33.98 stations only with a PL of 127.3)

C-MED/AMBULANCE/ RESCUE/ REACT NETWORKS

Special C-MED/Ambulance Notes

Many communities across the state employ municipal ambulance services run by the police or fire departments or private contractors. Typically, the community ambulance will be dispatched over the town police or fire frequency, but when the EMTs or paramedics wish to speak with a hospital (usually through a C-MED), many town ambulances will communicate over the following frequencies:

155.340	Primary Medical Channel (and C-MED)
155.280	Primary Medical Channel (and C-MED)
155.160/155.220/155.265	Secondary Medical

American Red Cross

47.420	National Primary Channel
47.580	Central Zone: Greater Boston
47.500	North Zone: north of Boston
47.660	South Zone: south/southwest of Boston
47.660	West Zone: west/northwest of Boston
145.230R	Ham-Emergency (448.975 backup)
472.1875	Boston Area (Administration/Blood Delivery)

Miscellaneous Emergency/Rescue Systems

155.280	BOSTON HOSPITALS DISASTER NET (Boston C-MED CSQ; Hospitals 151.4)
155.235	Boston Med Flight (Air Ops.) (91.5)
155.160	New England Life Flight (Worcester) (118.8)
155.175	Boston Med Flight (Ground Ops.) (91.5)
462.675/151.625/154.570/GMRS	REACT Radio
GMRS-MED	Mass. Emergency Unit (Waltham)

Massachusetts C-MED Regional Networks

C-MED Centers direct ambulance to hospital radio by assigning frequencies.

MED	BASE	MED	BASE	MED	BASE
#1	463.000	#5	463.100	#9	462.950
#2	463.025	#6	463.125	#10	462.975R
#3	463.050	#7	463.150	HEAR	155.340
#4	463.075	#8	463.175	HEAR	155.280

Note: Ambulances may be monitored on the frequency exactly 5 MHz above base, unless repeaterized.

STATEWIDE PL: 192.8

WESTERN MASS. C-MEDS: (PL: 167.9)
　　HEAR + 155.385/155.355/155.40
HAMPSHIRE C-MED CENTER: (PL: 173.8)
　　HEAR + 155.385/155.366/155.400
SPRINGFIELD C-MED CENTER: (PL: 151.4)
　　MED 4　Calling　　MED 6, 8, 7, 1　Backup
　　MED 3　Critical　　155.280/155.340, also
WORCESTER C-MED CENTER: (PL:186.2)
　　MED 4　Calling　　MED 5, 7, 8　Backup
　　MED 2　Critical　　155.340/155.280, also
MERRIMACK VALLEY C-MED CENTER: (PL: 156.7)
　　MED 4　Calling　　155.340　Primary
　　MED 1　Critical　　MED 8, 6, 5　Backup
METRO BOSTON C-MED CENTER: (PL:151.4)
　　MED 4　Calling　　MED 6, 8, 5　Backup
　　MED 3　Critical　　- Repeaterized
　　155.340　Ambulances out of greater Boston
　　155.280　Ambulances in greater Boston
SOUTH SHORE C-MED CENTER (Hanson): (PL:179.9)
　　MED 4　Calling　　MED 8, 6, 5　Backup
　　MED 7　Critical　　155.340/155.280, also
FALL RIVER C-MED CENTER: (PL: 156.7)
　　MED 4　Calling　　MED 3, 8, 6　Backup
　　MED 1　Critical　　No VHF
CAPE COD C-MED CENTER: (PL: 173.8)
　　MED 4　Calling　　MED 5, 6, 8, 3　Backup
　　MED 2　Critical　　155.280
NORTH SHORE C-MED CENTER: (PL: 162.2)
　　MED 4　Calling　　155.340　Primary
　　MED 7　Critical　　MED 5, 8, 2, 6　Backup

<u>Various Community and Company Radio Frequencies:</u>
155.160/155.175/155.220/155.235/155.265/155.280/155.34

BOSTON MARATHON
(frequencies subject to change yearly)

464.925	Boston Athletic Assoc.-race timers	D-156
464.100	Boston Athletic Assoc.-operations	186.2
462.675	Finish Line -security	
461.5125	Finish Line -first aid/medical	
464.550	Hancock Staff Operations	
472.9625	Interstate Rentals (staging,tents)	167.9
462.700	Capron Lighting Operations	
147.150R	Ham operators- First Aid (western course)	
147.360R	Ham operators- First Aid (eastern course)	
145.230R	Ham operators- Red Cross (net/finish line)	
146.640R	Medical buses (transport of injured runners)	
146.610R	Medical buses (alternate) also 145.270	
147.550	Ham operators- Copley Square Operations	

NEWS MEDIA

Note: Much of the media now also use cellular phones. Inputs are either 5 MHz up or down from listed repeaters unless otherwise noted.

Boston Television

WBZ TV 4		(PL: 146.2)	
450.0375R	(F-1)	Assignment/ENG and reporter	146.2
450.350R	(F-2)	IFB (program audio)/cars	146.2
450.5375R	(F-3)	ENG crews - live shots	146.2
450.0375M	(F-4)	Direct -off repeater	146.2
450.5375M	(F-5)	Direct -off repeater	146.2
450.650	(F-6)	WBZ Radio Traffic	82.5
455.475		IFB	
450.675	(NBC)	IFB (sports)	
455.8125	(NBC)	Miscellaneous network use	
450.1875	(NBC)	Miscellaneous network use	82.5

(Note: WBZ may scramble their communications.)

WCVB TV 5		(PL: 167.9)
455.0875	(F-1)	Engineering/Live shots/feeds
455.6125	(F-2)	Direct on Boston repeater output
455.5125	(F-3)	IFB/(reporters and cameras)
455.6125R	(F-4)	Assignment Desk (450.4125 in)
455.2875R	(F-5)	Backup/Special Events
455.2875	(F-6)	Direct

ABC NEWS & SPORTS Boston Remotes
450.1125, 455.0875, 450.5875R, 450.800, 455.5875, 455.675

WHDH TV 7		(PL: 136.5 base only)
450.6125	(F-1)	Assignment/ENG and reporter
450.0875	(F-2)	Engineering
450.5125	(F-3)	IFB/Backup

CBS SPORTS Remotes
450.5125, 450.2125. 161.640

Miscellaneous TV Stations

450.250R	WLVI TV 56	News at 10 Ops.	77.0
450.3875R	WGBH TV 2	News/Eng. (F-1)	167.9
455.4875R	WGBH TV 2	Inactive (F-2)	167.9
455.1875	WSBK/NESN	Sports Crews (F-1)	167.9
455.4125	WSBK/NESN	Sports Crews (F-2)	167.9
450.700R	WHSH TV 66	Repeater Down	85.4

Boston Area Press

453.000	Boston Globe	77.0
464.5625	Boston Globe (security)	
464.575	Boston Globe (security)	136.5

452.9625	Boston Globe (portables)	
452.9875	Boston Globe (portables)	
452.975	Boston Herald	156.7
173.375	Associated Press	127.3
173.375	Lowell Sun	103.5
463.600	Lawrence Eagle Tribune	162.2
173.225	Middlesex News	146.2
173.325	Salem News	
173.275	Quincy Patriot Ledger	114.8

Boston Radio

450.1125R	Metro Traffic Control (455.1125 input)	141.3
450.2125	Metro Traffic Control backup	141.3
461.300R	SmartRoute Traffic	167.9
121.750	Traffic Copters to Logan (& 123.075, 131.05)	
455.1125	WBOS FM 92.9 (F-1) Comms.	CSQ
450.1875	WBOS FM 92.9 (F-2) Comms.	CSQ
25.99	WCGY FM 93.5/WCCM AM 800 Comms.	
450.700R	WCGY/WCCM RPU (& 450.800)	
450.4625R	WCLB FM 105.7/WKOX AM 1200 (F-1)	179.9
450.5875	WCLB FM 105.7/WKOX AM 1200 (F-2)	179.9
26.43	WCLB FM 105.7/WKOX AM 1200	85.4
450.850R	WEEI AM Sports	74.4
450.750	WEEI AM Sports	74.4
450.900	WFNX FM 101.7 RPU (450.95, 455.9, 455.95)	
166.250	WFNX FM 101.7 RPU	
450.0875R	WHAV FM 1490/WLYT FM RPU (455.4125 in)	
166.250	WILD AM 1090 Remote Pick-up	
153.230	WJDA AM 1300 Comms. (Quincy)	
161.640	WJDA AM 1300 RPU (& 161.670)	
484.3375	WJDA AM 1300	
464.325	WJUL FM 91.5 Comms. (Lowell) (& 461.90)	
455.3125	WJUL FM 91.5 RPU (& 455.3875)	
455.800R	WLLH AM 1400 (Lowell)	CSQ
455.700	WLLH AM 1400 (& 455.3875)	CSQ
154.600	WODS FM	
455.950	WXKS FM 107.9 IFB (Medford)	
450.950	WZLX FM 100.7 Remote Pick-up (& 455.90)	

Former WHDH Radio Frequencies (also see WEEI freqs.)

450.5875R	AM 850 (F-1) News, Traffic	94.8
450.3125R	AM 850 (F-2) Backup	94.8
450.150	AM 850 RPU link from Newton	94.8
161.670	AM 850 RPU (& 161.730, 450.900, 455.900)	

WBCN FM 104.1

450.4375R	(F-1)	Comms., Traffic, Cues	82.5
455.4375M	(F-2)	Simplex -repeater input	82.5
455.4125	(F-3)	Engineering, Remote set-up	82.5
455.1875	(F-4)	Backup, On-ste IFB	82.5
161.640	RPU	(& 161.67, .70, .73, .76)	
450.700		RPU (& .75, .90, .95, +455.70, .75 etc.)	
153.350R		Mobile repeater off 450.4375	

WBZ AM 1030
450.650R	(F-1)	News, Traffic	82.5
455.650	(F-2)	Repeater input	82.5
455.450	(F-3)	RPU and portables	82.5
455.925	(F-4)	RPU and portables	82.5
161.640		RPU (& 161.67, 161.70, 161.73, 161.76)	

WRKO AM 680/WBMX FM 98.5
450.0625R	(F-1)	WRKO News, Traffic	94.8
455.350	(F-2)	WBMX Comms., Traffic	94.8
455.150	(F-3)	Unknown use	94.8
450.5625R	(F-4)	Unknown use	94.8
161.670		RPU (& 161.70, 161.76, 450.70, 450.80)	

Southeast Massachusetts Media

173.225	Brockton Enterprise	123.0
173.325	Cape Cod Standard Times	131.8
483.7875	Media Broadcasting (Somerset)	
173.375	Standard Times (New Bedford)	156.7
461.875	Sun Publishing (Attleboro)	
153.350R	WATB FM 103.9 Comms. (Yarmouth)	CSQ
455.925	WATB FM 103.9 RPU (& 161.700, 161.760)	
166.250	WATB FM 103.9 IFB	
153.350R	WATD FM 95.9 Comms. (Marshfield) (170.15 in)	
455.925	WATD FM 95.9 RPU from U-Mass.(161.70 in)	
450.925	WATD FM 95.9 RPU (& 450.7, 161.76, 166.25)	
161.640	WCIB Radio (Falmouth)	
161.730	WCOD Radio (Hyannis)	
450.3125R	WLNE TV 6 Dispatch (New Bedford)	
161.670	WLNE TV 6 Backup	
161.640	WPLM FM 99.1/AM 1390 RPU (Plymouth)	
161.670	WPLM FM 99.1/AM 1390 RPU	136.5
166.250	WQRC FM 99.9 Skyview Traffic (Falmouth)	
450.850	WQRC FM 99.9 (& 450.05, 161.70, 161.76)	
153.230	WSAR AM 1480 Comms. (Fall River)	74.4
450.450	WSAR AM 1480 RPU	

Central Massachusetts Media

455.700R	WAAF Radio RPU w/cues (Worcester)	CSQ
450.800R	WAAF Radio Backup (Worcester)	CSQ
450.5875	WAAF Radio (Worcester)	
153.230	WSRS/CVS Traffic Van (Worcester)	77.0
153.230	WEIM Radio (Fitchburg)	
161.760	WFTQ Radio (Worcester)	
461.700	WUNI TV (Worcester)	203.5
464.550	WUNI TV (Worcester)	
455.1125	WORC Radio (Worcester) Traffic	
455.1875	WORC Radio (Worcester) Traffic	
455.3875	WORC Radio (Worcester) Traffic	
173.325	Worcester Telegram & Gazette	100.0
450.700R	WHSH TV (Marlboro)	
450.2125R	WTAG Radio (Worcester)	100.0
464.2125	WXLO Radio (Worcester)	

Western Massachusetts Media

450.3125	WWLP TV (Springfield) (F-1)	127.3
450.950	WWLP TV (Springfield) (F-2)	127.3
161.640	WGGB TV (Springfield)	110.9
161.730	WSPR Radio (Springfield)	
173.375	Springfield Ledger	107.2
173.225	Berkshire Eagle (Great Barrington)	D-114
161.670	WFCR/WMUA remotes (UMass.)	
450.4875	WSPR Radio (Springfield)	
455.4875	WGBY TV (Springfield)	

UTILITY TROUBLE-EMERGENCY CREWS

<u>Boston Edison</u>

158.160	Distribution Dispatchers ("DD")	179.9
153.500	Pilgrim Nuclear Plant Operations	156.7
153.500	Underground Crews	
153.560	Underground Crews (mobiles 131.8)	CSQ
37.780	Power Generation	103.5
461.850	Security, Administration, Pagers	131.8
	OVERHEAD TROUBLE CREWS:	
484.8375	Walpole -south of Boston crews	156.7
484.8625	Waltham -west/nw of greater Boston	156.7
484.8875	Woburn -north of Boston	156.7
484.9125	Framingham -metrowest	100.0
484.9125	Somerville -greater Boston north	156.7
484.9375	Hyde Park -greater Boston south	156.7

Future Boston Edison System (Trunked):
936.3875 through 936.500 (every 12.5 KHz)
937.3875 through 937.500 (every 12.5 KHz)

<u>Boston Gas</u>

37.620	Construction Crews	CSQ
153.530	Trouble Calls	100.0
153.440	Data	CSQ
158.130	Trouble Calls	103.5
158.190	Operations	100.0
153.680	Construction (mobiles 179.9)	CSQ

<u>Commonwealth Electric</u>

37.540	New Bedford area	131.8
37.760	Plymouth area	131.8
451.025	F1-Cape & Vineyards meter dept	203.5
451.125	F2-Cape & Vineyards trouble calls	203.5
451.200	F3-Cape & Vineyard administration	203.5
451.250	F4-Cape & Vineyard trouble calls	203.5
451.675	Miscellaneous use	203.5
173.350	Administration	
37.660	Common Systemwide Channel	131.8

New England Power Service -trouble crews- (PL: 100.0)

FREQ.	DISTRICT	DISPATCHER LOCALE	
47.880	Central	Worcester	
48.120	So. Central	Hopedale/Marlboro/Franklin/Worc.	
48.220	No. Central	Leominster/Worcester	
47.880	No. Central	(same as above, secondary)	
48.500	Western	Gt. Barrington/N. Adams/Worc.	
48.280	Western	Northampton/Worcester	
48.060	North Shore	North Andover	
48.140	North Shore	Malden	
48.300	Merrimack	North Andover/Tewksbury	
48.540	Merrimack	(same as above, secondary)	
48.120	Attleboro	Attleboro/Hopedale	
48.080	South Shore	Weymouth (48.54 also)	
48.480	Systemwide	System Common Channel	
48.440	Systemwide	NEPS Construction	
456.150	Mobile repeater		CSQ
48.290	Systemwide	Emergency Operations	
	(also 48.43, 48.49)		
37.60	Systemwide	REMVEC Operations	123.0
173.395	Power Load Management Data		CSQ
	(also 173.205 173.315, 173.335)		

Commonwealth Gas

37.46	MetroWest area trouble calls	131.8
37.54	Plymouth area trouble calls	151.4
37.70	Construction Crews	131.8
37.72	New Bedford area operations	
48.02	Greater Worcester trouble calls	CSQ
451.100	New Bedford area trouble calls	
451.250	Cambridge area trouble calls	146.2

Eastern Utilities

451.075	Meter Department	203.5
451.175	Fall River area	203.5
451.375	Brockton/Norwell area	203.5

AT&T Longline Maintenance

451.325	Operations/Maintenance	103.5

New England Telephone/NYNEX

451.350	MetroWest	110.9
451.625	MetroWest	
451.300	North Shore	127.3
451.300	Western MA	
451.575	Central MA	141.3
451.350	Cape Cod	186.2
451.350	Greenfield Area	
451.400	Greenfield Area	
451.375	Springfield Area	
451.400	Brockton Area	100.0

Frequency	Location	Tone
451.450	Waltham area	
451.500	Plymouth Area	100.0
451.500	South Western Area	
451.500	North Central MA	110.9
451.425	Mobiles -systemwide	
851.0375	Administration	DPL
937.8875 - 939.000 future use (12.5 KHz steps)		

Bay State Gas
Frequency	Location	Tone
158.220R	Lawrence	100.0
158.145R	Lawrence	100.0
153.590R	Brockton	203.5
48.24	Springfield	186.2
464.150	Springfield	

Cambridge Gas & Electric Light
Frequency	Location	Tone
158.250	Cambridge	131.8

Colonial Gas Company (Cape Cod)
Frequency	Location	Tone
48.36	Operations/Trouble Calls	114.8
48.96	Future repeater input	

Essex County Gas
Frequency	Location	Tone
48.180	Amesbury	88.5

Fitchburg Gas & Electric Light
Frequency	Location	Tone
451.125	Operations/Trouble Calls	110.9

Lowell Gas Company
Frequency	Location	Tone
153.710	Operations/Trouble Calls	CSQ
153.500	Portables	CSQ

Western Massachusetts Electric
Frequency	Location	Tone
47.76	System common	
47.86	Amherst area	100.0
47.98	Springfield City area	131.8
47.98	Greater Springfield area	100.0
48.04	Pittsfield area	100.0
48.16	Greenfield area	100.0
48.34	Erving area	162.2
173.250	Administration	
173.350	Administration	

Miscellaneous Utilities
Frequency	Location	Tone
47.700	Berkshire Gas	167.9
153.470	Fall River Gas	167.9
153.605	Mass Wholesale Electric (Ludlow)	D-315

Dig Safe
Frequency	Location	Tone
462.125	Operations	114.8
464.350	Operations	118.8
472.3625	Operations	151.4

RAILROADS (all CSQ unless noted)

Amtrak/Conrail
160.920	Amtrak -Road (F-1)	
161.070	Amtrak -Road (F-2)	
160.800	Conrail -Road (F-1)	
160.800	Conrail -Hot Box Detectors	100.0
161.295R	Amtrak -Police	100.0
160.365	Amtrak -Police repeater input	
161.205	Amtrak -Police Car to car	
452.900	Amtrak -Terminal Services/police portables	
160.515	Amtrak -Maintenance	
160.560R	Conrail -Police	
161.550	Conrail -Police input to repeater	
160.860	Conrail -Hump Yards	
160.455	Conrail -Yard	
160.980	Conrail -Yard	
161.130	Conrail -Maintenance base	
160.710	Conrail -Maintenance mobiles	
161.055	Conrail -Special maintenance projects	
457.9375	Conrail -End of Train (EOT) Telemetry	

Boston & Maine
- 161.160   Dispatch to train
- 161.520   Train to dispatch
- 161.400   Road & Yard
- 161.190   Cars/Yardmen (160.230 also)
- 161.370   Maintenance of Way
- 160.350   Hump switcher
- 160.440   Piggy back vans/Weld rail plant
- 161.235R Railroad Police
- 160.260   Railroad Police -repeater input

Bay Colony (Marshfield/Bourne/Hyannis)
160.350R	Road/Dispatch	
161.355	Road/Dispatch -repeater input	
161.265	Maintenance	
163.4125	RR tie to Army Corps of Engineers	173.8
156.650	Cape Cod Canal Bridge tie	
160.485	New Channel	

Grafton & Upton (Hopedale)
- 160.245   Road

Grand Trunk (Palmer/Millers Falls)
- 160.770   Road (161.415 also)
- 161.040   Road/Phone Patch
- 160.935   Dispatcher (161.205 also)

Mass Central (Amherst)
- 160.470   Road

<u>Pioneer Valley (Westfield)</u>
160.335   Road (161.085, 161.025 also)

<u>Providence & Worcester Railroad   (Worcester/Uxbridge)</u>
160.650	Ch. #1	Road
161.100	Ch. #2	Yard
160.890	Ch. #3	Maintenance of Way
160.775	Ch. #4	Police/Comm. & Signal Dept.
161.235		Yard

<u>MBTA (Metropolitan Boston) PL Tone: 162.2</u>
470.6875	Blue Line Operations	
470.6375	Green Line Operations	
470.6125	Orange Line Operations	
470.4125	Red Line Operations	
470.6625	MBTA Police ch. #1	131.8
483.5625	MBTA Police ch. #2	131.8
470.7875	MBTA Police ch. #3 (BAPERN 3)	131.8
470.5625	MBTA Police ch. #4 (BAPERN 4)	131.8
472.5875	Buses/Trackless Trolleys	
472.5125	Buses (472.6125 also)	
472.6375	"The Ride" (van for the disabled) -- w/data	
31.140R	"Transportation"/Repair/Supervisors	
30.900	Input to repeater	
44.460	Maintenance/Engineering/Power	
160.920	Amtrak tie	
154.570	Wireless microphones	
153.755R	Riverside Station -car repair (156.775 input)	

<u>MBTA Commuter Rail</u>
161.490	Ch. #1 - System Emergency -TRAINS (alert)
160.590	Ch. #1 - System Emergency -DISPATCHER
160.320	Ch. #2 - General Operations -NORTH DISP.
160.800	Ch. #3 - General Operations -WEST/SOUTH
161.070	Ch. #4 - Yard Operations
160.695	Engineering Department
161.565	Maintenance/Utility (161.460 also)
160.875	Yards -North of Boston / 160.920 ops. South

CELLULAR & CORDLESS PHONE

Cellular phones can be found between 869 & 894 MHz. Cellular mobile phones can only be monitored on those scanners which have 800 MHz capability. Many of the scanners sold today also cannot receive 800 MHz and many of the 800 MHz radios which are sold have had the cellular portion electrically deleted by the manufacturer to prevent you from listening. There are federal regulations which prohibit the interception of telephone calls. Cordless phones may use many sets of frequencies from 1.6 MHz through 900 MHz. The most common frequencies are found between 46.61 through 46.97 MHz and 49.67 through 49.99 MHz.

AIRPORTS (also see Military section)

121.500	Air Emergency (also 243.000)
121.750	Helicopters (also 120.750 & 123.050)

Boston-Logan International Airport

128.800	Tower
128.200	Tower
119.100	Tower
134.050	Gate Control
121.900	Ground Control
120.600	Approach Control -South
118.250	Approach Control -North
127.200	Approach Control -West
133.000	Departure Control
121.650	Clearance Delivery/Pre-Taxi Clearance
121.750	Tower to Helicopters
123.075	Helicopters
135.000	ATIS
122.950	UNICOM
122.400	RCO
854.9625	Massport -Fire Dept. emergency channel
856.-860.4375	Massport Operations/State PD/Buses
858.-860.2625	Massport (as above)
855.-860.8125	Massport (as above)

Boston-Logan Ground Crews

460.650	Continental Airlines
460.825	Delta Airlines
460.875	Northwest Airlines
460.675	Trans World Airlines
460.700	US Air
460.725	United Airlines
463.8875	Marriott Flite-Services
461.175	Marriott Flite-Services
TRUNKED	Arinc (856-860.8875)

Boston-Logan Private Air Radio (plane to company office)

130.125	Air France
129.400	Airinc. (Northeast)
129.225	American Airlines
129.150	British Airways
130.400	Continental Airlines
130.525	Continental Airlines
131.850	Delta Airlines
131.900	Delta Airlines
131.450	Northwest Airlines
131.700	Northwest Airlines
130.125	Swiss Air
130.100	US Air (also: 936.250; 936.6375; 937.1375)
129.300	United Airlines

Boston-Heliport
122.900	Common Traffic

Barnstable-Hyannis
119.500	CTAF/Tower
121.900	Ground Control
125.150	Clearance Delivery
118.200	Cape Approach/Departure Control
132.900	Boston Center Approach/Departure Control
123.800	Hyannis ATIS
122.950	Hyannis UNICOM
123.300	Airport Services
126.425	Hyannis RCO
155.745	Airport Security/Operations

Bedford-Hanscom
118.500	CTAF/Tower
121.700	Ground Control
124.600	ATIS
124.400	Boston Approach/Departure Control
121.850	Clearance Delivery
122.950	UNICOM

Beverly
125.200	CTAF/Tower
118.700	ATIS
121.600	Ground Control
124.400	Boston Approach/Departure Control
122.950	UNICOM

Chatham
122.800	CTAF/UNICOM
118.200	Cape Approach/Departure Control
132.900	Boston Center Approach/Departure Control
127.300	Clearance Delivery

Edgartown
122.800	CTAF/UNICOM

Fall River
122.800	CTAF/UNICOM
128.700	Providence Approach/Departure Control
124.850	Boston Center Approach/Departure

Falmouth
122.800	CTAF/UNICOM

Fitchburg
122.700	CTAF/UNICOM
124.400	Boston Approach/Departure Control

<u>Gardner</u>
122.800   CTAF/UNICOM
123.750   Boston Center Approach/Departure

<u>Great Barrington</u>
122.800   CTAF/UNICOM
125.000   Albany Approach/Departure Control

<u>Hanson</u>
122.900   CTAF

<u>Haverhill</u>
122.800   CTAF/UNICOM

<u>Hopedale</u>
122.800   CTAF/UNICOM
119.000   Bradley Approach/Departure Control

<u>Lawrence</u>
120.000   Common Traffic
124.300   Ground Control
124.400   Boston Approach/Departure Control
122.800   UNICOM
126.750   ATIS

<u>Mansfield</u>
123.000   CTAF/UNICOM
118.250   Boston Approach/Departure Control

<u>Marlboro</u>
122.800   CTAF/UNICOM

<u>Marshfield</u>
122.800   CTAF/UNICOM
118.250   Boston Approach/Departure Control

<u>Marstons Mills</u>
122.900   CTAF

<u>Methuen</u>
122.800   CTAF/UNICOM

<u>Montague/Turners Falls</u>
123.000   CTAF/UNICOM
123.750   Boston Center Approach/Departure

<u>Nantucket</u>
118.300   CTAF/Tower
122.950   UNICOM
126.600   ATIS
126.100   Cape Approach/Departure Control

132.900	Boston Center Approach/Departure
121.700	Ground Control
128.250	Clearance Delivery

New Bedford
118.100	CTAF/Tower
121.900	Ground Control
124.850	Boston Center Approach/Departure Control
128.700	Providence Approach/Departure Control
122.950	UNICOM
126.850	ATIS

Newburyport/Plum Island
123.000	CTAF/UNICOM
124.400	Boston Approach/Departure Control

Norfolk
122.800	CTAF/UNICOM

North Adams
122.800	CTAF/UNICOM

Northampton
122.700	CTAF/UNICOM
125.350	Bradley Approach/Departure Control
133.600	Clearance Delivery

Norwood
126.000	CTAF/Tower
121.800	Ground Control/Clearance Delivery
124.100	Boston Approach/Departure Control
122.950	UNICOM
119.950	ATIS
123.500	Wiggins Airways

Orange
122.800	CTAF/UNICOM
123.750	Boston Center Approach/Departure

Palmer
122.800	CTAF/UNICOM
123.950	Bradley Approach/Departure Control

Pepperell
123.050	CTAF/UNICOM

Pittsfield
122.700	CTAF/UNICOM
125.000	Albany Approach/Departure Control
128.600	Clearance Delivery
122.050	RCO

Plymouth
123.000	CTAF/UNICOM
126.300	Cape Approach/Departure Control
127.750	Clearance Delivery
132.900	Boston Center Approach/Departure

Provincetown
122.800	CTAF/UNICOM
118.200	Cape Approach/Departure Control
120.650	Clearance Delivery
132.900	Boston Center Approach/Departure

Shirley
122.800	CTAF/UNICOM

Southbridge
122.800	CTAF/UNICOM
123.950	Bradley Approach/Departure Control

Spencer
123.000	CTAF/UNICOM

Stow
122.800	CTAF/UNICOM
124.400	Boston Approach/Departure Control

Taunton
122.700	CTAF/UNICOM
128.700	Providence Approach/Departure Control
124.850	Boston Center Approach/Departure

Tewksbury
122.800	CTAF/UNICOM
124.400	Boston Approach/Departure Control

Vineyard Haven
121.400	CTAF/Tower
126.250	ATIS
122.950	UNICOM
124.700	Cape Approach/Departure Control
124.700	Clearance Delivery (when tower closed)
121.800	Ground Control

Worcester
120.500	CTAF/Tower
121.900	Ground Control
124.350	Clearance Delivery
119.000	Bradley APP/DEP & Clearance Delivery
122.950	UNICOM
126.550	ATIS
122.200	RCO

Rhode Island

Barrington
155.490	KCC348	Police	114.8
158.970	KCC348	Eastern New England Intercity	CSQ
153.950	KNFF614	Fire - E. Bay Net -PD Disp.	CSQ
153.950	KNFF614	Fire - HQ-Rumstick Road	CSQ
153.950	KNFF616	Fire - MIddle Highway Sta.	CSQ
153.950	KNFF613	Fire - Sowams Rd. Station	CSQ
154.280	KCE265	Intercity Fire	CSQ
154.980	WPEH315	Highway Department	167.9
173.2375	WGJ330	Water Department Data	CSQ

Bristol
155.130R	KCB268	Police	114.8
453.200	KCB268	Police	
154.890	KCB268	Police - repeater input	114.8
155.370	KCB268	Police	
158.970	KCB268	Intercity Police	CSQ
154.145R	KDU510	Fire	
159.450	KDU510	Fire -repeater input	
153.950	KDU510	Fire - East Bay Net	CSQ
155.805	KNEK333	Highway Department	
151.685	WNJP823	Public Schools Department	
153.020	WNIJ691	Turnpike & Bridge Authority	107.2
451.050	KEM239	Bristol County Water	123.0
153.665	KGT720	Bristol & Warren Gas	
155.265	WNKF762	Paramed Systems	
155.400	KNBC423	Veteran's Hospital	

Burrillville
155.565	KRV409	Police	
156.090	KRV409	Police - northwest Police net	
154.725	KRV409	West Law Enforcement-rare use	
158.970	KRV409	Eastern New England Intercity	
154.190	KCE481	Glendale Dist. -No. League	CSQ
154.190	KJY654	Harrisville Dist.-No. League	CSQ
154.190	KLG492	Nasonville Dist. -Northern Lge.	
154.190	KNCP417	Oakland/Mapleville-No. Lge.	CSQ
154.325	KNCP417	Oakland/Mapleville-No. Lge.	CSQ
154.190	KNEA882	Pascoag Dist -Northern Lge.	CSQ
151.040	KRJ723	Highway Department	
155.805	KNCE716	Municipal Services	
151.745	WNZE493	School Department	
151.835	WNZE493	School Department	
151.865	WNZE493	School Department	
48.000	KCT459	Pascoag Water Department	

Central Falls
156.210	WPEK304	Police - Blackstone Valley Net
155.430	WPEK304	Police - tactical

155.760	KDR366	Police - detectives/Highway	
155.655	KJN311	Police	
158.970	KSN311	Eastern New England Intercity	
154.415	KTC812	Fire	
154.280	KTC812	Intercity Fire	
155.760	KDR366	Highway Dept./Police Detectives	
453.2125	WPDR895	Municipal Svcs. (453.5375, 453.8625)	
468.6875	WPDT344	Don Wyatt Detention Facility	

Charlestown

154.650	KGV254	Police	118.8
154.815	KGV254	Washington County Net	118.8
155.190	KGV254	Police -RISPERN	
46.500	KCD444	So. Fire Lge.-Westerly Disp. "X"	127.3
46.500	KXQ956	So. Fire Lge-Cross Mills VFD	127.3
46.420	WZY355	Fire mobile tie to So. Kingstown	
46.220	WZY355	Fireground working channel	
46.280	WZY355	Fire alert tones	
46.280	KNCZ343	Fire alert tones	
460.625	WYZ355	Fire -repeats 46.28	
155.235	KBG351	Ambulance	
158.925	WNSV365	Municipal Services	
156.165	WPDN537	Public Works Department	

Coventry

154.725R	WNJT650	Police - West RI Law Enf.	123.0
159.345	WNJT650	Police - repeater input	123.0
155.190	WNJT650	Police - RISPERN -F2-	
155.475	KCB258	Police - state tie -F3-	118.8
155.625	KCB258	Police - E. Greenwich tie	88.5
460.0125	WNJT650	Police - mobile repeater	
158.970	KCB258	Eastern New England Intercity	
45.200	KLW278	Fire Alarm-Fl-dispatch	CSQ
45.200	KDK673	Central Coventry Fire Dist.	CSQ
46.400	WNCS440	Central Coventry Fire Dist.	CSQ
45.200	KJR201	Harris Fire District	CSQ
45.200	KFD55	Hopkins Hill Fire District	CSQ
45.200	KGN529	Tiogue Fire District	CSQ
45.200	KGK719	Washington Fire District	CSQ
45.200	KDZ496	West Coventry Dist.-Greene Sta.	
45.200	KAY971	West Coventry Dist.-Summit Sta.	
45.160	KDK672	Fire - Anthony	
45.200	KDK672	Fire - Anthony	CSQ
45.480	KDK672	Fire Alarm-F2-disp. Anthony	
154.280	KLS466	Fire Alarm-Intercity Fire	CSQ
45.720	KLP784	Highway Department	
45.140	WNVQ877	Municipal Services	
153.740	KUQ835	Housing Authority	
151.895	KCM722	School Department	

Cranston

482.4125	KXN403	Police	127.3
482.4625	KXN403	Police - Channel #2	127.3
482.5625	KXN403	Police - Channel #3	127.3
155.190	KXN403	Police - RISPERN	
158.970	KXN403	Police - E. New England	CSQ
154.010R	KCD447	Fire	192.8
460.600	WNQZ568	Fire -dispatch only	192.8
159.405R	KCD447	Fire	192.8
159.465	KCD447	Fire -fireground	
154.280	KCD447	Intercity Fire -Net HQ	CSQ
158.820	KBB969	Building Departments	
159.135	WNWG978	Highway Department	
154.085	KJY766	Senior Citizen Van	
151.835	KTA652	School Department	
155.220	KNCQ764	School Department	D-606
453.775	WPBT980	Housing Authority	
155.400	KNBU364	State Mental Health Hospital	
155.295	WPEE364	Rhode Island Medical Center	
154.680	WPCE399	State Correctional Services	
453.600	WNFT949	State Juvenile Correctional Svcs.	

Cumberland

155.430	KNAJ380	Police	
155.655	KNAJ380	Police - town tactical -F2-	
156.210	KNAJ380	Police - Blackstone Valley Net	
484.7375	WIL513	Police - Future use	
482.3875	WIL513	Police - Future use	
158.970	KNAJ380	East New England Intercity - F4-	
154.205	WNCL994	Fire - Ashton Fire District	94.8
154.205	KNEM436	Fire - Berkley Fire District	94.8
154.205	KNFW529	Fire - Control -PD Dispatch	94.8
154.205	KCD609	Fire - Cumberland Hill Fire	94.8
154.205	KCF567	Fire - N. Cumberland Dist.	94.8
154.205	KCD818	Fire - Valley Falls Fire District	94.8
154.205		Fire - Cumberland Rescue	94.8
154.280	KNFW529	Intercity Fire -at Police Disp.	CSQ
151.130	KGL555	Highway Department (& KBQ228)	
154.570	WNRX276	High School	

East Greenwich

155.625	KRV415	Police	88.5
155.190	KRV415	Police -F2- RISPERN	
155.085	KRV415	Police -F3- Highway tie	
154.725	KRV415	Police - Regional network	
158.970	KRV415	E. New England Intercity	CSQ
151.475	KCA713	Fire	131.8
151.190	KCA713	Fire -F2-	
154.280	KCA713	Intercity Fire -F3-	
151.280	KCA713	Fire - new channel	
155.085	KEM675	Highway Department	
155.115	KNGS337	Narragansett Bay Commission	

SCANNER MASTER
Massachusetts, Rhode Island & Southern New Hampshire Pocket Guide –6th Edition
Errata & Update Sheet

Page 101	461.025 is <u>not</u> the South Shore Sparks Club. (It is a private business Community Repeater and should not be used without the proper licensing.)
Page 5	460.325 is now Avon Police Operations
	453.9625 is now used by the town Civil Defense
Page 8	150.790 repeats 45.48 Beverly Fire, PL 131.8
Page 19	Chicopee Police are switching to 800 MHz
Page 23	Dunstable Highway 150.995 PL is 151.4
Page 25	Fall River Fire – New Radio System
	453.375R F-1 Operations
	453.850M F-2 Fireground
	471.5125R F-3 Backup/Emerg. Mngmt. tie
Page 28	156.165 (179.9) is now Gardner DPW
Page 31	47.740 (100.0) is Harwich Water Department
Page 35	486.0625 (131.8) is Ipswich Police Car to Car
Page 35	Kingston Fire 460.600 PL is 203.5
Page 35	Cranes Beach 159.420R/151.220 PL is 88.5'
Page 42	Mattapoisett Fire is to change frequencies
Page 54	Norton PD *reportedly* switching to 800 MHz.
Page 59	464.575 (127.3) Wachusett Ski Area Parking
Page 70	160.080 is a Stow Police new mobile channel
Page 73	852.5875 (100.0) is Tyngsboro Police
Page 77	W. Bridgewater is using mobile data terminals for dispatching and other communications.
Page 78	156.135 is a new Westhampton DPW channel
Page 82	485.3875 (146.2) is Wilmington Police "Tac 5"
Page 82	Woburn Fire Department is now using 131.8 PL
Page 86	State PD Western MA trunk system now testing on 858.7875, 859.7875, 860.7875.

If you have any further updates or corrections, or any questions, please call Scanner Master at 800-722-6701.

East Providence
154.770R	KNFQ464	Police	103.5
155.310	KNFQ464	Police -input to repeater	103.5
155.010	KNFQ464	Police - Ch.#2 - Seekonk tie	
153.800	KCI290	Police - Ch.#3 - detective/hgwy.	
158.970	KNFQ464	E. New England Intercity	CSQ
154.070	KCB723	Fire - Police dispatch	127.3
154.280	KCB723	Intercity Fire	CSQ
153.800	KCI290	Highway Department/PD detec.	
153.845	WZM944	Public Buildings Department	
155.115	KNGS357	Sewer District	

Exeter
155.580R	WZC581	Police	118.8
154.950	WZC581	Police -input to repeater	118.8
155.190	WZC581	Police -RISPERN	
154.815	WZC581	Police - Washington Cty. tie	
46.380	WNQO861	Fire -Dispatch	107.2
460.5875	WNQO861	Fire -Emergency Dispatch Ctr.	
46.380	KNFC542	Fire - Exeter No. 1	107.2
46.380	KLI377	Fire - Exeter No. 2	107.2
46.460	WXK614	Fire - Ladd School VFD	
45.280	WPEK568	Fire - Emergency Dispatch Ctr.	
46.500	KLI377	Southern Fire League - mobiles	
154.280	KNFC542	Fire - Intercity Fire Net	CSQ
154.280	KNCM554	Fire - Intercity Fire Net	CSQ
460.525	reported	Fire - future system	
155.220	KNCM554	Ambulance	118.8
159.075R	KSI566	Highway Department	
155.865	KSI566	Highway Department -input	

Foster
155.535	KWO599	Police - Johnston/ Scituate	CSQ
154.725	KWO599	Police -West Law Enforcement	
155.190	KWO599	Police -RISPERN	
158.970	KWO599	Eastern New England Intercity	
154.190	KDA658	Fire - Foster Ctr.-Wnsqtckt.	CSQ
154.190	KBA630	Fire - So. Foster -Wnsqtckt.	CSQ
154.190	KBA630	Fire - Moosup Vlly.-Wnsqtckt.	CSQ
156.180	KIB977	Highway Department	

Gloucester
156.090	WXB704	Police - Northwest Station	CSQ
158.970	WXB704	E. New England Intercity	CSQ
154.725	WXB704	Police -West Law Enforcement	
154.190	WQW527	Fire - Chepachet - Wnsqtckt.	127.3
154.190	KCD235	Fire - Harmony -Wnsqtckt.	127.3
154.190	KSV685	Fire - W. Gloucester Station	127.3
154.295	KSV285	Fire - W. Gloucester Station	127.3

Hopkinton

154.800R	KWQ544	Police	118.8
159.300	KWQ544	Police - Repeater input	118.8
156.210	KWQ544	Police - Westerly tie/mobiles	
154.815	KWQ544	Police - Washington County Net	
158.970	KWQ544	E. New England Intercity	CSQ
155.190	KWQ544	Police -RISPERN	
46.500	KNFE836	Fire -Ashaway "X4"-S. League	
46.500	KGU237	Fire -Hope Valley	
46.280	KGU237	Fire -Hope Valley (also 46.38)	
460.6375	KGU237	Fire -Hope Valley mob. repeater	
46.500	KNGU698	Fire -Wyoming "X9" (also 46.28)	
46.500	mobiles	Fire - Camp Yawgoog - S. League	
46.240	WNRO555	S.W. RI Emerg. Disp. (also 46.50)	
37.900	KVA917	Highway Department	
47.580	WPDZ586	Hope Valley Ambulance	

Jamestown

155.070	KLK534	Police	118.8
155.580	KLK534	Police -F2- N. Kingstown tie	118.8
155.685	KLK534	Police - Newport County Net	
155.190	KLK534	Police -RISPERN	
153.950	KCE673	Fire - East Bay Fire Net	
45.680	KSN284	Highway Department	CSQ
153.020	KNIJ691	Turnpike & Bridge Authority	107.2

Johnston

155.535	KCC347	Police - w/Foster-Scituate	118.8
155.700	WPBY569	Police - town operations	
154.725	KCC347	Police - regional network	CSQ
158.970	KCC347	E. New England Intercity	CSQ
154.175	KCE738	Fire	CSQ
154.190	KCE738	Fire - Woonasquatucket Lge.	CSQ
154.190	KNDL869	Fire - Cameroon Parish	CSQ
154.280	KCE738	Intercity Fire	CSQ
151.040R	KEV422	Highway Department	118.8
159.075	KEV422	Highway Dept. -repeater in	118.8
155.205	reported	Universal Ambulance	85.4

Lincoln

151.265	KCC646	Police - new channel	CSQ
156.210	KCC646	Police - Ch.#1-Blkstne Vlly.	CSQ
156.060	KFI491	Police - secondary/Highway	118.8
158.970	KCC646	Police - Ch.#2-East N.E.	CSQ
155.655	KCC646	Police - Ch.#3 - town tactical	118.8
155.430	KCC646	Police - Ch. #4 - area tactical	
154.160	KBA752	Fire - Police Dispatch	71.9
154.160	KTP332	Fire - Albion District	71.9
154.160	KRF363	Fire - Fairlawn District	71.9
154.160	KDF568	Fire - Lonsdale District	71.9
154.160	KEA752	Fire - Lime Rock District	71.9

154.160	KNBJ668	Fire - Manville District	71.9
154.160	WNQU227	Fire - Quinville District	71.9
154.160	KLP900	Fire - Saylesville District	71.9
154.190	KBA752	Woonasquatucket Fire League	tie
154.280	KBA752	Intercity Fire - at police disp.	CSQ
156.060	KFI491	Highway Dept./PD backup	CSQ
154.570		Water Commission - portables	
154.570	KB30665	Lincoln Mall	
464.475	KB53139	Burrillville Racing Association	
154.650	WQW866	Rhode Island Community College	
151.955	KD51582	Blackston Valley Tourism Cncl.	

Little Compton

155.415R	KQT988	Police	118.8
155.745	KQT988	Police -repeater input	118.8
155.685	KQT988	Newport County Police Net	
158.970	KQT988	E. New England Intercity	CSQ
46.060	KCC573	Fire-Newport Cty. Fire League	
453.625	WPEF894	Municipal Services	

Middletown

155.790	KCE213	Police	118.8
155.970	KCE213	Police	
155.685	KCE213	Newport County Police Net	
155.190	KCE213	Police -RISPERN	
158.970	KCE213	E. New England Intercity	CSQ
46.100	KCC635	Fire	CSQ
46.060	KCC635	Newport County Fire League	
151.115	KBA205	Highway Department	118.8
464.325	WPTD566	Municipal Services	
461.7625	WPDT566	Municipal Services	
154.570	WNUB282	Meadowland Park	
151.925	WRF248	St. George's School	

Narragansett

154.875R	KCC925	Police	118.8
151.400	KCC925	Police - repeater input	118.8
154.815	KCC925	Washington Cty. Police Net	
155.190	KCC925	Police -RISPERN	
453.100	KCK787	Fire	107.2
46.260	KCK787	Fire - Tone Alert/Simulcast	
46.420	KCK787	Fire	107.2
46.040	KKL886	Volunteer Rescue	
154.280	KCK787	Intercity Fire	CSQ
156.180	KNBA272	Highway Department	
154.600	KB67925	Nuclear Science Center	
464.3125	KB94742	State Services	

New Shoreham

158.790	WNDQ941	Police -F1-
154.205	WNFH289	Police -F2- Fire Dispatch
154.815	KWQ545	Police -F3- Washington Cty. Net

155.190	KWQ545	Police -F4- RISPERN	
154.515	WNFI960	Police -F5- Island Alarms Inc.	
156.210	KWQ545	Police -F6- Westerly Police tie	
154.875	KWQ545	Police -F7- Narragansett tie	
156.800	KWQ545	Police -F8- Coast Guard tie	
157.620	KWQ545	Police -F9- Utility Co. tie	
156.015	WNDQ941	Police - new channel	
154.205	WNFH289	Fire -F2- Police Dispatch	
33.600	KYS833	Fire	
159.015	WNDQ941	Highway Department	
158.745	WNLY890	Municipal Services	
157.620	WNFD907	Block Island Light Co.	
39.060	KVV994	State of R.I.	

Newport

155.730R	KCB245	Police	118.8
154.755	KCB245	Police - input to repeater	118.8
155.685	KCB245	Newport County Police Net	
155.100	KLL981	Newport County Sheriff	
46.060	KCD292	Fire - Newport Cty. Fire League	
46.480	KCD292	Fire - Channel #2	
154.220	KCD292	Fire	
154.400	KCD292	Fire	
154.280	KCD292	Fire - Intercity Fire Network	CSQ
158.760	WNQU306	Public Works Department	
453.8875	WNQU306	Water Department data	
453.325	WPCG348	Housing Authority	
158.460	WPEF240	School Department - paging	
155.325	KNCH643	Edgehill Newport	
151.805	WNAP266	Newport Restoration Foundation	
151.895	KD21340	Newport Yachting Center	
151.955	WNLJ439	Newport Condo Management	
160.395	WNPB254	National Railroad Fndtn. Museum	
463.7875	WPDS672	Marriott Hotel	
154.600	WNUM923	Treadway Hotel & Resort	
464.825	KNEU399	Inn on the Harbor	
464.750	KNIJ872	Newport Islander Doubletree Hotel	
464.775	KNIJ872	Newport Islander Doubletree Hotel	
151.775	KNIS320	Viking Tours	
461.575	WNNA303	Mall at Newport	

North Kingstown

155.580R	KCB259	Police	118.8
154.950	KCB259	Police-input to repeater	118.8
154.815	KCB259	Washington Cty. Police Net	
155.190	KCB259	Police -RISPERN	
158.970	KCB259	E. New England Intercity	CSQ
154.235	KDO275	Fire - Headquarters	118.8
154.235	KJN702	Fire - Sta. #2 - School St.	118.8
154.235	KJN703	Fire - Sta. #3 - Saunderstown	
46.380	KDO275	Fire -regional net	

46.420	KDO275	Fire -regional net	
154.280	KDO275	Intercity Fire	CSQ
155.220	KNCR752	Ambulance	
155.820	KLP935	Town Hall to Highway & Water	
155.820	KLP935	Highway Department	
155.820	KBH346	Water Department	
155.040	WXF904	Quonset State Airport -ops.	
153.920	WXF904	Quonset State Airport -backup	
154.995	WXF904	Quonset State Airport	
153.020	WPDS582	Port Authority	

North Providence

154.800R	KCA235	Police	167.9
158.730	KCA235	Police - input to repeater	167.9
155.190	KCA235	Police - detec./cycles/RISPERN	
154.725	KCA235	Police - special ops. -F2-	
155.895	WPDP829	Police - mobiles	
158.970	KCA235	E. New England Intercity	CSQ
154.250R	KCD488	Fire	167.9
153.890	KCD488	Fire - input to repeater	167.9
154.115	KCD488	Fire - Ch. #2/Civil Defense Van	
154.400	WPDS872	Fire - new channel	
460.6125	KCD488	Fire - mobile repeater	
154.280	KCD488	Intercity Fire	167.9
154.115	WXT570	Seniors Van/Fire Ch.#2/CD	
156.240	KFB907	Highway Department	123.0
158.970		State Fire Marshal to Police	CSQ

North Smithfield

156.090	KRV410	Police -W. RI Law Enfrcmnt.	146.2
155.190	KRV410	Police -RISPERN	
155.430	KRV410	Police -Area Tactical	
158.970	KRV410	E. New England Intercity	CSQ
154.190	KCD501	Fire -Main Sta.-No. League	CSQ
154.190	KBD913	Fire -Primrose -No. League	CSQ
154.190	KNFW805	Fire -Slatersville Station	CSQ
154.280	KBD913	Intercity Fire - at Primrose	CSQ
159.165	WPEJ396	Highway Department	
154.600	WPBP406	School Department	

Pawtucket

154.830R	KNFT991	Police -Fl-	100.0
159.090	KNFT991	Police -input to repeater	136.5
155.655	KNFT991	Police -F2-city tactical	
155.430	KNFT991	Police -F3-area tactical	
159.090	KNFT991	Police -special operations	
155.835	KNFT991	Poilice -mobiles	
158.970	KCB277	E. New England Intercity	CSQ
154.445	WQJ318	Fire	74.4
154.280	WQJ318	Intercity Fire	CSQ
155.955	KZR526	Municipal Services	

453.750	WNNB424	Highway Department	
461.1125	WNRN301	Public Library	
155.175	KRJ880	Costigan Ambulance	
469.2875	WPCF513	Pawtucket Red Sox Baseball	

Portsmouth

154.845R	KBE504	Police	118.8
155.850	KBE504	Police - input to repeater	118.8
155.685	KBE504	Newport County Police Net	
155.190	KBE504	Police -RISPERN	
158.970	KBE504	E. New England Intercity	CSQ
154.325R	WPBW830	Fire - new system	D-032
153.890	WPBW830	Fire - repeater input	D-032
46.060	KCC453	Fire - Newport County League	
46.060	KNFW936	Fire - Newport County League	
154.280	as above	Intercity Fire	CSQ
155.100	KSU429	Water Dept./Newport Cty.Sheriff	
159.120	KLR457	Highway Department	

Providence

460.100	KRG855	Police -F1- Operations/traffic	179.9
460.200	KRG855	Police -F2- DVP detectives	
460.425	KRG855	Police -F3- East Side Ops.	179.9
460.275	KRG855	Police -F4- Records/Tow	179.9
460.325	KRG855	Police -F5- Detectives	179.9
158.970	KCA574	E. New England Intercity	CSQ
155.100	WZZ274	Providence Cty. Sheriff-court	
154.370R	KCB660	Fire - Primary Dispatch	118.8
153.830	KCB660	Fire - input to repeater	118.8
159.360	KCB660	Fire - fireground	118.8
465.100	WNO97	Fire - Fire to Police tie	179.9
154.280	KCB660	Intercity Fire	CSQ
463.075	MED 4	Ambulance operations	
453.950	KCE432	Highway Department	146.2
453.425	WNKC266	Park Department	
453.575	WZZ270	Housing Authority	123.0
453.625	WPED375	State Services	
155.985	WRE293	Civic Center/Pagers	118.8
469.8125	KB45408	Civic Center	
31.240	WQQ861	School Department Buses	107.2
153.710	KCE465	Water Dept./Fire Dept. tie	103.5
153.740	KTK738	Elderly Affairs	
45.440	KWL311	State Drug Control	131.8
45.440	KXA242	State Civil Defense-Health tie	
461.5875	WPDE579	Eastside Marketplace	
463.2625	WPDE579	Eastside Marketplace	
464.925	WNZR718	Roger Williams Zoo	
461.275	KWN902	Providence College	
453.150	KNDL382	Rhode Island College	

State Services: 453.0375, 453.0625, 453.0875, 453.3375
Convention Center: 464.575, 471.8875, 472.9625, 484.0375, 484.3625, 484.4625, 484.6375

Richmond

154.800	KNGQ547	Police -F1- w/Hopkinton	118.8
155.190	KNGQ547	Police -F2- RISPERN	
154.815	KNGQ547	Police -F3- Wash. Cty. Net	
46.500	KNGU700	Fire - Alton Dist. "X2"	127.3
46.500	KNGU698	Fire - Carolina D. "6"	127.3
154.100	WNKK378	Highway Department	118.8
453.6875	KPD385	Municipal Services	

Scituate

155.535R	WPBR802	Police - w/Foster-Johnston	110.9
159.045	WPBR802	Police -repeater input	123.0
155.190	KCD851	Police -F2- RISPERN	
158.970	KCD851	Police -F3- Eastern New England	
154.190	KCC506	Fire - Chopmist Hill - Wnsqtckt.	
154.190	KCC508	Fire - Hope Jackson	CSQ
154.190	KCA474	Fire - North Scituate	CSQ
154.190	KCC507	Fire - Potterville	CSQ
154.040	KNHF500	Fire - Dispatch	CSQ
154.040	WPCE497	Fire - Cranston tie at Hope Jacksn	
154.040	KNHF500	Fire - North Scituate	CSQ
154.280	KCC508	Intercity Fire	CSQ
37.960R	KVG763	Highway Department	
39.180	KVG763	Highway Dept. -repeater in	136.5
153.710	KKH974	Prov. Water Supply Board	103.5

Smithfield

156.090	KRV411	Police -West RI Law Enf.	CSQ
155.190	KRV411	Police -RISPERN	
154.725	KRV411	Police -West RI Law Enforcement	
158.970	KRV411	E. New England Intercity	CSQ
154.190	KNBG232	Fire -Sta.#1 Greenville-Wnsqtkt.	CSQ
154.190	KNBG355	Fire -Sta.#2 Georgiaville	CSQ
154.190	KLK634	Fire -Sta.#3 Log Rd. -Wnsqtckt.	CSQ
154.250R	KCD894	Fire -No. Providence tie	167.9
154.340	as above	Fire -new channel	
154.400	as above	Fire -new channel	
154.280	as above	Intercity Fire	CSQ
453.700	KNBG232	Fire -tone dispatch	
150.995	KCH951	Highway Department	CSQ
463.5625	WPEU365	Bryant College	

South Kingstown

155.550R	KCB260	Police -F1- Operations "K"	118.8
158.835	KCB260	Police - repeater input	118.8
154.815	KCB260	Police -F2- Washington Cty. HQ	
155.190	KCB260	Police -F3- RISPERN	
158.970	KCB260	E. New England Intercity	CSQ
46.420	KBO581	Fire - police dispatch "K"	
46.340	KBO581	Fire -	
46.260	WNKB269	Fire - Kingston Fire District	
154.280	KOB833	Intercity Fire	CSQ

46.500	mobile	Southern Fire League mobile tie	
460.5875	WNKB269	Fire -mobile repeater	
159.165	KDX466	Highway Department	
47.920	KKH972	Water Department	
158.895	WNUT425	Municipal Services	
158.775	WPEG956	Municipal Services	
155.160	KDL573	South County Ambulance	
155.295	WNMI220	Ocean State Ambulance	
155.040	KNAO534	University of Rhode Island	
155.970	KNEY909	University of Rhode Island	

(& 151.895, 154.515, 154.540, 154.815, 155.160, 155.19)

Tiverton

155.415R	KCF295	Police	118.8
155.745	KCF295	Police -secondary	118.8
45.660	KCF295	Police -old channel	
45.700	KCF295	Police -old channel	
154.680	KCF295	Police - input to repeater	118.8
155.685	KCF295	Police - Newport Cty. Net	
155.190	KCF295	Police -RISPERN	
158.970	KCF295	E. New England Intercity	CSQ
46.200	WXK634-7	Fire	CSQ
46.060	KNGS468	Newport Cty, Fire League	
154.280	WXK636	Intercity Fire	CSQ
45.120	KRA511	Highway Department	
155.745	KNCK635	Municipal Services	118.8

Warren

155.370	KCA704	Police - shared with Bristol	114.8
158.970	KCA704	E. New England Intercity	CSQ
153.950	KCD890	Fire - East Bay Fire Net	CSQ
154.280	KCD890	Intercity Fire	CSQ
156.120	KSJ258	Highway Department	114.8

Warwick

453.675	WNKB204	Police - operations	141.3
453.825	WNKB204	Police - NCIC/license cks.	141.3
453.975	WNKB204	Police - detectives	141.3
155.130	KCB246	Police - old channel	
154.890	KCB246	Police - old repeater input	
155.550	KCB246	Police - unknown use	
155.190	KCB246	Police - RISPERN	
158.970	KCB246	Eastern New England Intercity	CSQ
154.310R	KCA716	Fire - Unit Operations	162.2
154.310R	WRZ305	Fire - Unit to Kent Cty. Hosp.	162.2
155.055	KCA716	Fire - Input to Repeater	162.2
153.770	KCA716	Fire - Tone /Disp.	103.5
153.770	WQD350	Fire - Apponaug Station 1	103.5
153.770	WQD349	Fire - Lakewood Station 2	103.5
153.770	WQE633	Fire - Oakland Station 3	103.5
153.770	WQE632	Fire - W. Shore Rd. Sta. 4	103.5
153.770	WQE631	Fire - Cowessett A. Sta. 5	103.5

153.770	WQD351	Fire - Conimicut Station 6	103.5
153.770	WQD352	Fire - State Airport Sta. 8	103.5
153.770	WQD348	Fire - Comm. Ave. Sta. 9	103.5
154.280	KCA716	Intercity Fire	CSQ
159.000	KCF260	Highway Department	162.2
453.475	KNJC285	City Services Interagency	141.3
155.040	KNEY913	T.F. Greene Airport Security	100.0
154.995	KST251	T.F. Greene Airport Maint.	100.0
154.355	WNRJ823	T.F. Greene State Airport Fire	
453.225	WNZQ806	Housing Authority	
30.960	WPAI939	School Department	
31.240	WPAI939	School Department	
154.650	KYO315	RI Community College	
464.875	WNSN972	RI Special Olympics	
464.375	WNSN972	RI Special Olympics	
464.575	WNSN972	RI Special Olympics	
154.600	KA96103	Warwick Mall	
464.775	KB90858	Rocky Point Park	
464.825	KNHA601	Rocky Point Park	
464.725	KB82885	Rocky Point Park	
151.775	KK9817	Warwick Country Club	
46.000	KJU848	Midland Amb. (461.175, 463.6, 464.3)	

West Greenwich

155.760R	KOB262	Police -F1-	82.5
153.995	KOB262	Police -input to repeater	82.5
155.190	KOB262	Police -F2-RISPERN	
158.970	KOB262	E. New England Intercity	CSQ
46.380	expired	Fire-W. Greenwich Fire Assn.	
154.280	KOB262	Intercity Fire-police dispatch	CSQ
46.520	KQU306	Highway Department	

West Warwick

156.150	KCB265	Police -F1-	123.0
155.190	KCB265	Police -F2-RISPERN	
153.815	KCB265	Police -F3-and Highway Dept.	
453.300	WPCS971	Police -New frequency	
154.725	KCB265	Police -Coventry tie	123.0
155.625	KCB265	Police -East Greenwich tie	88.5
158.970	KCB265	E. New England Intercity	CSQ
154.430	KCB769	Fire	173.8
154.280	KCB769	Intercity Fire	CSQ
153.815	KMK204	Highway Dept./Police use	
451.250	KRF225	Kent County Water Dept.	

Westerly

156.210R	KCC361	Police -Blackstone Vlly Net	118.8
153.785	KD42535	Police -input to repeater	118.8
154.815	KCC361	Police -F2- Wash. Cty. Net	
155.190	KCC361	Police -F3- RISPERN	
154.950	KCC361	Police -unknown use	

158.970	KCC361	E. New England Intercity	CSQ
46.500	KCD444	Fire -So. League Dispatch "X"	
46.360	KUV824	Fire -Westerly Fire District	
46.500	KUY824	Fire -Westerly Fire District	
46.260	KUV824	Fire -Westerly Fire District	
154.130	WPER340	Fire -Westerly Fire District -new	
154.160	WPER340	Fire -Westerly Fire District -new	
46.240	WSY542	Fire -Misquamicut Fire District	
46.500	WSY542	Fire -Misquamicut Fire District	
46.240	KAW628	Fire -Watch Hill District	
46.500	KAW628	Fire -Watch Hill District	
46.240	KCD444	Fire-future Southern League use	
46.280	KCD444	Fire-future Southern League use	
154.025	WNCT817	Highway Department	
47.460	KCH354	Westerly Ambulance	
47.580	KCH354	Westerly Ambulance	

Woonsocket

156.330R	KCR261	Police	146.2
155.430	KW5888	Police - repeater input	146.2
482.8375	KXK720	Police - detectives	127.3
155.190	KCR261	Police -F4-RISPERN	
155.475	KCR261	Police -National Tactical	146.2
155.655	reported	Police -mobiles	
158.970	KCR261	E. New England Intercity	CSQ
154.130	KCE997	Fire Alarm	146.2
154.130	KXR846	Fire -Providence St. Station	146.2
154.130	KXR848	Fire -Cumberland Hill Sta.	146.2
154.130	KXR845	Fire -North Main St. Station	146.2
154.130	KXR850	Fire -Mendon Rd. Station	146.2
154.130	KXR851	Fire -Social St. Station	146.2
154.130	KXR849	Fire -Fairmount St. Station	146.2
154.280	KCE997	Intercity Fire	CSQ
159.060	KCE996	Highway Department	
453.900	WNAE230	Municipal Services	
153.875	KLK515-9	Woonsocket EMS	CSQ
153.875	KLK515	Civil Defense/Rescue/City Hall	
153.875	KLK516	Police tie to City C.D. network	
153.875	KCE997	Fire Alarm tie to C.D. network	
153.875	KLK5180	Fire Station ties to C.D. net	
153.875	KLK517	Woonsocket Hosp. tie on C.D. net	
472.8375	WII493	ParaMed Ambulance	107.2

RHODE ISLAND STATE POLICE

Base Station Channelization (PL: 118.8)

Channel 1	155.505	Statewide Administration "ADMIN"
Channel 2	155.610	Statewide Records/Information
Channel 3	154.935	North Zone Operations "NZ"
Channel 4	154.905	South Zone Operations "SZ"
Channel 5	155.445	Statewide Tactical Operations
Channel 6	155.190	RISPERN Statewide Intercity
	158.970	Eastern New England Intercity
(KTL541/2)	155.475	Local PD Tie/Radar Squads

Mobile Unit Channelization (PL: 118.8)

Channel 1		155.445R Statewide Repeater
Channel 1	154.695	input to repeater
Channel 2	155.475	Local PD tie
Channel 3	154.935	North Zone Operations
Channel 4	154.905	South Zone Operations
Channel 5	155.445	Tactical Channel #1
Channel 6	155.505	Statewide Administration
Channel 7	155.610	Statewide Information
Channel 8	155.190	RISPERN Statewide Intercity
Channel 9	159.150	Tactical Channel #2

Portable Unit Channelization

Channel 1	154.935/154.905	North or South Zone Ops.
Channel 2	155.445	Tactical Channel 1
Channel 3	155.505	Statewide Administration
Channel 4	155.190	RISPERN Statewide Intercity

Zones & Barracks

NORTH ZONE:
X1 Scituate Headquarters
X3 Chepachet Barracks
X4 Lincoln Barracks

SOUTH ZONE:
K1 Portsmouth Barracks
K3 Hope Valley Barracks

Radio Signals

Signal 01	Call barracks		Signal 10	Hit & Run
Signal 02	Return to barracks		Signal 15	Hold-up
Signal 05	Accident		Signal 20	Stolen car
Signal 06	Don't transmit		Signal 30	Missing person
Signal 08	Clears Signal 6		Signal 50	Drunken Driver

R.I.S.P.E.R.N.

In conjunction with the establishment of the State Police VHF Mobile System has been the establishment of the Rhode Island State Police Emergency Radio Network (RISPERN). 155.190 is the RISPERN frequency and is to be used only in times of emergency and is to be used only in mobiles and portables of all the law enforcement agencies in the state.

DIVISION OF FIRE SAFETY (State Fire Marshal)

158.805	Repeater Output	118.8
153.860	Mobile Input	118.8
153.980	Mobile Input	118.8
158.970	Intercity (used for contact with State Police)	

DEPARTMENT OF CORRECTIONS

155.880	Prison Guards	118.8
453.600	Division of Juvenile Corrections	
39.280	Old Channel - Phased Out	
155.100	County Sheriff's /transport between local PD's, one of 8 court houses and the prisons.	

DEPT. OF ENVIRONMENTAL MANAGEMENT

Enforcement Division (CSQ)

31.540	Control (KCH723)
31.540	Via microwave to Chopmist Hill (KCA475)
31.580	Park Police Cars
158.970	Intercity Police (KYS831)

The Enforcement Division is charged with enforcing fish and wildlife laws, DEM rules and regulations as well as helping to insure proper forest management.

Fish & Wildlife Division (CSQ)

31.540	Operations

Division office stations:

Wickford Marine Base	"M"
Great Swamp	"S"

With its headquarters located at Government Center in Wakefield, the Fish & Wildlife Division maintains wildlife food patches and stocks streams and rivers with trout (it has three fish hatcheries). Federal land is managed by:

34.810	National Fish & Wildlife Svc. (Ninigret Base)
34.830	National Fish & Wildlife Svc. Charlestown)
163.225	National Marine Fisheries Svc.(Narragansett)

Forest Environment Division (CSQ)

31.620	Operations -channel 1-
31.740	Secondary -channel 2-
31.660	Portables
31.700	Portables
154.280	Division tie to Statewide Intercity Fire
154.190	Division tie to Northern Fire League

Forest fire towers:

Buck Hill, Chopmist Hill, Escoheag, Mowry, Pine, Shannock, Tiverton

Based in North Scituate, the Forest Environment Division is responsible for forest fire detection, suppression, etc.

Parks & Recreation Division (CSQ)

31.540	Enforcement, Adm., Parks, Fish-Wildlife
31.580	Park Police -channel 2-
31.620	Forestry and Fire Control
31.740	Forestry -channel 2-
151.175	Park Ranger Portables
151.385	Park Ranger Portables
159.285	Park Ranger Portables

The Parks and Recreation Division maintains all state parks, state beaches and Fort Adams.

D.E.M. Radio Signals
- Signal 01 Report to........in person
- Signal 02 Call by phone
- Signal 03 Closing in 15 minutes
- Signal 30 All clear, fire is out
- Signal 31 Smoke, fire, under control
- Signal 32 Fire
- Signal 33 Fire permit
- Signal -- Plane crash
- Signal 55 Weather forecast
- Signal 77 Channel for message

D.E.M. 10-codes
- 10-03 Affirmative
- 10-12 VIP's are present
- 10-30 Violation of F.C.C. rules
- 10-41 Switch on channel two
- 10-42 Out of service at home
- 10-97 Arrived at scene

DEPARTMENT OF TRANSPORTATION

Radio Frequencies

856.3125-860.3125	Operations -statewide
856.3375-860.3375	Operations -statewide

47.22	Ch. #1 Old system/car to car/Bridges	131.8
47.34	Ch. #2 Old system	131.8

Station locations and ID's

PROVIDENCE HQ
Base 1/10	Maintenance HQ
Base 2	Traffic Maintenance
Base 3	Bridge Maintenance
Base 4	Construction
Base 5	Chief Highway Spvr.
Base 6/11	Defense Civil Prep.

Weather ("W") & Road ("R") Conditions Reporting Code:

2A	Johnston		6B	Westerly
2B	Lincoln		7AE	Providence
3A	Scituate		8A	Portsmouth
3B	Glocester		8B	Middletown
4A	Coventry		8C	Little Compton
4C	Howard-Call Box Com		9B	Charlestown
5A	Bellville		12	T.F. Green Airport
6A	Hope Valley		13	Weather Bureau

W-1	Clear
W-2	Partly Cloudy
W-3	Cloudy
W-4	Raining
W-5	Freezing Rain
W-6	Sleeting
W-7	Light Snow (give accumulation in inches)
W-8	Heavy Snow (give accumulation in inches)
W-9	Storm Over

R-1	Pavement Bare and Dry
R-2	Pavement Bare and Wet
R-3	Snow on Pavement
R-4	Ice on Pavement
R-5	Slush on Pavement
R-6	Pavement Partly Bare
R-7	Slippery in Spots

Aid to Motorist Call Box Control Center, Howard

158.970	Control Center to state/local police (after call has been received via a call box by a motorist requesting police assistance)
154.280	Control Center to local fire departments (after call has been received via a call box by a motorist requesting the fire service)
75.58	Call boxes
75.64	Call boxes

PUBIC TRANSIT AUTHORITY

FREQ.	USAGE	
452.675	Telemetry (Security/Maintenance)	CSQ
452.750	Buses	118.8
452.800	Buses	
452.850	Supervisors, Mechanics (telemetry)	CSQ

RHODE ISLAND MEDICAL RADIO SYSTEM

Standard UHF Radio System (see MA C-MED section)

HEAR Radio Channels (also known as RIMCOM):

155.340	Primary (many ambulances w/o UHF)
155.280	Hospital to Hospital Emergency Radio Net
155.160	South County Hospital and Ambulance

GREENVILLE C-MED CENTER CHANNELS:

MED 4	Calling
MED 6	Assigned Ambulance to Hospital Channel
MED 8	Assigned Ambulance to Hospital Channel

PROVIDENCE C-MED CENTER CHANNELS:

MED 4	Calling
MED 1	Assigned Ambulance to Hospital Channel
MED 5	Assigned Ambulance to Hospital Channel
MED 7	Assigned Ambulance to Hospital Channel

NORTH KINGSTOWN C-MED CHANNELS:

MED 4	Calling
MED 6	Assigned Ambulance to Hospital Channel
MED 8	Assigned Ambulance to Hospital Channel

STATE CIVIL PREPAREDNESS

45.440   State Civil Prep. (ops./emerg van) (131.8)
(also used by State Health & drug strike-force teams)
148.025   CD ("CID") STARS Radio Network (CSQ)

MISCELLANEOUS STATE AGENCIES

153.740	Eldery Affairs Vans
155.850	State Property

AIR & ARMY NATIONAL GUARD

Army National Guard Radio System

49.900	Repeater Output - Primary (Coventry site)
49.600	Input to Repeater (also 49.400)
49.160	Police Security
49.800	Helicopters/Police
49.700	Engineering

Air National Guard Radio System

41.450	Operatons
149.475	Fire Protection
141.800	Miscellaneous

DIVISION OF AIRPORTS (a division of the D.O.T.)

Division Radio Frequencies

154.995	T.F. Greene State Airport Operations	100.0
155.040	Quonset Point State Airport Operations	
173.2375	Runway Condition Sensors -telemetry	
153.920	State Airports (portable channel two)	
171.925R	FAA Operations	136.5

Air Radio Frequencies

FREQ.	AIRPORT	LOCATION	USE
123.000	Block Island	Block Island	Unicom
119.450	Block Island	Block Island	Prov. App./Dep.
124.850	Block Island	Block Island	Boston Ctr App./Dep
122.800	Newport State	Newport	Unicom/CTAF
128.700	Newport State	Newport	Prov. App./Dep.
127.250	Newport State	Newport	Clearance Delivery
124.850	Newport State	Newport	Boston Ctr App./Dep
126.350	Quonset State	No. Kingstown	Tower/CTAF
122.950	Quonset State	No. Kingstown	Unicom
135.400	Quonset State	No. Kingstown	Prov. App./Dep.
124.850	Quonset State	No. Kingstown	Boston Ctr App./Dep
134.500	Quonset State	No. Kingstown	Ground Control
122.700	North Central	Pawtucket	CTAF/Unicom
124.850	North Central	Pawtucket	Boston Ctr App./Dep
135.400	North Central	Pawtucket	Prov. App./Dep.
124.350	North Central	Pawtucket	Quonset Clearance
123.950	North Central	Pawtucket	Boston Ctr App./Dep
120.025	North Central	Pawtucket	Weather Data

122.900	Providence Heli	Providence	CTAF
122.950	T.F. Green	Warwick	Unicom
124.200	T.F. Green	Warwick	ATIS
122.600	T.F. Green	Warwick	Flight Service
122.200	T.F. Green	Warwick	Clearance Delivery
135.400	T.F. Green	Warwick	Ocean App. Control
118.600	T.F. Green	Warwick	Ocean App. Control
127.900	T.F. Green	Warwick	Ocean Dep. Control
124.850	T.F. Green	Warwick	Boston Ctr App./Dep
120.700	T.F. Green	Warwick	Tower ("Prov.")
121.900	T.F. Green	Warwick	Ground Control
126.650	T.F. Green	Warwick	Clearance Delivery
122.800	West Kingston	Richmond	CTAF/Unicom
123.000	Westerly State	Westerly	CTAF/Unicom
125.750	Westerly State	Westerly	Prov. App./Dep.
124.850	Westerly State	Westerly	Boston Ctr App./Dep

UNITED STATES COAST GUARD

For Marine Radio channelization: see page 110.

Rhode Island Coast Guard stations: Point Judith Sta., Narraganset / Castle Hill Sta., Newport; Block Island Sta.

Radio Frequencies

CHANNEL	FREQ.:	USE:
14	156.700	Port Operations
16	156.800	Calling/Distress
21	157.100	Coast Guard Operations
23	157.150	Coast Guard Operations
83	157.175	Coast Guard Operations
	164.550	Cape Cod Air Sta. -rescue helos
	171.2375	Coast Guard ANRAC (& 165.3125)

Marine Radiotelephone

NARRAGANSETT OPERATOR:
161.825 (ch. 84)/161.875 (ch. 85)

PROVIDENCE OPERATOR:
161.950 (ch. 27)/162.000 (ch.28)

NOAA WEATHER

162.400   Providence

RAILROADS

Amtrak/Conrail (CSQ)

FREQ.	CHANNEL	USE
160.800	Channel #1	Conrail ROAD
160.920	Channel #1	Amtrak ROAD
161.070	Channel #2	YARD
160.515	Channel #3	Communications & Signal
160.635	Channel #4	Maintenance of Way
161.295R	Channel #5	Amtrak Railroad Police
161.205	Channel #6	Police (car to car)
160.560		Conrail Police
452.900		Station Services (Provi.)

Seaview Railroad (Davisville/Quonset)

| 160.845 | Channel #1 | Operations (WNDE831) |

Providence & Worcester Railroad (CSQ)

FREQ.	CHANNNEL	USE
160.650	Channel #1	Road/Yard
161.100	Channel #2	Yard
160.890	Channel #3	Maintenance
160.755	Channel #4	Police/Communications

NEWS MEDIA

WJAR -Channel 10- Television (PL: 127.3)
- 450.3875   -channel 1- Operations
- 450.2125   -channel 2- Engineering
- 153.230   -channel 3- Reporters

WLNE -Channel 6- Television
- 450.3125R Dispatch
- 161.670   Backup (PL: 167.9)
- 462.125   Unknown use
- 464.750   Unknown use

WPRI -Channel 12- Television (PL: 162.2)
- 450.4875R -channel 1- News & Engineering
- 450.5875   -channel 2- Portables
- 455.4875   -channel 3- News & Engineering
- 26.250   Primary Low Band
- 26.100   Van IFB

Other Outlets
- 450.1875R WPRO Radio -Traffic reports
- 450.250   WEAN Radio -Traffic reports

455.2125	WEAN Radio - News/Traffic reports	
455.2125R	WALE Radio	146.2
450.250	WALE Radio (input)	
173.325	New England Newspapers (Pawtucket)	
173.275	Providence Journal	CSQ
463.850	Providence Journal	
464.325	Providence Journal	
173.375	Woonsocket Evening Call	
450.750	Traffic Net -channel 1- (CSQ)	
455.250	Traffic Net -channel 2- (CSQ)	

UTILITIES

Narragansett Electric (PL: 103.5)
48.070	Providence Trouble Calls	
48.540	Providence Meter Department	
48.500	North Kingstown Trouble Calls	
47.960	North Kingstown Meter Department	
48.480	Common Dispatch	
48.440	New England Power Svc. Construction	100.0
154.600	Providence Office operations	

Ocean State Power (Burrillville)
37.600, 451.1125, 451.1375, 451.3625, 451.6875

Providence Gas Co. (136.5)
153.410R, 153.545, 153.575, 153.665, 153.725R,
158.175, 158.220, 158.265

Providence Water Co.
153.575, 153.605 (D-051), 153.710 (103.5), 158.220R

Miscellaneous Utilities
49.020	Algonquin Gas Co.
151.985R	NYNEX (100.0)
451.425	NYNEX (Providence)
451.500	NYNEX (Woonsocket)
451.025	Valley Gas (123.0)
451.175	Valley Gas (Cumberland)

EUA Service Corp.
47.860, 47.900, 451.075, 451.225, 451.475, 451.525,
451.5625, 451.625, 462.4625, 462.5125

Southern New Hampshire

Section Notes:
The format for the New Hampshire communities in this section differs from the Massachusetts format. Because the county police/sheriff departments in New Hampshire patrol throughout the state, it is important to monitor the county as well as the local and state police. The letters in the parenthesis following the town names indicate the county in which the town is located:

- (C) Cheshire County
- (H) Hillsboro County
- (M) Merrimack County
- (R) Rockingham County

Some of the larger cities located to the north of these counties were included in the listings below. Note that the numbers in quotes following the call signs are town radio identifiers. An * after the number in quotes indicates that the PL tone is 136.5, the standard tone used in the state.

See the *SCANNER MASTER Maine, New Hampshire and Vermont Pocket Guide* for more information on New Hampshire and for coverage of the entire state.

Allenstown (M)
155.565	Police	KZG259	136.5
155.685R	Police -Merrimack Cty.	KZG258	136.5
460.5625	Police -mobile repeater	WNZU271	
465.5625	Police -mobile repeater	WNZU271	
155.040	Fire	WQA717	136.5
154.355	Fire -Capital Area	KDO290	"50"*
154.235	Fire -Capital Area	KDO290	"50"*
453.1875	Fire -mobile repeater	WPBH202	
458.1875	Fire -mobile repeater	WPBH202	
46.100	Fire -new channel	KDO290	
45.48	Highway Department	KSZ739	

Amherst (H)
154.875	Police -Milford dispatch	KNAC253	136.5
33.64	Fire -dispatch	KEG401	CSQ
33.90	Fire -mobiles	KEG401	CSQ
155.160	Ambulance	KNAQ910	136.5
39.50	Highway Department	KCH465	CSQ
39.50	Civil Defense	KCH465	CSQ

Antrim (H)
155.760	Police	WRE212	146.2
154.430R	Fire -SW Mutual Aid	KUQ336	"2"*

154.430R	Fire -North Branch Station	KUQ355	"2"*
153.770	Fire -repeater input	KUQ335-6	136.5
155.880	Municipal Services	mobiles only	

Atkinson (R)
154.755	Police	KFI605	136.5
154.815R	Rockingham County	WRV34	136.5
154.190	Fire -Seacoast Net	KBT790	"57"*
154.190	Fire -Atkinson Disp.	WXT674	"57"*
460.6375	Fire -mobile repeater	KO34333	
154.160	So. Rockingham Cty. Net	KBT790	136.5
154.160	Atkinson Dispatch	WXT674	136.5
154.010	Haverhill-Methuen tie	KBT790	136.5
154.010	Atkinson Dispatch tie	WXT674	136.5
154.280	Seacoast Fireground	KBT790	136.5
154.280	Seacoast Fireground	WXT674	136.5
153.965	Highway Department	KIB285	

Auburn (R)
155.565	Police	WNCM785	136.5
155.640	Police -F2- Raymond tie	WNCM785	136.5
154.845R	Police -Manchester tie	WNCM785	136.5
155.790	Police -new channel	WNWM413	136.5
154.815R	Rockingham County	WNBH430	136.5
154.130	Fire -Derry Dispatch	KZH934	CSQ
154.190	Fire -Seacoast Net	KZH934	
154.280	Seacoast Fireground	KZH934	

Bedford (H)
155.310	Police	KUY641	136.5
155.520R	Hillsboro County	WRG20	136.5
33.78	Fire -Dispatch	KNGS387	CSQ
33.64	Fire -MACC mobiles	KNGG387	CSQ
33.90	Fire -MACC secondary	KNGG387	
156.195	Highway Department	KUO996	
46.58R	Civil Defense	KNEK302	156.7
46.56	Civil Defense	KNEK302	
464.8125	Bedford Mall	reported	

Bennington (H)
154.430R	Fire -SW Mutual Aid "4"	KDL959	136.5
153.770	Fire -repeater input	KDL959	136.5
154.965	Municipal Services	KB47076	136.5

Boscawen (M)
155.760	Police	KNJK336	136.5
155.685R	Merrimack County	KKD479	136.5
155.700	Merrimack County	KGL485	136.5
155.730	Merrimack County	WNRR478	136.5
154.355	Fire -Capital Area	KMA754	"51"*
154.235	Capital Area	KMA754	"51"*
155.760	Highway Department	KEC394	

Bow (M)
155.760	Police/Ambulance	KCH727	136.5
155.685R	Merrimack County	KKD479	136.5
155.700	Merrimack County	KGL485	136.5
154.355	Fire -Capital Area	KGP771	"52"*
154.235	Fire -Capital Area	KGP771	"52"*
461.950	School District	WNVI200	

Bradford (M)
154.355	Fire -Capital Area	WXP391	"82"
154.235	Fire -Capital Area	WXP391	"81"
154.130	Fire -Lebanon/Hanover tie	WXP391	141.3
154.430R	Fire -SW NH Mutual Aid	WXP391	136.5
154.295	Fire -Twin Mtn. Mutual Aid	WXP391	CSQ
154.265	Fire -spare	WXP391	CSQ
159.135	Highway Department	KD41671	156.7

Brentwood (R)
154.815R	Rockingham Cty. Rptr.	KCG672	136.5
154.815R	Rockingham Cty. Rptr.	KCG958	136.5
154.950	Rockingham Cty. Sheriffs	KCB958	136.5
155.415	Rockingham Cty. Towns	KCB958	136.5
154.815R	Rockingham Cty. Jail	KQD34	136.5
154.250	Fire	KNBS858	
154.190	Fire -Seacoast Fire Net	KNBS858	136.5
154.280	Seacoast Fireground	KNBS858	
155.340	County Ambulance Disp.	KNBA836	CSQ
46.58R	Civil Defense	KNIM373	156.7
46.58R	Rockingham County	KNBB241	156.7
155.055	Rockingham County	KB25228	
453.550	Rockingham Cty. Jail	KUS521	156.7
852.3625	Rockingham County	WPCM491	

Brookline (H)
154.875	Police -"Base 500" disp.	KCD938	136.5
155.490R	Police -repeater	WNDM757	CSQ
154.890	Police -repeater input	WNDM757	146.2
33.74	Fire -MACC base/mob.	KDA385	CSQ
33.64	Fire -dispatch	KDA385	136.5
33.90	Fire -secondary	KDA385	CSQ
153.785	Fire	reported	136.5
155.220	Ambulance	WNGW200	136.5

Candia (R)
154.815	Rockingham Cty. Rptr.	KCB958	136.5
154.130	Fire -Regional Net	WXB966	CSQ
154.190	Fire -Seacoast Net	WXB966	"50"
154.280	Seacoast Fireground	WXB966	

Canterbury (M)
154.355	Fire -Capital Area	KVN514	"53"*
154.235	Fire -Capital Area	KVN514	"53"*
156.010	Public Works Department	WPDX479	

Chester (R)

153.995	Police	KNIG885	136.5
154.815R	Rockingham County	KCB958	136.5
154.130	Fire -Derry Dispatch	KIL262	CSQ
154.190	Fire -Seacoast Fire Net	KIL262	"47"/CSQ
154.280	Fire -Seacoast Fireground	KIL262	

Chichester (M)

154.355	Fire -Capital Area	KGR238	"54""
154.235	Fire -Capital Area	KGR238	"54""
151.010	Highway Department	KNIH351	

Concord (M)

155.625R	Police	KCA792	136.5
154.800	Police -input to repeater	KCA792	136.5
155.565	Police -Allenstown tie	KCA792	136.5
155.700	Police -county tie	KCA792	136.5
155.820	Police -simplex	KNJK423	136.5
453.0375	Police -mobile repeater	KB87826	203.5
453.1125	Police -mobile repeater	KB87826	179.9
453.1375	Police -mobile repeater	KB87826	192.8
453.2375	Police -mobile repeater	KB87826	186.2
453.7375	Police -mobile repeater	KB87826	
155.625R	Merrimack County	KRK930	136.5
155.700	Merrimack County	KMA591	136.5
155.655	House of Correction	KWF785	141.3
154.355	Fire -Central Station	KFF285	"55""
154.235	Fire -Central Station	KFF285	"55""
154.355	Fire -Manor Station	KFF286	"55""
154.235	Fire -Manor Station	KFF286	"55""
154.355	Fire -Heights Station	KFF287	"55""
154.235	Fire -Heights Station	KFF287	"55""
154.355	Fire -N. State St. Station	KNFB836	"55""
154.235	Fire -N. State St. Station	KNFB836	"55""
154.355	Fire -Broadway Station	KNAW606	"55""
154.235	Fire -Broadway Station	KNAW606	"55""
460.5875	Fire -154.355 link	KVF642	151.4
460.6375	Fire -154.235 link	KVF642	186.2
453.7375	Fire -154.355 Link	reported	186.2
154.355	Capital Area Dispatch	KVF642	136.5
154.235	Capital Area Dispatch	KVF642	136.5
154.355	Capital Area Dispatch	WRA223	136.5
154.235	Capital Area Dispatch	WRA235	136.5
154.220	Capital Area Fireground F3	KVF642	136.5
154.280	Capital Area Fireground F4	KVF642	136.5
154.355	CD Tie -Capital Area	KFT552	136.5
154.430	CD Tie -SW Mutual Aid	KJF871	136.5
453.475	Fire -Fire Alarm maint.	WNHW542	141.3
158.805	Parks Department	KWQ574	
159.120	Highway Department	KNCW676	136.5
451.2625	Water Department Data	WPDV438	

153.860	Public Health Service	KB77600	
153.935	Concord Airport	KT9125	
153.965	State Technical School	KNJP369	
155.805	Corrections Department	WNGV356	
453.325	State Technical School	KNJP369	
453.175	Dept. of Human Service	WNGX284	
453.825	State Government	WNXZ583	
453.2125	State Government	KB78364	
453.2625	State Government	KD34284	
156.030	State Government	WNJX720	
453.875	State Government	WNPH822	
45.08	Manchester CD tie	KZQ655	
46.52	Merrimack County CD	KNEN767	
45.36	Massachusetts CD tie	KNAT731	162.2
45.52	Vermont CD tie - in	WSQ990	118.8
46.54	Civil Defense	KNJL962	
46.56	Civil Defense - mobile	WSQ990	
46.58R	Civil Defense	KUX264	156.7
47.66	Concord Union Schools	KNDV825	
155.085	State Hospital Security	KNIM408	
155.385	Concord Hospital	KSZ467	146.2
155.340	Concord Hospital	KSZ467	
155.340	NRH Tri-State Medical	WYH483	
464.475	Concord Hospital Security	KNHL338	
155.220	Raceway Ambulance	WNPE605	
155.295	Raceway Ambulance	WNPE605	
461.375	Concord Area Transit	WNPP727	
469.5125	Ramada Inn	KB93491	

Danbury (M)

158.835	Police/Fire	KNJC647	136.5
33.90	Lakes Region	KP8074	"36"
33.96	Lakes Region	KP8074	"36"
43.00	Ragged Mtn. Ski Area	WNKD358	
464.925	Ragged Mtn. Ski Area	WNKJ933	

Danville (R)

154.815	Rockingham County	WNCF885	136.5
154.190	Fire -Seacoast Fire Net	KJF794	"13"/CSQ
154.190	Fire -Long Pond Rd. Sta.	WRY683	"13"/CSQ
154.160	S. Rockingham Cty. Net	KJF794	
154.280	Seacoast Fireground	KJF794	
158.985	Highway Department	WZU393	
155.235	Southeast NH EMS	WZT968	136.5

Deerfield (R)

153.815	Police/Fire	KYQ364	
154.190	Seacoast Fire Net	KXM834	CSQ
151.745	Deerfield Fair Association	WNLH750	
464.875	Deerfield Fair Association	WNJX315	

Deering (H)
155.370	Police	KNHM413	
154.310	Fire	WYC727	136.5
155.520R	Hillsboro County	KQQ582	136.5
156.210	Highway Department	WNAV246	
158.775	Municipal Services	WNBV202	

Derry (R)
453.525	Police	WNKT923	D-244
460.275	Police -new frequency	WNKT923	
153.995	Police -Chester tie	WZX667	136.5
154.130	Fire -East Broadway Sta.	KBD339	CSQ
154.190	Fire - East Derry Station	WNPZ624	CSQ
460.575	Mobile Repeater	KBD339	
154.190	Seacoast Fire Net tie	KBD339	
453.375	Highway/Water Depts.	WNPU985	103.5
453.800	School Department	WNMK726	127.3
46.58R	Civil Defense	WNPU328	156.7
453.8625	Water Department	KD30281	data
155.340	Parklane Medical Center	KNEM443	91.5
155.385	Parklane Medical Center	KNEM443	91.5

Dover
154.680	Police	KCA352	136.5
154.385	Fire	KCA769	136.5
153.950	Fire	KCA769	
154.190	Fire -Seacoast Fire Net	KCA769	"14"
154.280	Fire -Seacoast Fireground	KCA769	
154.310	Fire -Rollingsford tie	KCA769	
150.995	Highway Department	KNGG383	CSQ
45.96	School Department	KIL305	
46.58R	Civil Defense	KNIM373	156.7
453.350	Parks Department	WNRX896	
463.950	Housing Authority	WNMV654	
464.575	Cochecho Country Club	KD23383	

Dublin (C)
155.070	Police -Cheshire County	WNAW950	136.5
155.640	Police -west Hillsboro tie	WNAW950	136.5
155.640	Police -west Hillsboro tie	WNAW950	136.5
155.520R	Hillsboro County	WNAW950	136.5
154.430R	Fire -SW Mutual Aid	KDO291	"8"*
153.770	Fire -repeater input	KDO291	136.5
151.115	Highway Department	WNVA887	

Durham
155.775R	Police -Durham/UNH PD	KQS749	136.5
153.755	Police -repeater input	KQS749	136.5
154.725R	Strafford County	KTG679	136.5
155.595	Strafford County -input	KTG679	136.5
154.415	Fire and Ambulance	KCF395	CSQ

154.190	Seacoast Fire Net	KCF395	"15"
154.190	Seacoast Fire Net	WRA216	
158.745	Highway Department	KNCJ393	
46.58R	Civil Defense -state tie	KNIM373	156.7
155.670	UNH -Tactical -F2-	KNIM754	136.5
155.940	UNH -Special Events	KB23827	
156.000	UNH -Maintenance	KGP686	136.5
158.895	UNH -Shuttle Vans	WPDQ324	
453.800	UNH -WENH TV Ch. #11	KJY633	110.9
453.325	UNH	WNJR885	
463.200	UNH	WPAU454	

East Kingston (R)

154.100	Police/Fire/DPW	KSJ347	136.5
154.190	Fire -Seacoast Net	WNWN534	"16"CSQ
154.280	Seacoast Fireground	WNWN534	
46.58R	Civil Defense	KNIM373	156.7

Epping (R)

154.815R	Rockingham County	KCB958	136.5
155.250	Rockingham County	KCB958	136.5
154.190	Fire -Seacoast Net	KNBX749	"18"
154.190	Fire -W. Epping	KNBX769	CSQ
154.280	Fire -W. Epping fireground	KNBX769	CSQ
154.280	Fire -Seacoast fireground	KNBX749	
151.040	Highway Department	WPET768	
151.685	New England Dragway	WNCW869	D-134

Epsom (M)

155.700	Police	WNFW543	136.5
155.685R	Merrimack County	WZG268	136.5
155.700	Merrimack County	WZX712-4	136.5
154.355	Fire -Capital Area	WZJ334	"56"*
154.235	Fire -Capital Area	WZJ334	"56"*
153.920	Highway Department	WPCY412	

Exeter (R)

155.250	Police	KCB760	136.5
154.815R	Rockingham County	WJU74	136.5
154.400	Fire	KQP561	136.5
154.190	Seacoast Fire Net	KQP561	"19"*
154.280	Seacoast Fireground	KQP561	136.5
155.115	Town Manager	KIZ613	
155.115	Highway Department	KNCA740	103.5
155.115	Municipal Services	KZR602	
155.295	Exeter High School	KNEQ263	
46.58R	Civil Defense	KNBB241	156.7
155.340	Exeter Memorial Hospital	KQP471	85.4

Fitzwilliam (C)
155.070	Cheshire County	KZB374	136.5
155.640	West Cheshire County	KYY946	136.5
465.075	Police -mobile repeater	KA7743	
154.430R	SW Mutual Aid-Depot Sta.	KCD360	"10"
154.430R	SW Mutual Aid-Village Sta.	WYV316	"10"
154.980	Highway Department	WXP374	136.5
154.980	Highway-PD tie	KKV583	136.5

Francestown (H)
154.430R	Fire -SW Mutual Aid	KCO366	"37"*
153.770	Fire -repeater input	KCO366	136.5
154.540	Crotched Mtn. Ski Area	KNDV732	
155.205	Crotched Mtn. Ski Patrol	KNEQ386	
155.220	Crotched Mtn. Ski Patrol	KNEQ386	
155.340	Crotched Mtn. Ski Patrol	KNEQ386	

Franklin (M)
154.785	Police	WNSL326	136.5
155.685R	Merrimack County	KKL605	136.5
155.700	Merrimack County	KCD461	136.5
33.84	Fire -Lakes Region	WZU255	173.8
33.76	Fire -Lakes Region	WZU255	173.8
33.84	Fire -Lakes Region	KRS394	173.8
33.76	Fire -Lakes Region	KRS394	173.8
33.90	Fire -Lakes Region	WZU255	"7"
33.96	Fire -Lakes Region	WZU255	"7"
33.90	Fire -Lakes Region	KRS394	"7"
33.96	Fire -Lakes Region	KRS394	"7"
159.165	Highway Department	KNEN339	136.5

Fremont (R)
154.815R	Rockingham County	KCB958	136.5
154.190	Fire -Seacoast Net	KVG897	"20"/CSQ
154.280	Seacoast Fireground	KVG897	
155.925	Municipal Services	WNUH806	

Goffstown (H)
155.190	Police	KLJ222	136.5
158.880	Fire -Dispatch	KIZ289	136.5
158.880	Fire -Church St. Station	KCG481	136.5
158.880	Fire -Terrill Hill Road	KGX289	136.5
158.880	Fire -Pinardville Station	KTZ239	136.5
155.520R	Hillsboro County SD	WGW52	136.5
155.520R	Hillsboro County tie	WGW53	136.5
155.520R	Hillsboro County Jail	KNDL925	136.5
155.115	Police mobile	mobiles	
155.520R	Hillsboro County repeater	KWQ659	136.5
159.105	Highway Department	KNBJ261	136.5
155.340	Town Ambulance	WSZ234	

Greenfield (H)
154.430R	Fire -SW Mutual Aid	KIZ389	"13"*
153.770	Fire -repeater input	KIZ389	136.5
151.895	Crotched Mtn. Rehab Ctr.	WQN893	167.9
151.955	Crothced Mtn. Rehab Ctr.	WQN893	167.9
156.240	Highway Department	WPCV686	

Greenland (R)
155.985	Police	KDC683	136.5
155.520R	Rockingham County	WFE759	136.5
154.190	Fire -Seacoast Net	KCG654	"21"/CSQ
154.145	Fire -area regional	KCG654	
154.280	Seacoast Fireground	KCG654	
46.58R	Civil Defense	KNIM373	156.7

Greenville (H)
155.565	Police	KNFJ320	136.5
155.565	Police -"Base 500" Dispatch	KXD211	136.5
155.490R	Police -repeater	WNDM755	CSQ
154.890	Police -repeater input	WNDM755	146.2
155.715	Police -Ashby, MA tie	KNFZ692	CSQ
155.520R	Hillsboro County	KNFF860	136.5
33.74	Fire -dispatch	KNHN570	CSQ
33.64	Fire -MACC mobiles	KNHN570	CSQ
33.90	Fire -MACC secondary	KNHN570	CSQ
39.50	Highway Department	KNFZ692	CSQ
155.220	Ambulance	WNGW200	186.2

Hampstead (R)
154.755	Police	KNAP567	
154.190	Fire -Derry Dispatch	KWF904	CSQ
458.600	Fire -mobile repeater	KWF904	
151.070	Highway Department	WNUB921	
155.265	Ambulance	WNQA828	
151.895	Central School	WNVE719	

Hampton (R)
460.150	Police	WNEC690	203.5
154.755	Police -old frequency	WNKR694	
154.815R	Rockingham County	WHLL74	136.5
154.190	Fire -Seacoast Net	KLO459	"22"*
154.145	Fire -area regional/disp.	KLO459	136.5
46.58R	Civil Defense	KNIM373	156.7
46.58R	Civil Defense	KNCG416	156.7
155.745	DPW/Waste Water Plant	KJB972	136.5
48.20	Hampton Water Works	KCX924	

Hampton Falls (R)
158.850	Police	WNHV842	
154.815R	Rockingham County	KCB958	136.5
154.190	Fire -Seacoast Net	KNFQ722	"23"*

154.145	Fire -area regional	KNFQ722	136.5
46.58R	Civil Defense	KNIM373	156.7

Henniker (M)
155.760	Police	WRE213	146.2
155.685R	Merrimack County	WKQ310	136.5
154.355	Fire -Capital Area	KVF804	"58"*
154.235	Fire -Capital Area	KVF804	"58"*
156.120	Highway Department	KCL823	

Hill (M)
33.90	Fire -Lakes Region	KP8074	"11"
33.90	Fire -Lakes Region	KP8074	"11"
33.84	Fire -Lakes Region	KP8074	"11"
33.76	Fire -Lakes Region	KP8074	"11"

Hillsboro (H)
155.760	Police	KDG231	146.2
155.520R	Hillsboro County	WFE612	136.5
154.310	Fire	WZS934	
154.355	Fire -Capital Area	KUZ970	"59"*
154.235	Fire -Capital Area	KUZ970	"59"*
156.120	Highway Department	KCU851	
155.205	Ambulance	KIL652	

Hollis (H)
153.785	Police/Ambulance/DPW	WNBK820	136.5
154.875	Police -area net	KSX310	136.5
155.520R	Hillsboro County	WCU954	136.5
33.64	Fire -dispatch	KDC288	136.5
33.68	Fire -secondary	KDC288	CSQ
33.90	Fire -mobiles	KDC288	CSQ
33.74	Fire -mobiles "Base 500"	KDC288	CSQ
39.50	Civil Defense	KNAO337	CSQ
159.015	Highway Department	WNRD741	136.5
155.340	Ambulance	WNBP898	

Hooksett (M)
155.565	Police	KLM579	136.5
155.685R	Merrimack County	KVP563	136.5
158.760R	Fire -repeater	KNHZ809	136.5
153.845	Fire -repeater input	KNHZ809	136.5
46.100	Fire	KCD880	
154.355	Capital Area tie	KR2990	"63"*
154.235	Capital Area tie	KR2990	"63"*
154.370	Fire -mobiles	KB50158	
154.385	Fire -mobiles	KB50158	
154.040	Tri-Town Ambulance	KVX852	136.5
154.040	Highway/Water Cmsn.	KVX852	136.5
151.655	Hookset School District	WRM629	

Hopkinton (M)

39.44	Police	KIZ636	
155.685R	Merrimack County	KXK431	136.5
155.700	Merrimack County	WZU399	136.5
154.160	Fire -Kearsage Net	KBG347	136.5
154.355	Capital Area	KBG347	"60"*
154.235	Capital Area	KBG347	"60"*
33.06	Highway Department	KNJS444	

Hudson (H)

460.425	Police	WNNI577	136.5
460.425M	Police -car to car	WNNI577	136.5
155.955	Fire -Headquarters	KKC978	CSQ
155.955	Fire -Robinson Road	WZC695	CSQ
155.955	Fire -Musquash & Wason	KRA416	CSQ
154.280	Fire -Seacoast Fireground	KCD795	CSQ
153.950	Fire/Rescue	KCD795	136.5
154.190	Seacoast Fire Net	KCD795	
37.26	Highway Department	KNHH329	136.5
151.925	School Department	WNUD231	
154.600	Nottingham W. Elementary	WNXL840	
158.205	Southern NH Water Co.	KLU609	146.2
151.775	State Services	WNSV474	

Jaffrey (C)

155.070	Cheshire County	KVT716	136.5
154.710	Police -backup	KVT716	
154.430R	Fire -SW Mutual Aid	KCF416	"16"*
153.770	Fire -repeater input	KCF416	136.5
155.775	Highway Department	KRA330	

Keene (C)

155.250	Police	KCA758	136.5
155.535	Police	KCA758	136.5
155.070	Cheshire County SD	WXP483	136.5
155.070	Cheshire County SD	KNFS532	136.5
155.070	Cheshire County SD	KNBP853	136.5
155.640	Hillsboro County towns	KNIK655	136.5
155.640	Hillsboro County towns	KKW230	136.5
460.3125	Hillsboro Dispatch link-up	KNIK655	136.5
465.3125	Hillsboro Dispatch link-dn.	KNIK655	136.5
155.070	Cheshire County Dispatch	KNFS532	136.5
154.430	Fire -SW Mutual Aid -main	KCF415	"19"*
154.430	Swanzey tx for Keene	KZE511	"19"*
154.430	SW Mutual Aid at Keene	KZB373	136.5
154.430	SW Mutual Aid at Gilsum	KIL506	136.5
154.430	SW Mutual Aid at Stod.	KNAX703	136.5
154.430	SW Mutual Aid at Lmpstr.	KCF415	136.5
154.430	SW Mutual Aid at Unity	WNXS528	136.5
33.54	Tri-State Mutual Aid	KCE579	123.0
33.78	SW Mutual Aid	KCE579	123.0

33.54	Tri-State Mutual Aid	KNFN788	123.0
33.78	SW Mutual Aid -backup tx	KNFN788	123.0
154.430	SW Mutual Aid	KIU830	136.5
154.385	Fireground	KIU830	136.5
155.220	SW NH Mutual Aid Amb.	WQD390	136.5
155.205	RJ DiLuzio Ambulance	KNGY306	
46.58R	Civil Defense	KNGS457	156.7
462.275	Civil Defense	KNGD371	
158.895	Highway Department	WNAZ567	
39.060	Municipal Services	KB30889	
155.025	Municipal Services	KB36811	
155.880	Municipal Services	WNPL342	
158.820	Municipal Services	KAS423	
158.985	Water and Sewer Dept.	WNAZ567	
155.865	Cheshire Voc. School	WZU371	
151.925	Cheshire Voc. School	KAM923	
155.055	Keene State College	KJR361	
154.600	Keene State College	KB70934	
151.715	Keene State College	WNZR522	
153.470	Keene Gas Corp.	KSV467	
151.805	Cheshire Fair Assoc.	WNMK699	
154.515	Cheshire County YMCA	KB93630	

(SW NH Fire Links: 460 & 465.6375, .5875, .6375-136.5)

Kensington (R)

154.055	Police/Fire/DPW	KNBN574	136.5
154.190	Seacoast Fire Net	KUX411	"24""
154.190	Seacoast Fire Net	KIB220	"24""
154.280	Seacoast Fireground	KUX411	
154.280	Seacoast Fireground	KIB220	
154.145	Fire -area regional	KUX411	
154.145	Fire -area regional	KIB220	

Kingston (R)

154.040	Police/Fire	KAN889	136.5
154.815R	Rockingham County	WFE760	136.5
154.190	Fire -Seacoast Fire Net	KTV665	"25"
154.280	Fire -Seacoast Fireground	KTV665	
46.58R	Civil Defense	KNIM373	156.7
155.205	Sanborn Reg. High School	KNFM350	

Laconia

155.790	Police	WQI966	136.5
155.010	Police -mobiles	WQI966	136.5
159.150	Police -marine patrol	KNIM239	
154.830	Belknap County	KCA946	136.5
154.740	Belknap County SD	WNAZ498	136.5
33.90	Fire -Laconia	KCA215	"13"
33.96	Fire -Laconia	KCA215	"13"
33.90	Fire -Lakeport Station	KCE410	"13"
33.96	Fire -Lakeport Station	KCE410	"13"
33.90	Fire -Weirs Stations	KNEP997	"13"

33.96	Fire -Weirs Station	KNEP997	"13"
153.830	Fireground Portables	KCA215	
460.6125	Fire -mobile repeater	(& 465.6125)	
33.90	Lakes Region Dispatch	KBZ283	173.8
33.96	Lakes Region Dispatch	KBZ283	173.8
33.90	Lakes Reg.Disp. -Backup	KNGB769	173.8
33.96	Lakes Reg.Disp. -Backup	KNGB769	173.8
33.54M	Tri-State Mutual Aid	KBZ283	
33.48M	Tri-State Mutual Aid	KBZ283	
33.84	Fire -Mutual Aid	KCA215	173.8
33.76	Fire -Mutual Aid	KCA215	173.8
154.355	Capital Area	KMK706	136.5
154.235	Capital Area	KMK706	136.5
451.475	Lakes Reg. Disp. Link -up	WDT317	118.8
456.475	Lakes Reg. Disp. Link -dn	WDT317	118.8
453.4125	Lakes Reg. Disp. Link -up	KBZ283	118.8
458.4125	Lakes Reg. Disp. Link -dn	KBZ283	118.8
460.5625	Lakes Reg. Disp. Link-up	KBZ283	179.9
465.5625	Lakes Reg. Disp. Link -dn	KBZ283	179.9
155.340	Lakes Region EMS	KNIT753	
156.180	Highway Department	KCE766	
153.680	Water Department	KDH542	
155.145	Laconia State School	KNBL822	
155.340	Laconia State Hospital	KNDS840	151.4
453.225	Belknap County Services	WPBP835	
467.925	Laconia Country Club	KD42917	

Litchfield (H)

154.905	Police -dispatch	WNSG386	136.5
155.130	Police -Nashua Regional	KM5952	
155.520R	Hillsboro County	WDT325	136.5
154.190	Fire -Seacoast Net	KWO615	136.5
154.280	Fire -Seacoast Fireground	KWO615	
159.165	Highway Department	WNVY927	

Londonderry (R)

155.865	Police	WNGY516	136.5
158.970	Eastern New England	KDQ322	CSQ
155.520R	Hillsboro County	KVI627	136.5
154.815R	Rockingham County	WRG48	136.5
151.175	Fire -dispatch	KQO260	136.5
154.190	Fire -Seacoast Net	KQO260	136.5
156.165	Highway Department	KTZ373	136.5
453.500	High School	KNFX450	
156.165	Building Inspector	KTZ373	151.4
158.745R	Municipal Services	WPCR905	
153.995	Municipal Services -input	WPCR906	
158.205	S. NH Water Commission	KLU609	146.2

Loudon (M)

155.700	Police -Merrimack County	KYY845	136.5
155.685R	Merrimack County	KZB392	136.5
155.685R	Merrimack County	KRK930	136.5
154.355	Fire -Capital Area	KVF486	"61"*
154.235	Fire -Capital Area	KVF486	"61"*
154.040	Highway Department	KVN625	
155.295	American Ambulance	KNEP969	

Lyndeboro (H)

154.875	Police -"Base 500" disp.	WNBH294	136.5
155.490R	Police -repeater	WNDM752	CSQ
154.890	Police -repeater input	WNDM752	146.2
33.64	Fire	WYR518	CSQ
33.68	Fire -secondary	WYR518	CSQ
33.74	Fire -"Base 500" mobiles	WYR518	CSQ
33.90	Fire -mobiles	WYR518	CSQ
39.50	Highway Department	reported	
155.100	Ambulance	reported	

Manchester (H) (See Trunked System listed below)

156.210R	Police - Dispatch	KCB226	136.5
158.910	Dispatch -repeater input	KCB226	136.5
155.475	Police -statewide	KCB226	136.5
154.845R	Alternate/Detectives	KCB226	136.5
155.970	Alternate/Detectives -input	KCB226	136.5
158.730	Police -simplex	KCB226	136.5
153.740R	Airport Security/Ops	KNAO324	D-703
158.940	Airport -repeater input	KNAO324	D-703
155.520R	Hillsboro County	WGW54	136.5
155.520R	Hillsboro County	WGW55	136.5
155.520R	Hillsboro County SD	WGZ746	136.5
155.430	Hillsboro County	KNBX710	136.5
460.050	County Jail	WNQU633	
460.625R	Fire -F1- dispatch	KCA695	D-445
460.625M	Fire -F2- simplex	KCA695	
460.600R	Fire -F3- fireground	KCA695	D-445
460.600M	Fire -F4- simplex	KCA695	
460.5125	Fire -F5- HazMat	KCA695	
460.5375	Fire -F6- HazMat	KCA695	
453.4125	Fire -mobiles	KCA695	
72.92	Call Boxes	WFQ980	CSQ
33.78	Fireground/Comms. Div.	KCA695	CSQ
154.965R	Ambulance	WNBC227	91.5
155.745	Ambulance -repeater input	WNBC227	91.5
468.1875	Ambulance -mobile use	WPEF695	
462.9875	Ambulance -mob. repeater	WNSP717	
453.150	Highway Department	KDQ942	136.5
453.150	Highway Department	KDT581	136.5
464.075	Guardian Angels	reported	D-631
45.08	Civil Defense HQ "EPO"	KCH919	

45.08	Amoskeag Amb. base	KNCL539	
45.08	Highway Dept. base	KZQ719	
45.08	Water Dept. base	KZQ720	
45.08	Fire Dept. base	KZQ721	
45.08	Health Dept. base	KZQ723	
45.08	Catholic Med. Ctr. base	KZQ724	
45.08	Elliot Hospital base	KZQ725	
45.08	Veterans Med. Ctr. base	KZQ726	
45.08	Red Cross base	KZQ727	
45.08	Police Dept. base	KZQ728	
45.08	Airport base	KZQ732	
45.08	School Dept. base	WQC311	
30.86	Parks Department	KNBD404	136.5
33.02	Traffic Department	KCA568	136.5
45.24R	Building Department	KBK706	136.5
453.450	Water Department	WNHP697	D-331
453.3375	Water Dept. Pumping Sta	KD39125	CSQ
153.740	Cemetery Department	KNAO296	
453.050	Environmental Protection	KDQ905	
453.050	Public Building Services	WNBV200	
453.450	Municipal Services	WNHP697	
452.800	Manchester Transit -base	WQJ983	136.5
457.800	Manchester Transit -buses	WQJ983	136.5
452.6375	Manchester Transit	WQJ983	
458.8875	Municipal Services	KD24528	
453.100	School Buses	KNFS837	123.0
453.950	Housing Authority	WNNK803	D-503
153.905	Youth Development Ctr.	KRB551	136.5
155.385	Elliot Hospital	KNEN587	167.9
155.340	Elliot Hospital	KNEN587	167.9
155.385	Veterans Hospital	reported	67.0
155.205	Chaulk Ambulance	reported	151.4
464.950	Mall of NH	WNBR773	
455.4875R	WMUR TV	KPH212	146.2
464.375	Holiday Inn	KNDU549	

Manchester City Services New Trunked System
856.4875, 857.4875, 858.4875, 859.4875, 860.4875, 856.2125

Marlboro (C)

155.070	Cheshire County	KCH716	136.5
154.430R	SW Mutual Aid	KCE889	"20"
153.770	Fire -repeater input	KCE889	136.5
151.115	Highway Department	WNUV989	

Mason (H)

155.565	Police -"Base 50" dispatch	WNBK693	136.5
155.490R	Police -repeater	WNDM753	CSQ
154.890	Police -repeater input	WNDM753	146.2
33.74	Fire -"Base 500" dispatch	KNCP221	CSQ
33.64	Fire -MACC mobiles	KNCP221	CSQ
33.90	Fire -MACC secondary	KNCP221	CSQ
39.50	Highway Department	WNBL288	CSQ

Merrimack (H)

155.550R	Police	KGY253	100.0
154.740	Police -input to repeater	KGY253	100.0
155.130	Nashua Regional	KGY253	136.5
153.980	Fire	KSR881	136.5
154.415	Fire -new frequency	WPCD590	
154.190	Seacoast Fire Net	KBF769	136.5
151.025	Highway Department	WPCC446	
153.875	Municipal Services	KSO922	136.5
156.000	Municipal Services -mob.	KD50343	
153.605	Village District Water	WNZZ962	
153.650	Village District Water	WNZZ962	
154.540	National Ambulance	WNGP292	
155.235	Merrimack Ambulance	KUY288	136.5
155.265	Care Ambulance	WPAF570	

Milford (H)

154.875	Police -ch.1 dispatch	KCD463	136.5
155.475	Police -ch.2 car-car	KCD463	136.5
155.520R	Hillsboro County	WDB352	136.5
33.64	Fire -MACC Base Disp.	WNKW865	CSQ
33.68	Fire -MACC Secondary	WNNV625	CSQ
33.74	Fire -"Base 500" mobiles	WNKW865	CSQ
453.1625	Fire -mobile repeater	WNKW865	100.0
453.0625	Fire -mobile repeater	WNPU388	
155.100	Ambulance/Town Admin	WNPU388	136.5
39.50	Highway Department	KNHB592	CSQ
39.18	Civil Defense	KNHC287	CSQ

Mount Vernon (H)

154.875	Police -Milford dispatch	KCD463	136.5
33.64	Fire -Souhegan Valley	KDA384$	CSQ
33.74	Fire -"Base 500" mobiles	KDA384$	CSQ
33.90	Fire -mobiles	KDA384$	CSQ
33.68	Fire -secondary	KDA384$	CSQ

($ and call sign WNJN970)

Nashua (H)

460.100	Police -F1- dispatch	KSM925	136.5
460.200	Police -F2- secondary	KSM925	136.5
460.325	Police -F3- detectives	KSM925	136.5
460.100M	Police -F4- simplex	KSM925	136.5
460.200M	Police -F5- simplex	KSM925	136.5
460.325M	Police -F6- simplex	KSM925	136.5
155.520R	Hillsboro County	WDB257	136.5
155.520R	Hillsboro County SD	WGT377	136.5
154.325	Fire -dispatch	KCA694	103.5
151.250	Fire -administration	KCA694	103.5
458.500R	Fire -officer's mob. rptr.	KCA694	103.5
154.190	Fire -Seacoast Fire Net	KCA694	CSQ
154.280	Fire -Seacoast Fireground	KCA695	CSQ

460.5125	Fire -HazMat	KCA694	
465.5125	Fire -HazMat	KCA694	
460.5375	Fire -mobiles	KCA694	
465.5375	Fire -mobiles	KCA694	
155.175	Rockingham Ambulance	WXY281	71.9
159.195	Highway Department	KDY361	123.0
155.025	Highway Department	KDY361	123.0
158.925	Municipal Services	WXY521	
453.7125	Municipal Services	KD44604	94.8
464.425	School Department	KNEC987	
154.570	School Department	KB65669	
33.400	Pennichuck Jr. High Schl.	WNRS285	
151.955	Daniel Webster College	KB75648	
151.955	Rivier College	WNKR355	
158.895	Nashua School Buses	WXY521	
153.470	Gas Service, Inc.	KCD520	114.8
153.425R	Pennichuck Water Works	KCH460	D-125
158.175	Pennichuck Water -input	KCH460	D-125
453.300	State Services	WNKL202	
155.340	Memorial Hospital	KVZ689	77.0
155.340	St. Joseph Hospital	KSM295	100.0
464.950	Pheasant Lane Mall	WNGJ501	D-174

New Boston (H)

155.310	Police	KVG840	136.5
155.520R	Hillsboro County	KQQ583	136.5
154.160	Fire -Kearsarge Net	KDY391	136.5
154.355	Capital Area	KP8074	"76"*
154.235	Capital Area	KP8074	"76"*
154.055	Public Works Department	KNGK764	

New Ipswich (H)

155.565	Police -"Base 500" disp.	KKR624	136.5
155.490R	Police -repeater	WNDM756	CSQ
154.890	Police -repeater input	WNDM756	146.2
33.74	Fire -dispatch	KDA381	CSQ
33.64	Fire -MACC mobiles	KDA381	CSQ
33.90	Fire -secondary	KDA381	CSQ
33.82	Fire -Ashburnham, MA tie	reported	118.8
39.50	Highway Department	KNJM515	CSQ
155.220	Ambulance	reported	
151.745	Wind Blown Ski Touring	KD20999	

New London (M)

154.995	Police	KMA297	
154.995	Police, Fire & Highway tie	KMA298	
155.010	Police	WNFI996	
155.685R	Merrimack County	KTZ214	136.5
155.700	Merrimack County	KGY294	136.5
156.150	Sullivan County	KNFL502	136.5
154.995	Fire/Highway Depts.	KYG548	
153.830	Fireground portables	KV5149	

154.160	Fire -Kearsage Net	reported	136.5
155.280	Ambulance Dispatch	WSV418	146.2
155.340	New London Hospital	KQM788	82.5

Newbury (M)
39.18	Police	KBI767	
154.160	Fire -Kearsage Net	WXY233	136.5

Newfields (R)
154.815	Rockingham County	KCB958	136.5
154.190	Fire -Seacoast Fire Net	KYO252	"32"
154.280	Seacoast Fireground	KYO252	
158.805	Municipal Services	WNWU204	

Newington (R)
154.115R	Police	KZR473	136.5
159.000	Police -input to repeater	KZR473	136.5
154.815R	Rockingham County	WGP693	136.5
154.115	Fire	KZR474	136.5
154.220	Fire -new frequency	WPCU963	
154.190	Seacoast Fire Net	KCC991	"33"*
154.280	Seacoast Fireground	KCC991	CSQ
46.58R	Civil Defense	KNEY901	156.7
152.420	Fox Run Mall	KA68790	
463.975	Fox Run Mall	WNBR772	D-025
464.925	Newington Mall	WNMH577	D-315

Newmarket (R)
155.370	Police	WNBM827	
154.815R	Rockingham County	WFE761	136.5
154.815R	Rockingham County	WPG47	136.5
155.085	Fire	KGL462	
154.190	Seacoast Fire Net	KCF575	"34"
155.160	Wadleighs Vet Clinic	WZM838	

Newton (R)
155.250	Police	KXB528	
154.815R	Rockingham County	WAL288	136.5
154.190	Fire -Seacoast Fire Net	KSU379	"35"*
154.145	Fire -area regional	KSU379	
154.010	Fire -Haverhill/Methuen tie	KUS379	136.5
154.160	So.Rockingham Cty. Net	KSU379	
46.58R	Civil Defense	KNIM373	156.7

North Hampton (R)
154.815R	Rockingham County	KCB958	136.5
154.190	Fire -Seacoast Net	WNAF231	"36"
154.145	Fire -area regional	WNAF231	136.5
465.5875	Fire -mobile repeater	WNAF231	
156.225	Highway Department	WRX797	136.5
46.58R	Civil Defense	KNIM373	156.7

Northfield (M)
155.700	Police -Merrimack County	KVS271	136.5
155.685R	Merrimack County	KWQ702	136.5
155.055	Municipal Services	WNID978	
37.98	Winnisquam Reg. Schools	WRE377	

Northwood (R)
154.785	Police	KNCP845	
154.815R	Rockingham County	KCB958	136.5
154.815R	Rockingham County	KRS227	136.5
154.950	Rockingham County	KCB958	136.5
155.415	Rockingham County	KCB958	136.5
154.415	Fire	KIU542	136.5
154.355	Capital Area	KIU542	"71"*
154.235	Capital Area	KIU542	"71"*
154.190	Seacoast Fire Net	KIU542	CSQ
154.280	Seacoast Fireground	KIU542	CSQ
155.340	Ambulance	KNBD703	

Nottingham (R)
155.310	Police	WNUZ514	
154.815R	Rockingham County	WRV36	136.5
154.190	Fire -Seacoast Net	KWV747	"37"
156.135	Highway Department	WNXT816	
158.730	Municipal Services	WPDE376	

Pelham (H)
154.770	Police	KDV653	146.2
155.520R	Hillsboro County	WCU955	136.5
154.235	Fire	WNQG635	146.2
154.190	Fire -Seacoast Net	KNHP376	CSQ
154.280	Fire -Seacoast Fireground	KNHP376	CSQ
158.745	Highway Department	WNSP673	146.2

Pembroke (M)
155.580	Police	WNQR592	
46.10	Fire	KCD338	
154.355	Capital Area	KWI736	"62"*
154.235	Capital Area	KWI736	"62"*
453.850	Highway Department	KNJY216	
155.880	Municipal Services	WNPM741	

Peterboro (H)
159.150	Police	KNAL832	
155.640	Police -also regional	KNAL832	136.5
155.565	Police -area net	KNAL832	136.5
155.520R	Hillsboro County	KNAL832	136.5
155.520R	Hillsboro County -repeater	KSV678	136.5
155.520R	Hillsboro County	WAC447	136.5
154.430R	Fire -SW Mutual Aid	KCF417	"24"*
153.770	Fire -repeater input	KCF417	136.5
155.055	Highway Department	WNJL374	110.9

Pittsfield (M)

155.685R	Merrimack County	KKL605	136.5
154.415	Fire	KZO330	
453.400	Fire -new frequency	WPCV617	
154.355	Fire -Capital Area	KZO330	"72"*
154.235	Fire -Capital Area	KZO330	"72"*
155.895	Highway Dept./PD backup	KNEN395	

Plaistow (R)

154.755	Police	KTE395	136.5
154.815R	Rockingham County	WAL289	136.5
453.400	Fire -new channel	WPCV963	
154.190	Fire -Seacoast Net	KUL738	"39"*
154.280	Fire -Seacoast Fireground	KUL738	"39"*
154.010	Fire -Haverhill/Methuen tie	KUL738	136.5
154.160	So. Rockingham Cty. Net	KUL738	
159.045	Highway Department	KNAJ363	136.5

Portsmouth (R)

154.740R	Police	KCA797	136.5
155.985	Police -repeater input	KQ7728	136.5
153.905	Police -secondary	KCB207	136.5
155.115	Police -Kittery tie	KCA797	192.8
154.815R	Rockingham County	WRG49	136.5
154.340	Fire	KCB207	173.8
154.190	Fire -Seacoast Fire Net	KCB207	"40"*
154.190	Fire -Seacoast backup tx	KLR393	"40"*
154.145	Area regional	KCB207	
153.905	Water Department	WNAF223	
154.055	Housing Authority	KIU436	136.5
155.025	Municipal Services	KB46165	136.5
453.725	Municipal Services	WNLZ723	
155.715	Highway/Water/Buildings	KCI218	136.5
155.835	Pease Development Auth.	WPAR994	
158.835	Pease Development Auth.	WPAR994	D-431
155.715	Police Department tie	KLR321	136.5
155.715	Fire Department tie	KNFZ569	136.5
155.715	Madbury tie	KRX605	136.5
155.715	Civil Defense tie	KTL490	136.5
155.715	Waste Water Plant	KTL491	136.5
158.925	Municipal Services	WQJ235	
155.340	Portsmouth Hospital	KNBU324	107.2
153.230	WHEB Radio	varies	82.5

Raymond (R)

155.640	Police	KNCD578	136.5
154.815R	Rockingham County	WRG50	136.5
154.190	Fire -Seacoast Net	KSO992	"41"*
154.130	Fire -regional net	KSO992	
154.280	Seacoast Fireground	KSO992	
45.52	Highway/Water Dept.	KNCG396	118.8
462.9625	Ambulance	WNSE827	
151.655	Pine Acres Recreation	(& 154.570)	

Rindge (C)
155.070	Cheshire County	KWX371	136.5
154.430R	Fire -SW Mutual Aid	KDL958	"26"*
153.770	Fire -repeater input	KDL958	136.5
156.180	Highway Department	KFP400	156.7

Rochester (Strafford County)
159.030R	Police	KCA804	136.5
154.890	Police -repeater input	KCA804	136.5
154.725R	Police -Strafford County	KRG709	136.5
154.980	Fire	WNVV305	103.5
33.980	Fire -Farmington tie	KCR901	
154.190	Fire -Seacoast Net	KCR901	
154.965	Municipal Services	(& 39.90)	

Rye (R)
155.250	Police	KCD686	136.5
154.815	Rockingham County	KCB958	136.5
154.145	Fire -area regional	KCD685	
154.190	Fire -Seacoast Net	KCD685	"42"*
156.240	Highway Department	WNIG249	
153.545	Water District	WNVM438	
453.425	University of NH	WNGC726	

Salem (R)
156.015	Police -ch.1	WNQJ331	136.5
155.730	Police -ch. 2	KTK619	136.5
155.130	Nashua Regional	KXC724	136.5
158.970	Eastern New England Net	KXC724	CSQ
154.815R	Rockingham County	WJU73	136.5
154.385	Fire	KCB774	136.5
154.190	Fire -Seacoast Fire Net	KCB774	
458.500	Fire -mobile repeater	KCB774	192.8
153.800	Highway Department	KTI547	
153.545	Water Department	WNVM438	
46.58R	Civil Defense	KNIM373	156.7
461.5625	Rockingham Park Mall	WNWV464	D-311
151.805	Rockingham Park Track	KNIY296	118.8
151.835	Rockingham Park Track	KNIY296	
151.955	Rockingham Park Track	KNIY296	

Canobie Lake Park
154.625	F1 -Maint./Operations	WNPM508	114.8
154.570	F2 -Security	WNPM508	114.8
154.540	F3 -Ride operations	WNPM508	114.8
151.715	Food Concessions	WRT970	97.4
151.745	Food Concessions	WRT970	97.4

Salisbury (M)
155.685R	Merrimack County	KKL605	136.5
154.160	Fire -Kearsarge Net	KQG679	136.5
154.355	Fire -Capital Area	KQG679	"74"*
154.235	Fire -Capital Area	KQG679	"74"*
33.90	Fire -Lakes Region Net	KQG679	"38"*

Sandown (R)
154.815R	Police/Rockingham Cty.	KCB958	136.5
154.190	Fire -Seacoast Net	KNAT699	"56"*
154.280	Fire -Seacoast Fireground	KNAT699	
154.160	Fire -Kearsarge Net	KNAT699	136.5
154.040	Municipal Services/PD	WNUD274	141.3

Seabrook (R)
155.250	Police	KCH504	136.5
154.815R	Rockingham County	WOM42	136.5
154.950	Rockingham County SD	KCB958	136.5
154.815R	Rockingham County SD	KCB958	136.5
154.145	Fire -area regional	KCQ311	
154.190	Fire -Seacoast Net	KCQ31	"43"*
155.145	Highway Department	KBZ374	136.5

South Hampton (R)
154.815R	Rockingham County	KCB958	136.5
154.145	Fire -area regional	KZF205	
154.190	Fire -Seacoast Net	KZF205	"49"

Stratham (R)
154.085	Fire	KTO488	
154.190	Seacoast Fire Net	KTK632	"44"
154.280	Seacoast Fireground	KTK632	

Sutton (M)
154.160	Fire -Kearsarge Net	WXF743	136.5
154.025	Highway Department	WQU418	

Swanzey (C)
155.070	Police -Cheshire County	KKW230	136.5
155.640	Police -Cheshire County	KKW230	136.5
33.78	SW Mut. Aid -W. Swanzey	KCE789	"43"***
33.78	SW Mut. Aid -E. Swanzey	KCP574	"27"***
33.78	SW Mut. Aid -Swanzey Ctr.	KCL206	"28"***
154.430	SW Mutual Aid	KF8311	136.5
154.385	SW Mutual Aid	KF8311	136.5
33.54	Tri-State Mutual Aid	KF8311	"28"***
45.76	Highway Department	KFP398	
46.58R	Civil Defense	KNGS453	156.7

** indicates a PL tone of 123.0

Temple (H)
155.565	Police -"Base 500" disp.	KKR624	136.5
155.490R	Police -repeater	WNDM754	CSQ
154.890	Police -repeater input	WNDM754	146.2
33.74	Fire -dispatch	WNCM663	CSQ
33.64	Fire -MACC mobiles	WNCM663	CSQ
33.90	Fire -MACC secondary	WNCM663	CSQ

Troy (C)
155.070	Cheshire County	KGX510	136.5
154.430	Fire -SW Mutual Aid	KCN691	"34"*
155.985	Highway Department	KNAE997	
154.570	Inn at East Hill	WNYN595	

Warner (M)
155.685R	Merrimack County	KKL605	136.5
154.100	Fire	WYR589	
154.355	Capital Area	KFP260	"80"*
154.235	Capital Area	KFP260	"80"*
154.160	Fire -Kearsarge Net	KFP260	136.5

Weare (H)
158.850R	Police	KNCA538	136.5
155.595	Police -input to repeater	KNCA538	136.5
155.520R	Hillsboro County	WDB258	136.5
154.310	Fire	KZB475	136.5
154.355	Capital Area	KR2990	"75"*
154.235	Capital Area	KR2990	"75"*
154.160	Fire -Kearsarge Net	KZB475	136.5
156.195	Highway Department	KNFP356	
158.955	Municipal Services	KNCH518	

Webster (M)
155.685R	Merrimack County	KKL605	136.5
154.160	Fire -Kearsarge Net	KNGN573	136.5
154.355	Capital Area	KNGN573	"65"*
154.235	Capital Area	KNGN573	"65"*
153.920	Municipal Services	WNSU376	
460.750	School District	WNUD889	

Wilmot (M)
154.160	Fire -Kearsarge Net	WQN260	136.5
151.055	Highway Department	WNZU803	

Wilton (H)
154.875	Police -Milford dispatch	WJZ449	136.5
155.565	Police -Regional network	KKR624	136.5
155.520R	Hillsboro County	WDT339	136.5
33.64	Fire -dispatch	KDA380 or	CSQ
33.68	Fire -secondary	WNKW865	CSQ
33.90	Fire -mobiles	KDA380	CSQ
33.74	Fire -"Base 500" mobiles	KDA380	CSQ
155.220	Ambulance	WNGW200	186.2
39.50	Highway	KCA262	CSQ

Windham (R)
155.610	Police	KWN961	136.5
154.815R	Rockingham County	WRG51	136.5
156.015	Police -Salem tie	KWN961	136.5
154.055	Fire/Highway	KNJX263	CSQ
154.190	Fire -Seacoast Net	KKV835	

NEW HAMPSHIRE STATE POLICE

Channel/Frequency Plan   (PL: 136.5)

Ch.	Freq.	Troop	Station	County	Car #
1	44.94	HQ	Concord	statewide	001-099
2	44.82	-	statewide	car-to-car	all
3	45.26	F	Twin Mtn.	Grafton/Coos	600-699
4	45.30	A	Epping	Rockingham/ Strafford	100-299
5	45.22	C	Keene	Cheshire/ Sullivan	300-399
6	45.46	E	Tamworth	Carroll/ No. Belknap	500-599
7	45.18	-	statewide	Aircraft/Radar	-
8	45.02	B	Milford	Hillsboro	200-299
9	44.98	D	Bow	Merrimack/ So. Belknap	400-499
10	44.86	-	statewide	car to car #2	all
-	44.78	-	statewide	crime task force	
	856.2125			MarinePatrol - Laconia	
	155.655			Corrections Department (141.3)	
	154.920			Mobile Repeater	

VHF Hi-band system (PL: 136.5)

155.475	statewide interagency
155.910	towns to state police -north
156.090	towns to state police -south

Digital System

151.400R	repeater out
159.225	repeater input

Statewide Police Radio 10-codes

- 10-1   In service
- 10-2   Out of service
- 10-3   Go ahead with message
- 10-4   Repeat
- 10-5   Message received
- 10-6   Standby
- 10-7   Unable to copy message
- 10-8   Transporting subject
- 10-9   Call by phone
- 10-10 Phone where you can be reached
- 10-11 Report in person
- 10-12 Disregard last information
- 10-13 Assist motorist
- 10-14 Request to take meal
- 10-15 Off at court
- 10-16 Abandoned vehicle

10-17	Arrest log information
10-18	Your location
10-19	DWI
10-20	Motor vehicle listing
10-21	Motor vehicle record check
10-22	Motor vehicle license check
10-23	NCIC check
10-24	Criminal record check
10-25	Traffic accident
10-25X	Traffic accident - hit and run
10-26	Fatal accident
10-27	Ambulance needed
10-28	Wrecker needed
10-29	Fire Department needed
10-30	Construction in road/traffic tie-up
10-31	Notify County Attorney
10-32	Medical Referee needed
10-33	Need assistance
10-34	Officer needs help
10-35	Road block
10-36	Use caution - subject dangerous
10-37	Mental person
10-38	Blood relay
10-39	Escort
10-40	Surveillance - don't stop
10-41	Check suspicious car
10-42	Stop where you are
10-43	In pursuit
10-44	Suspicious person
10-45	Stolen/wanted vehicle
10-46	Breathalyzer needed
10-47	Explosion
10-48	Fire
10-49	Flooding
10-50	Homicide
10-51	Rape
10-52	Burglary
10-53	Abduction
10-54	Untimely death
10-54A	Accidental
10-54D	Drowning
10-54N	Natural causes
10-54S	Suicide
10-55	Armed robbery
10-56	Assault
10-57	Drug case
10-58	Larceny
10-59	Drunk
10-60	Brawl
10-61	Domestic disturbance
10-62	Bomb threat
10-63	Request explosive disposal unit
10-64	Barricaded subject

10-65	Request SWAT Team
10-66	Shots fired
10-67	Request canine unit
10-68	Send additional help
10-69	Plane crash
10-70L	Lost person
10-70M	Missing person
10-70W	Wanted person
10-71	Fish and Game Officer notified
10-72	Transporting mental person
10-73	Escape - Jail - Prison
10-74	Use scrambler
10-75	Resume your patrol
10-76	Request to leave patrol area
10-77	Report existing conditions
10-78	Meet party at...
10-79	All Clear
10-80	Prison Alert - report to Concord N.G. Armory
10-81	ETA destination
10-82	Will be late
10-83	Vehicle repair
10-84	Request radio repair
10-85	Road courtesy
10-86	Road and weather
10-87	Administrative relay
10-88	See complainant
10-89	Traffic check - scales/radar
10-90	Subject has monitor
10-91	Oil spillage
10-92	Bank alarm
10-93	Prowler
10-94	Prisoner in custody
10-95	Female in custody
10-96	Shoplifter
10-97	Motor vehicle complaint

Code 1 At your convenience
Code 2 Without delay
Code 3 Expedite - Emergency with lights and siren
Code 4 Expedite - Emergency without lights and siren
Code 1000 -- Emergency in progress
Code 2000 -- Emergency in progress at prison

NEW HAMPSHIRE CIVIL DEFENSE

46.58R	various	Civil Defense rptr. & car to car (156.7)
45.44	various	Repeater input (PL input varies)
45.52	WSQ 990	Concord CD HQ tie with VT (118.8)
46.54	KNJL 962	Concord CD HQ tie w/Rockingham
46.56	WSQ 990	Concord CD HQ and car-to-car
46.36	KNAT 731	Concord CD HQ tie w/ MA (162.2)
451.675	various	Seabrook Alert

NEW HAMPSHIRE EMERGENCY MEDICAL SERVICES

Some towns and cities are set up very well using the present VHF high-band system. Others are also using the UHF communications MED channels.

The statewide EMS frequency plan is as follows:

Channel	Frequency	Use
1	155.340	Ambulance to Hospital - primary
2	155.385	Ambulance to Hospital - secondary
3	155.280	Hospital to Hospital
4	155.175	Tactical on-scene
5	155.400	Ambulance to Hospital - backup
6	155.160	Catholic Medical Center, Mnchstr.
7	153.755R	Upper Conn. Valley area (output)
7	155.055	Upper Conn. Valley area (input)
8	155.220	SW Mutual Aid and Cheshire Hos.
8	155.220	Androscoggin Valley Hos., Berlin
9	155.235	Beatrice D. Weeks Hos.l, Lncaster
10	155.355	Littleton Hospital, Littleton

Southern NH Hospital PL tones on 155.340 MHz

67.0	Veteran's, Manchester	100.0	St. Josph, Nashua
71.9	Monadnock, Peterboro	107.2	Portsmouth
77.0	Memorial, Nashua	136.5	Milford Medical Center
91.5	CMC, Manchester	167.9	Elliot, Manchester

Statewide Medical Codes

1	Heart attack		19	Gunshot wounds
2	Difficult breathing		20	Stab wounds
3	Reaction to drugs		21	Stroke
4	Head injury		22	Reaction to surgery
5	Dizziness or fainting		23	Eye injury
6	Fractures		24	Multiple injuries
7	Abdominal pain		25	Dislocations/sprains
8	Neck/back injuries		26	Diabetic coma
9	Cardiac arrest		27	Old age
10	Dead on arrival		28	Unknown problem
11	Epilepsy/convulsions		29	Check-up from acc.
12	Lacerations/abrasions		30	Accident
13	Hemorrhaging		31	Severe infection
14	Childbirth		32	Drowning
15	Miscarriage		40	Private ambulance
16	Burns		45	Service needed
17	Punctures		60	Med Referee needed
18	Shock		100	Police assist

DEPARTMENT OF TRANSPORTATION

The state is divided into six districts. Each district has a radio frequency it uses, along with the statewide channel, plus the older VHF low-band system. The districts are divided into patrol sectors, of which there are 92 statewide, as well as four turnpike district patrol sectors. All UHF PL tones are 131.8.

Dist.	HQ Location	Frequency	Area
1	Lancaster	453.925	Coos County, North Grafton County, North Carroll County
2	Enfield	453.775	Lake Sunapee Region
3	Gilford	453.775	Lakes Region
4	Swanzey	453.625	Southwest
5	Hooksett	453.675	Central /Merrimack Vly.
6	Durham	453.625	Southeast Seacoast
All	Statewide	453.975	Statewide
8	Turnpikes/Adm.	37.94	Turnpikes/Adm. (118.8)

Mobile units have the capability to select channels from the list below. They switch to the nearest repeater site (identified by a letter) and then choose the frequency for their area. Radios with four channels use their channels 3 and 4 for the statewide repeater.

Ch. #	Frequency	Mode	Dist.
1	453.925	Car to car	1
2	453.925	Repeater	1
3	453.775	Car to car	2, 3
4	453.775	Repeater	2, 3
5	453.675	Car to car	5
6	453.675	Repeater	5
7	453.625	Car to car	4, 6
8	453.625	Repeater	4, 6
9	453.975	Car to car	statewide
10	453.975	Repeater	statewide

FISH AND GAME DEPT. - LAW ENFORCEMENT DIV,

The New Hampshire Fish and Game Department is responsible for the protection, preservation and conservation of the wildlife resources of the state of New Hampshire; more specifically, fish and game enforcement, fish hatcheries, animal problems and search and rescue operations in the woods and inland waters of the state, as well as the registration and implementation of safety training programs for off-highway recreational vehicles. The State Fish and Game Department, Law Enforcement

Division, works closely with the New Hampshire State Police, which dispatches Fish and Game units nights and weekends. Each repeater site is identified by a letter, which is used by the dispatcher and mobile unit during their communications. Mobile units are identified by a three-digit number, 200's being conservation and enforcement units, 300's being biologists and fishery operation, and 900's being Parks and Recreation, Bureau of Off-Highway Recreational Vehicles. Statewide PL tone is 131.8 for repeater outputs, inputs vary depending on the repeater site selected.

Primary Repeater Output	151.340
Primary Repeater Input	159.345
Primary Repeater Talk-Around	151.340
Simplex Car-to-Car	159.465

A secondary repeater system is set up at some locations, with some sites licensed. It is little used, as few radios have been upgraded with new frequencies.

Secondary Repeater Output	151.325
Secondary Repeater Input	159.315
Secondary Repeater Simplex	151.325
Simplex Car-to-Car	159.465

NEW HAMPSHIRE FOREST SERVICE

The New Hampshire Forest Service deals with forest fire observation and control, forestry conservation and management. Its radio system is made up of VHF high-band repeaters, as well as VHF low-band and VHF high-band simplex frequencies.

The state is divided up into two areas (at Concord), north and south, each served by its own radio system. Most forestry service radios are set up as follows:

Ch. 1	Southern Forest Service	151.445	(repeater out)
Ch. 1	Southern Forest Service	159.285	(repeater in)
Ch. 2	Northern Forest Service	151.295	(repeater out)
Ch. 2	Northern Forest Service	159.270	(repeater in)
Ch. 3	Fish and Game	151.340	(repeater out)
Ch. 3	Fish and Game	159.345	(repeater in)
Ch. 4	Car-to-car, aircraft	159.225	(simplex)
	Tower to tower	31.90	(simplex-AM)

Statewide PL tone is 131.8 except for 31.90 which is CSQ.

NEW HAMPSHIRE PARKS AND RECREATION

The Parks and Recreation Department has its own radio communications system with a PL tone of 131.8.

> Repeater Output 151.385
> Repeater Input 159.375
> Beaches simplex 159.375 (136.5)

COUNTY POLICE & SHERIFF DEPARTMENTS

The State of New Hampshire, unlike its neighbor Massachusetts, relies heavily on county communications. Each county has a police/sheriff's department that serves both the county and each town and city within it. These radio systems are also used by county sheriffs, State Police, some state agencies, federal agencies and local PD's for inter-department communications. It is for these reasons that counties were indicated next to each city and town in the Community Section: when monitoring one of these towns it is important to also monitor the county agencies. Note that most police radio systems in New Hampshire follow a four-channel radio plan. This plan is below, but note that the plan may not be used everywhere. County police and sheriff departments use a PL tone of 136.5.

Channel 1   State Police to Towns (155.910 or 156.090)
Channel 2   Statewide (155.475 MHz)
Channel 3   County Police or Sheriff Department
Channel 4   Local Police

County Police/Sheriff frequencies are as follows:

County	County Police	Local Use	Sheriff
Belknap	154.830		154.740
Carroll	154.860		155.535
Cheshire	155.070	155.640	
Coos	155.595		
Grafton	154.770R		
Hillsboro	155.520R	155.640*	155.430
Merrimack	155.685R	155.700	
Rockingham	154.815R	155.415	154.950
Strafford	154.725R		156.030
Sullivan	156.150		

General Southern NH area PD's: 155.490R (CSQ)

*Western Hillsboro County town police dispatch by S.W. District Mutual Aid.

COUNTY/REGIONAL FIRE NETWORKS

Many communities in New Hampshire are part of various county and regional fire networks. These regional nets provide not only centralized dispatch for local fire operations of the cities and towns in a wide area, they also coordinate mutual aid responses for all communities in the net during a major incident.

Capital Area Mutual Aid (Concord area) (PL: 136.5)
154.355	ch. #1	Primary Operations and Mutual Aid
154.235	ch. #2	Secondary/Fireground Operations
154.220	ch. #3	Moultonboro use (not on network)
154.280	ch. #4	Seacoast Regional Fire tie

Claremont Area Fire Network (PL: 136.5)
154.205	ch. #1	Primary operations

Lakes Region Mutual Aid Fire Assn. (Laconia area) (173.8)
33.900	ch. #1	Primary operations & dispatch
33.960	ch. #2	Fireground
33.840	ch. #3	Fireground
33.760	ch. #4	Fireground
33.480	ch. #5	Lakes Region mobiles
33.540	ch. #6	Lakes Region mobiles

Mt. Washington Valley Mutual Aid (PL: 136.5)
154.145	ch. #1	Primary operations

Ossipee Valley Mutual Aid (PL: 136.5)
154.175	ch. #1	Primary operations
154.340	ch. #2	Secondary operations

Seacoast Regional Fire Network (PL: 136.5 for many)
154.190	Mutual Aid and Operations
154.280	Secondary, Fireground

Southwestern New Hampshire Dispatch
154.430R	Primary operations	136.5
154.430M	Simplex primary	136.5
154.385	Fireground	136.5
154.430M	Simplex fireground	136.5
33.780	Low-band net (Keene area)	123.0

Additional Networks
33.540	ch. #1	Tri-State Net Primary	123.0
33.480	ch. #2	Tri-State Net Secondary	123.0
154.400		Twin State Fire -primary disp.	136.5
154.295		Twin State Fire -secondary	136.5
153.950R		Upper Conn. Valley -primary	141.3
154.160		Kearsarge Net	136.5

SELECTED AIRPORTS

Concord Municipal
122.700	Common Traffic/UNICOM
122.900	Civil Air Patrol Search & Rescue
123.100	Civil Air Patrol Rescue Training
127.350	Manchester Approach/Departure Control

Keene -Dillant-Hopkins
123.000	Common Traffic/UNICOM

Laconia Municipal
123.000	Common Traffic/UNICOM
134.750	Manchester Approach/Departure Control
119.850	Clearance Delivery

Manchester -Grenier Field
121.300	Tower/Common Traffic
119.550	ATIS (automated Terminal Information Svc.)
122.950	UNICOM
121.900	Ground Control
135.900	Clearance Delivery
124.900	Approach/Departure Control
134.750	Approach/Departure Control

Nashua -Boire Field
134.900	Tower/Common Traffic
125.100	ATIS
122.950	UNICOM
121.800	Ground Control Clearance Delivery
124.900	Manchester Approach/Departure Control

Portsmouth -Pease International Tradeport
122.950	UNICOM
118.800	Manchester Approach/Departure Control
128.400	Tower
120.950	Ground Control

RAILROADS

Boston & Maine Railroad
161.160	Dispatch to Train
161.250	Police
161.370	Maintenance of Way
161.400	Road & Yard
161.520	Train to Dispatch

Grand Trunk Railroad
160.935	Dispatcher
161.040	Road/Phone patch
161.205	Dispatcher
161.415	Road

Maine Central
161.620	Road
161.340	Yard

UTILITIES

Granite State Electric
48.42	Trouble Crews	103.5
48.48	Common Channel	100.0
48.44	New England Power Svc. Construction	100.0

Public Service of New Hampshire
158.250	Trouble Crews -base	D-073/D-351
158.130	Trouble Crews -mobile	D-073
158.265	Trouble Crews -base	D-023
153.515	Control Centers -base	D-025
153.455	Control Centers -mobiles	D-025
855.1125	Southern New Hampshire service calls	

Seabrook Nuclear Power Station
464.325	Security (may be scrambled)
451.025	Security (may be scrambled)
451.175	Pagers
451.225	Maintenance
451.675	Sirens (Massachusetts)
451.050	Sirens (New Hampshire)
851.1625	Evacuation
852.1625	Transportation
853.1625	Maintenance
854.1625	Tactical
855.1625	Radiological Units

NYNEX (Primary PL: 156.7)
451.425	Common
151.985	Dover
451.350	Gilford
451.375	Goffstown
461.600	Goffstown
451.575	Goffstown
451.375	Nashua
451.500	Northwood
451.300	Ossipee
451.625	Somersworth

Other Utilities
451.400	Chester Telephone Co.	107.2
37.580R	Concord Electric Co.	114.8
37.580R	Exeter & Hampton Electric	114.8
153.590	Manchester Gas	114.8

MISCELLANEOUS FREQUENCIES

162.400	NOAA Continuous Weather (Concord)	CSQ
171.525R	White Mountain National Forest	CSQ
463.950	Mt. Washington Observatory	123.0
463.950	Appalachian Mountain Club	107.2
168.125R	US Army Corps of Engineers	CSQ

VERMONT Major Systems

STATE POLICE (PL: 118.8)

TROOP	FREQUENCY	BARRACKS
A	460.225	Colchester
A	460.225	St. Albans
B	460.150	Derby
B	460.150	St. Johnsbury
C	460.375	Middlebury
C	460.375	Rutland
C	460.375	Shaftsbury
D	460.425	Bethel
D	460.475	Brattleboro
D	460.475	Rockingham
E	460.425	Middlesex
-	458.950	Investigative
	42.860	Special Operations

TROOP	COUNTIES COVERED
A	Chittenden, Franklin, Grand Isle, Lamoille
B	Caledonia, Essex, Orleans, part of Orange
C	Addison, Bennington, Rutland
D	Windham, part of Winsor, part of Orange
E	Washinton, part of Windsor, part of Orange

COUNTY SHERIFF

COUNTY	POLICE/SHERIFF	COUNTY DISPATCH	
Addison	155.415	Middlebury	
Bennington	155.580	Bennington	
Calendonia	460.450	St. Johnsbury	
Chittenden	460.450	Burlington	
Essex		State Police	
Franklin	155.700	Saint Albans	
Grand Isle		State Police	
Lamoille	460.450	Hyde Park	
Orange*	460.450	Orange	
Orleans	460.450, 460.275	Newport	118.8
Rutland	460.250	Rutland	118.8
Washington	45.50	Montpelier	
Windham	460.450	Newfane	118.8
Windsor	460.125	Windsor	118.8

Many county police radio systems also have the capability to communicate with the Vermont State Police and/or local cities and towns on statewide frequencies:

F1	460.—	State Police - area troop frequency
F2	460.500	Common cars and cruisers (statewide)
F3	460.025R	Statewide Repeater (465.025 input)
F4	460.275	Statewide State Police

BUREAU OF CORRECTIONS

460.325	Statewide	118.8

CIVIL DEFENSE

45.52	Statewide	118.8
45.44	NH Civil Defense tie	varies

DEPARTMENT OF HIGHWAYS

159.195R	(151.040 in) Districts 1, 4, 5, 7	88.5
159.180R	(151.070 in) Districts 2, 3, 6, 8, 9	179.9
159.075M	Simplex car to car	CSQ
161.490	Survey Teams	CSQ

DISTRICT	AREA SERVED	HQ
1	south west	Bennington
2	south east	Brattleboro
3	central SW	Rutland
4	central SE	White River Junction
5	central NW	Colchester
6	central NE	Berlin
7	northeast	St. Johnsbury
8	northeast	St. Albans
9	north central	Newport

ENVIRONMENTAL CONSERVATION

151.475R	Forestry statewide (151.160 input)	103.5
151.475	Forestry simplex	
151.460	Forestry -Washington County	
159.405R	Fish & Wildlife Statewide (151.19 in)	94.8
159.405	Fish & Wildlife Statewide Simplex	
151.190	Fish & Wildlife Simplex	

FIRE NETS

Addison County	154.175
Bennington County	154.340
Capitol Area	154.190 (107.2)
Chittenden County	154.385
CT River Valley	46.08 (CSQ)
Franklin County	154.265
Lamoille County	154.190 F1 / 154.070 F2
Orleans County	45.32 (110.9)
SW New Hampshire	154.430 F1 /154.385 F2 (136.5)
Tri-State Mutual Aid	33.540 F1 / 33.480 F2 (123.0)
Tri-Mountain	154.145R (154.445 input) (CSQ)
UpperValley Region	153.950R (154.415 input) (141.3)

CONNECTICUT Major Systems

STATE POLICE

LOW-BAND SYSTEM (PL: CSQ)

42.040	Ch. 1	Troop E	Montville; Groton	
		Troop G	Westport (Turnpike)	
		Troop H	Hartford (HQ)	
42.360	Ch. 2	Troop C	Stafford Springs	
		Troop D	Danielson; Brooklyn	
		Troop K	Colchester	
42.480	Ch. 3	Troop F	Westbrook;Kllngwrth	
		Troop I	Bethany; New Haven	
42.520	Ch. 4	Troop A	Southbury	
		Troop B	Canaan	
		Troop L	Litchfield	
42.180	Ch. 5	DN	Investigative	
42.300	Ch. 6	Investigative		
42.200	Ch. 7	Radar/Truck Wght Sqds		
42.240	Ch. 8	Radar/Truck Wght Sqds		
42.320		Crime Task Force		
42.580		Tactical Operations		
42.MHz		Fully Programmable		
45.860		Statewide Police Hotline		
154.875R		Dept. of Motor Vehicles		203.5

HI-BAND SYSTEM (Portables)

Ch. 1	154.6425	repeats 42.04	141.3
Ch. 2	154.7025	repeats 42.36	141.3
Ch. 3	154.6875	repeats 42.48	141.3
Ch. 4	154.6575	repeats 42.52	141.3
Ch. 5	154.830	standard mobile extender	141.3
Ch. 6	154.665	troop to troop	141.3
Ch. 7	154.695	Capitol Division/Armory	141.3
Ch. 8	156.210R	Bradley Field "Troop W"	141.3
	154.650	Bradley Field -input	141.3
Ch. 9	155.475	Tactical/Intersystem	141.3
Ch. 10	155.340	C-MED/HEAR	
Ch. 11	154.695R	Capitol Security Patrol	141.3
	155.475	Capitol Security Patrol	
Ch. 12	154.100R	Faifield City Hotline South	151.4
Ch. 13	154.100	Faifield City Hotline North	179.9
Ch. 14	154.875R	Dept. of Motor Vehicles	203.5
Ch. 15	151.355	Sheriffs Prisoner Transport	141.3
Ch. 16	154.860	Corrections Department	114.8
Ch. 17	162.400	Nat'l Weather Svc. - Meriden	
Ch. 18	162.475	Nat'l Weather Svc. - Hartford	
Ch. 19	162.550	Nat'l Weather Svc. - New London	

PROPOSED 800 MHz RADIO SYSTEM

Connecticut State Police has applied for the following trunked radio frequencies. Only testing has occurred.

866.0125, 866.1375, 866.2750, 866.3000, 866.5125,
866.6125, 866.6375, 866.7125, 866.7500, 866.8625,
867.0125, 867.0750, 867.1375, 867.2000, 867.2250,
867.5125, 867.5875, 867.7000, 868.0125, 868.1625,
868.2000, 868.3125, 868.5625, 868.6125, 868.7500

STATE/COUNTY SECURITY FREQUENCIES

453.9875	State Courts, Hartford	162.2
453.225	State Library, Hartford	114.8
453.550	Capitol Security - other than capitol	114.8
154.860	State Corrections Department	114.8
45.500	Windham County Sheriff	118.8
151.355	County Sheriff's Prisoner Transports	114.8

County Sheriff's Low Power Portables (often used inside courthouse: 465.1875, 465.2625, 465.4375, 465.4625)

REGIONAL POLICE HOTLINE NETWORKS

45.860	Statewide Police Hotline	CSQ
154.100R	Fairfield County Hotline (158.925 in)	179.9
460.075	"RAFS" Hartford Area Hotline - F1	114.8
460.175	"RAFS" Hartford Area Hotline - F2 main	114.8
460.150	"SCAN" South Central Area Network	114.8
460.300	"WARN" Waterbury Area Radio Network	114.8
460.225	"WEMLAC" Western MA/N. Central CT. 1	173.8
460.475	"WEMLAC" Western MA/N. Central CT. 2	173.8

BRADLEY FIELD (WINDSOR LOCKS)

156.210R	Airport State Police - Troop W	141.3
154.650	Airport State Police - input to repeater	141.3
453.300	Crash, Fire, Rescue operations	186.2
453.500	Maintenance	186.2

DEPARTMENT OF TRANSPORTATION

47.380	F1/District 1	Highway Maintenance	146.2
47.300	F2/District 2	Highway Maintenance	146.2
47.320	F3/District 3	Radio Repair/Survey	146.2
151.025	(Rocky Hill Base)	Supervisors/Inspectors	146.2
151.115	(Rocky Hill Base)	Supervisors/Inspectors	146.2

STATE CIVIL DEFENSE

45.520	State Civil Defense	114.8
45.600	State Civil Defense	114.8
161.640	At State Armory Emergency Broadcast Sys.	

CIVIL PREPAREDNESS

153.755	Area 1	Newtown headquarters	162.2
153.800	Area II	Meriden Headquarters	162.2
153.935	Area III	Rocky Hill Headquarters	162.2
153.965	Area IV	Colchester Headquarters	162.2
153.740	Area V	Torrington Headquarters	162.2

DEPARTMENT OF ENVIRONMENTAL PROTECTION

This department is responsible for environmental protection, state land fire protection and the maintenance of state parks. The system PL tone is 114.8.

44.680	Channel 1	Fire Control
44.920	Channel 2	HazMat
44.760	Channel 3	Parks
44.720	Channel 4	Law Enforcement
151.475		Mobile Repeaters

REGIONAL FIRE NETWORKS

State/County/Regional Fire Networks & Frequencies

46.160	Statewide Fire Network - county coordinators	141.3
33.780	Statewide Fire Network -mobiles/ground	179.9
33.860	Fairfield County - Local & Intercity Operations	CSQ
33.940	Hartford County - Local Fire Operations	CSQ
33.500	Hartford County - Fireground Operations	CSQ
154.265	Hartford Area Intercity Fire Network	107.2
154.145	Hartford Area Intercity Fireground/HAZMAT	107.2
33.700	Litchfield County - Local & Intercity Ops.	CSQ
46.180	Middlesex County - Local & Intercity Ops.	CSQ
46.220	Middlesex County - Secondary/Mobile Ops.	CSQ
46.180	Valley Shore Mutual Aid - Local and Intercity	141.3
46.260	Valley Shore Mutual Aid - Secondary Ops.	141.3
33.700	New London County - Local Ops.s	CSQ
33.900	New London County - Intra-County Ops.	CSQ
33.920	New London County - E. New London Cty.	CSQ
33.960	New London County - W New London Cty.	179.9
33.940	New London County - Waterford Area	179.9
154.295	South Central Intercity Fire Net	107.2
33.900	Tolland County - Local and Inter-County	CSQ
33.800	Tolland - Tone Dispatch	CSQ
33.900	Windham County - Local & Intercity Ops.	CSQ
33.800	Windham County- Tone Dispatch	CSQ
155.385	LifeStar Helicopter	123.0

MASSACHUSETTS AMBULANCE FREQUENCIES

Frequency	Tone	Name	Location
33.080	131.8	Spencer Rescue	Spencer
45.960	114.8	Stavis Ambulance	Brookline
46.040		Shore Ambulance	Rockland
47.460	146.2	Armstrong Ambulance	Stoneham
47.540	146.2	Armstrong Ambulance	Arlington
47.580	114.8	Marlboro-Hudson Amb.	Hudson
47.620		Reardon Ambulance	Boston
47.620		Trans-Med Ambulance	Attleboro
47.660	146.2	Armstrong Ambulance	Stoneham
47.660		Curtis Ambulance	Reading
153.650	91.5	Brewster Ambulance	Boston
153.995	CSQ	AmCare Ambulance	Newburyport
153.995	146.2	Chaulk Amb. -chat	Systemwide
154.540	110.9	Ruggerio Chair Cars	Milford
155.160	107.2	Berkshire Ambulance	Lenox
155.160		Boston Community Amb	Boston
155.160	DPL	EMT Corp.	Lawrence
155.160		Gold Cross Ambulance	Springfield
155.160	107.2	Leonard-Morse Hospital	Natick
155.160	118.8	New England Life Flight	Worcester
155.160	D-125	Trinity Ambulance	Lowell
155.175		Alert Ambulance	Fairhaven
155.175		Beauport Ambulance	Gloucester
155.175		Boston Ambulance	Boston
155.175	192.8	Frontline Ambulance	Worcester
155.175	91.5	Brewster Ambulance	Boston
155.175		Mercy Chair Cars	Greenfield
155.175		Transcare	Methuen
155.205	151.4	Bay State Ambulance	Malden
155.205	107.2	Bay State Ambulance	Springfield
155.205		Bay State Ambulance	Weymouth
155.205		Charter Ambulance	Springfield
155.205		Commonwealth Amb	Springfield
155.205		Paramedic Ambulance	Springfield
155.220		Adams Ambulance	Adams
155.220		Bellingham Ambulance	Bellingham
155.220		Bristol County Amb	Taunton
155.220		Huntington Lions Club	Huntington
155.220		Kiwanis Trauma Unit	Boston
155.220	179.9	Life Line Ambulance	Everett
155.220		Quaboag Valley Amb	Spencer
155.220		Shore Ambulance	Rockland
155.220		Village Ambulance	Williamstown
155.235	91.5	Boston Med Flight	Boston
155.235	97.4	Enos Ambulance	Burlington
155.235		Northampton Amb	Northampton
155.235		Trans-Med Ambulance	Attleboro
155.265	179.9	Life-Line Ambulance	Everett
155.265	192.8	Merrimack Valley Amb	Lwrnce/Lowell
155.265		Nordstroms Ambulance	Lynn

155.265	127.3	Norfolk-Bristol Amb	Brockton
155.265	127.3	Norfolk-Bristol Amb	Foxboro
155.280		County Ambulance	Pittsfield
155.295		Boston Ambulance Sqd	Boston
155.295	91.5	Charter Ambulance	Springfield
155.295		O'Brien's Ambulance	Beverly
155.295	192.8	Woods Ambulance	Gardner
155.325	114.8	Cataldo Ambulance	Everett
155.355	179.9	Enos Ambulance	Burlington
155.355		Life-Line Ambulance	Wakefield
155.355		Mt. Washington Rescue	Mt. Wshington
155.385	131.8	Boston Med Flight	Boston
155.385	91.5	Brewster Ambulance	Boston
155.385		Emergency Med Svcs	Pittsfield
155.385	136.5	Mercy Ambulance	Greenfield
155.400	91.5	Brewster Ambulance	Boston
161.220	CSQ	Fallon Ambulance	Boston
220.ACSB		Worcester-Himmer	Worcester
461.800	141.3	Patriot Ambulance F1	Fitchburg
461.925	186.2	Worcester-Himmer	Fitchburg
462.950	136.5	Action Ambulance	Melrose
462.950		North Shore Ambulance	Salem
462.950	186.2	Worcester City Amb	Worcester
463.000	167.9	Marlboro Hospital EMS	Marlboro
463.600	173.8	Cape Cod Ambulance	Yarmouth
464.250	136.5	Action Ambulance	Melrose
464.600	167.9	Woods Ambulance	Athol
464.700	82.5	Patriot Ambulance F2	Concord
472.0125	82.5	North Shore Ambulance	Salem
472.1875	127.3	Cataldo Chair Cars	Cambridge
472.8625	146.2	Professional Ambulance	Cambridge
483.8125	151.4	Valley Ambulance Svc	Billerica
852.9125		Trans Med Ambulance	Attleboro
856.5875	CSQ	Alves-Ruggerio	Mlfrd/Wstboro
856.8375	CSQ	Alves-Ruggerio	Mlfrd/Wstboro
861-5.837	CSQ	Bay State Ambulance	Springfield
800 Trunked		Chaulk Ambulance	New System

No. Suburban Paramedic: 851.2625, 851.8125, 852.2125, 853.1125, 853.9125, 854.8125, 855.5625, 855.5875, 856.2875, 857.2875, 856-860.6625, 861-865.4625

CTCSS "PL" TONE CODES

The capability to discrminate Continuous Tone Coded Squelch System (CTCSS) signals is a new feature to selected models of the Uniden/Bearcat line of police scanners. The 3 digit numbers, generally in the far right hand column of this guide (or signified by "PL:") enumerate the PL tone code known to be modulated on the listed frequency. This is a continuous sub-audible tone which which is added to the voice or data signal on a particular channel. When a receiver, be it a scanner or a two-way radio, has been programmed to recognize a certain tone, the receiver will become "unsquelched" and the voice or data will be heard. This allows numerous businesses or governmental agencies to license on the same frequency within a region and still not hear one another as they may use different PL tones. From a hobbyist perspective, this allows you to hone in on a certain agency and not be bothered with others on the same channel. It is also useful for blocking out intermodulation and skip. The tone list below includes codes designators used by various receiver and transceiver manufacturers.

Digital codes, a variation on PL, are listed in this guide as either "DPL" or "D-023" or another number.

EIA STANDARD CTCSS "PL" TONES

Tone No.	Code	Freq.	Tone No.	Code	Freq.
1	XZ	67.0	17	2B	118.8
2	XA	71.9	18	3Z	123.0
3	WA	74.4	19	3A	127.3
4	XB	77.0	20	3B	131.8
5	SP	79.7	21	4Z	136.5
6	YZ	82.5	22	4A	141.3
7	YA	85.4	23	4B	146.2
8	YB	88.5	24	5Z	151.4
9	ZZ	91.5	25	5A	156.7
10	ZA	94.8	26	5B	162.2
11	ZB	97.4	27	6Z	167.9
12	1Z	100.0	28	6A	173.8
13	1A	103.5	29	6B	179.9
14	1B	107.2	30	7Z	186.2
15	2Z	110.9	31	7A	192.8
16	2A	114.8	32	M1	203.5

others: 210.7, 218.1
225.7, 233.6, 241.8, 250.3

NEW ENGLAND FIRE & NEWS NET, INC.

P.O. Box 387   Newton Centre, MA 02159   617-327-6077

When it comes to pager alert systems,

NEW ENGLAND FIRE AND NEWS NETWORK

is the oldest, largest and most reliable.

NEFNN's UNIQUE system provides up-to-date fire and news information via state-of-the-art paging units including the Motorola Advisor and the NEC. The easy to read screen reports data promptly and continuously - 24 hours daily - 7 days a week.

NEFNN's FLEXIBLE system lets you choose only the information that interests you most from across all of New England and the New York City/New Jersey areas.

NEFNN's AFFILIATED with more fire and news paging systems across the United States and Canada than any other paging network!!

NEFNN's LOW COST system charges include a low monthly pager rental fee to a major paging service (with credit approval). There is also a **LOW** membership fee to **NEFNN**.

What's more, in addition to fire and news information, your pager can be used for personal messages with your own toll free pager number.

"The original Fire Pager - for the real fire buff"[SM]

Metro Radio System – Incident Codes (462.725, PL: 167.9)

- 10-01 Responding
- 10-02 Cancel response
- 10-03 Arrived on scene
- 10-04 Acknowledgement
- 10-05 Repeat
- 10-06 Stand by
- 10-07 Verify address or info
- 10-08 Call
- 10-09 Meet
- 10-10 Your location?
- 10-11 Radio test (R1 to R9)
- 10-12 Preliminary report
- 10-13 Need Help
  - Code 1-Urgent
  - Code 2-Not urgent
- 10-14 Disregard previous info
- 10-15 False call / No incident
- 10-16 Freq. request (fire only)
- 10-17 Fire box # request
- 10-18 Activity update
- 10-19 Monitor freq. for activity
- 10-20 Incident under control
- 10-21 Brush/woods fire
- 10-22 Motor vehicle fire
- 10-23 HazMat incident
- 10-24 Gas leak
- 10-25 Electrical fire
  - Code 1-Manhole
  - Code 2-Vault
  - Code 3-Under control
- 10-26 Ship fire
- 10-27 Subway/RR incident
- 10-29 Incident is photo-worthy
- 10-30 Fire/smoke showing
  - Code 1-Heavy fire/smoke
  - Code 2-Light fire/smoke
  - Code 3-Nothing showing
- 10-31 Explosion/bomb incident
  - Code 1-Explosion
  - Code 2-Bomb incident
- 10-32 High rise incident
- 10-33 Structural collapse
- 10-34 Construction accident
- 10-35 Working fire
- 10-36 Search for person
  - Code 1-Missing
  - Code 2-Lost
- 10-37 Water incident
- 10-38 Drowning search
  - Code 1-Confirmed victim
- 10-39 Aircraft incident
  - Code 1-Serious injury
  - Code 2-Not serious
- 10-40 Motor vehicle accident
  - Code 1-Jaws requested
  - Code 2-Photo/recon req.
  - Code 3-Not reportable
- 10-41 Emergency Vehicle MVA
- 10-42 School Bus Accident
- 10-43 MedFlight requested
- 10-44 Tractor trailer accident
- 10-45 Fatality/injuries
  - Code 1-Fatality
  - Code 2-Serious injury
  - Code 3-Minor injury
- 10-46 Weather alert
- 10-47 Avoid area/congestion
  - Code 1-Flooding
  - Code 2-Wind damage
  - Code 3-Accident
- 10-48 Report/road weather
- 10-49 Wrong-way traffic
- 10-50 Police operation
  - Code 1-Pursuit/Auto
  - Code 2-Manhunt/search
  - Code 3-Raid
  - Code 4-Other (specify)
- 10-51 Suicide
  - Code 1-Jumper
  - Code 2-Other (specify)
- 10-52 Demonstration
  - Code 1-Riot
  - Code 2-Civil disturbance
  - Code 3-Volatile situation
  - Code 4-Peaceful
- 10-53 SWAT Team response
- 10-54 Homicide
  - Code 1-Firearm
  - Code 2-Knife
  - Code 3-Other (specify)
- 10-55 Officer shot/stabbed
- 10-56 Officer in trouble
- 10-57 Shots fired
- 10-58 A&B/Dangerous weapon
  - Code 1-Firearm
  - Code 2-Knife
  - Code 3-Other (specify)
- 10-59 Armed subject
  - Code 1-Barricaded
  - Code 2-With hostage
  - Code 3-Other (specify)
- 10-60 Bank robbery
- 10-61 Armored car robbery
- 10-62 Armed robbery
  - Code 1-Home invasion
  - Code 2-Business
  - Code 3-Other (specify)
- 10-63 Kidnapping
- 10-64 Burglary
- 10-65 Body found
- 10-66 Rape
- 10-67 Selective enforcement
- 10-68 Prison/Jail incident
  - Code 1-Riot/disturbance
  - Code 2-Escape
- 10-69 Request for K-9 unit
- 10-70 VIP Arrival/escort
  - Code 1-Secret Svc. prot.
  - Code 2-State/local prot.
- 10-71 Sensitive incident
  - Code 1-Landline only
  - Code 2-Radio discretion
- 10-90 Essential radio traffic only
- 10-91 Request emergency notification
- 10-95 Unauthorized radio user
- 10-97 Hold radio traffic
- 10-98 Resume normal ops.
- 10-99 Restrict talk to incident
- 10-100 Major Emergency